C000060435

ALTRINCHAM

a history

EDITED BY DON BAYLISS

Willow
PUBLISHING

CONTENTS

List of Illustrations

FOREWORD

Charles Nickson's *Bygone Altrincham* and Alfred Ingham's *Altrincham and Bowdon* are interesting and valuable books, but the first was published over fifty years ago and the second over one hundred years ago. That in itself should be a sufficient reason for a new history of Altrincham, for there has been an enormous amount of change and development in the town since 1935, let alone 1885. It has grown in size and in some areas its outward appearance has been completely altered. It has had two major re-constitutions of its form of government. Additional sources of information concerning its past have been discovered or made available. But there is more to it even than this. What Don Bayliss and his team have produced is in effect the first real history of the town ever to be printed. For Nickson's volume made little pretence of being this. He did not call it a history but chose as a title *Bygone Altrincham* which suggests a series of reminiscences. This is, in fact, what it is: a series of reminiscences grouped geographically rather than chronologically in chapters named after different areas of the town, the Old Market Place, George Street, Goose Green. Only in the first chapter concerning the origins of the settlement and the second dealing with the town charter and the Court Leet is there any attempt at historical narrative and, unfortunately, since the development of place-name study, the first of these must be regarded as myth rather than fact. It is unlikely that any Saxon named Tring ever existed. Ingham's approach is more historical and information on the general development of the town is given in places. But the greatest part of the book is not about Altrincham at all. Of the seventeen chapters in the second edition, four are devoted to Bowdon and its church, four to the lords of Dunham Massey, three to Sale and other neighbouring places and only six to Altrincham itself. The present volume, however, because it has limited itself to the area of the old township (as explained by Dr. Bayliss in the Introduction) and because it is written by a team of authors of different interests and spheres of knowledge, has been able to combine a straightforward history of the town with many chapters on particular topics.

There are two further features which emphasise the gap between it and the works of Ingham and Nickson and both should make it more attractive to the late-20th century reader. One of the major developments in historical writing in the last hundred years has come from the realisation that places do not grow in isolation—that any village or town must be affected by what is happening, not only in neighbouring villages or towns, but in the country as a whole and even in surrounding countries. Ingham's and Nickson's books are almost totally devoid of any comparisons with outside developments. By contrast, in the present volume such comparisons are constantly made and in the early chapters often used to illuminate obscure periods in Altrincham's history. Finally, those who wish to pursue their newly acquired knowledge further will find the means to do it provided. In their writings on Altrincham Ingham and Nickson rarely did this. Both were journalists and it is known that these are often reluctant to reveal the sources of their information. Unfortunately, this means that a certain amount of what they wrote has to be relegated to the category of 'unverifiable hearsay'. But the readers of *Altrincham – A History* will find that in its concluding pages sources for what has been written are cited chapter by chapter. So, when the copious illustrations which accompany the text are also taken into consideration, the present volume (its publication shortly after the seven hundredth anniversary of the granting of the town charter) should be equally acceptable to serious students of the town's history or particular aspects of it and to those who simply wish to browse pleasantly among the wealth of information which is provided.

R. NORMAN DORE

INTRODUCTION

Altrincham, a town in the south-west corner of the Manchester conurbation, is attractively situated on a ridge overlooking pleasant countryside in north Cheshire. Today it has a population of 40,000 and forms part of Trafford Metropolitan Borough. For the last couple of centuries its chief landowners were the Stamford family of Dunham Hall, now a popular National Trust 'stately home' west of the town. This family exercised strong control over the size and quality of buildings in the district, resulting in large areas of imposing villas and mansions being built, especially in the western, high parts of the town and in neighbouring Bowdon and Hale to the south, some of which are now nursing or residential homes. There are several fine churches. Timperley to the east also has good properties. Altrincham and these adjunct places form a highly desirable area in which to live.

There is an attractive shopping centre in George Street, the north end of which is a 1970's pedestrianised precinct, and on parallel, but trafficked, Stamford New Road-Railway Street. Shops in and near the centre include a department store, a good range of high street multiples, two large supermarkets and also many small shops giving what the planners call a 'fine – grained', and, in most of the centre, a 'Victorian' atmosphere.

On Stamford New Road there is a new library and a bus-rail interchange with fast electric trains to Chester and Manchester. Behind the interchange is a popular leisure centre.

The main zone of modern office blocks has developed to the north of the shops; there are only a few office blocks elsewhere.

In the north-west of the present town centre is Old Market Place, the original centre of the town, with attractive buildings and market cross, but economically far less active than the streets mentioned above, and very noisy from the traffic which pounds along the A56 to and from Manchester.

South of Old Market Place is a small but fine area of Georgian residential property, now mainly converted to offices, down Market Street leading to the Town Hall. This was the seat of administration for the town when it was a Municipal Borough but now it is an outpost of Trafford MB, which is based in Stretford, five miles north-east. Opposite is the excellent Victorian 'listed' Market House, in and around which a bustling market is held three times a week. To the north-west is the Oldfield Brow area of council and private twentieth century housing.

To the north lies Broadheath, a major industrial area served by road, rail and canal. Formerly the home of machine-tool, printing machinery and other precision industries, the products of which were known world-wide, it suffered from post-World War II decline, but is now recovering, with many small firms and retail warehousing. Around Broadheath and in the eastern parts are areas of terraced property, some of great character.

Immediately east of the central shopping centre is a large area formerly occupied by railway sidings and old industrial premises, which is now mainly unsurfaced parking. Debate has raged for some years as to the future for this area.

This book has largely been written by local residents, with inputs also from a few contributors from outside the town. To all these, thanks are due. To other people who may well have been able to contribute, but whose expertise was not found in time, apologies are due. Apologies are also offered for any infringements of privacy through taking photographs.

The definition of the area studied was difficult because Altrincham started off as a small borough in AD1290 the middle of an agricultural township and then grew outwards not only to absorb the 630 acres of the township but eventually to coalesce with Bowdon, Hale and Timperley. It seemed sensible to avoid a study of an ever-expanding area so attention has been limited, as far as reasonably possible, to the ancient township which extended only from Broadheath to Spring Bank and from St. Margaret's to Stamford Park, as shown in the map. Details of Bowdon, Hale and Timperley are only touched upon when relevant to matters affecting this central area. The drawback is that while the old township boundary gives a useful limit for studies of early periods it becomes much less meaningful for studies of modern times.

The book has been produced with the blessing of Altrincham and Bowdon Civic Society and several members of this and Altrincham History Society have made written contributions or given other assistance.

Acknowledgements in respect of individual chapters are given at the end. Thanks are warmly given to the following: Trafford Leisure Services, for help in provision of sources and many illustrations; Trafford Planning Department and the Borough Surveyor and Engineer's Department; officers of the National Trust and Dr. P. McNiven of Rylands Library for illustrations, advice and archival and reprographic facilities; Mr. R. N. Dore, President of the Lancashire and Cheshire Antiquarian Society and Altrincham History Society for detailed help with historical fact and interpretation especially in chapters 1, 2, 4 and 5, for the foreword and for general overview; Mr. I. Sharman, Dr. S. Rigby and Dr. P. Booth for information, and help towards the understanding of mediaeval concepts; Dr. S. C. Bayliss, Dr. G. M. Swallowe, Dr. R. W. Bayliss, Mr. R. J. Rees, Mr. C.J. Hill and Mr. K. T. Howe for pointing out many errors and providing constructive suggestions on how to write English; and Mr. D. Rendell for a great deal of advice and help with selection and processing of many of the photographs. Finally I would like to thank my patient wife, who not only contributed two chapters but also added detailed information to several other chapters, and, as sub-editor, worked tirelessly with me to cut out overlap and achieve some continuity of style through the whole book.

DON BAYLISS

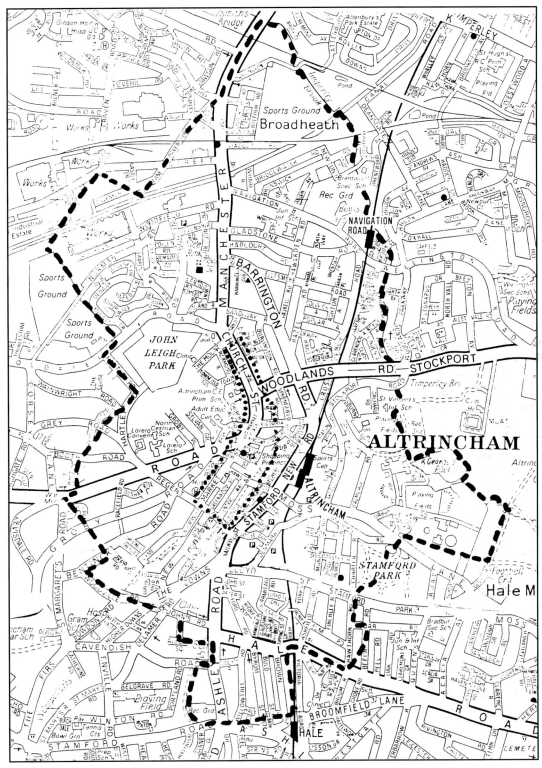

Trafford Borough Engineer's Department.

Modern road map of Altrincham showing the ancient township.

Mediaeval borough boundary • • • • • • • •

Township Boundary ▰▰▰▰▰▰▰

7

Chapter One

BACKGROUND

DON BAYLISS

The Royal Charter allowing the lord of Altrincham, Hamo de Masci, to hold a market and fair at Altrincham was sealed by Edward I on 10 July, AD1290 and was followed by Hamo's own charter creating Altrincham a market borough. The focus of this book is on the subsequent history of the town founded at that date. In this chapter, to set the stage, the earlier history of Altrincham will be discussed briefly. The nature of the site of Altrincham will first be considered.

THE PHYSICAL ENVIRONMENT OF THE ALTRINCHAM AREA

The Altrincham area contains (i) some lowland which is part of the surrounding north Cheshire plain, but its chief feature is (ii) a ridge of land rising to over 200' (over 60m) above sea-level, Fig 1.1.

(i) *The lowland.* The whole area is underlain by a solid basement of three layers of rocks of the Keuper Series of the Triassic period, over 100 million years old. The lowest strata consists of pinky-yellow Keuper Sandstones which made excellent building stones quarried in Timperley at Quarry Bank. The middle bed is a red sandstone which outcrops along Timperley Brook. The topmost bed of the series, the Keuper Marl, is a thick bed of sticky clay which contains valuable salt deposits. Salt from this bed was obtained locally from springs in the Bollin valley at Bowdon and at Dunham Woodhouses.

The Keuper rocks are veneered by a spread of boulder clay, several feet thick, deposited perhaps 25,000–18,000 years ago during the last major glacial advance of the last Ice Age. When the glaciers disappeared about 10,000 years ago, lakes developed in hollows in this impervious sheet of clay, and these

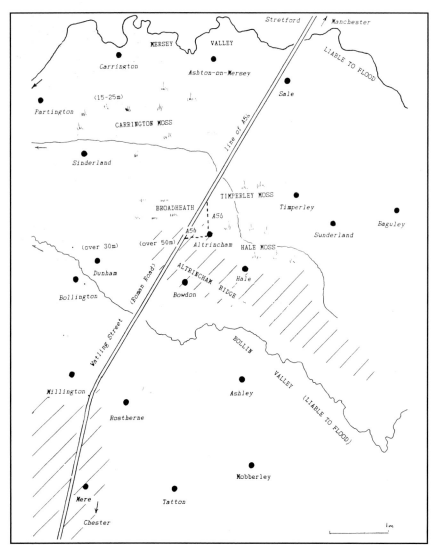

Fig. 1.1. Location of places mentioned, and environments which were significant in early times.

High ground over 50m shaded.

Heights in metres above sea level.

D.G.B.

were eventually colonised by sphagnum and other mosses, and a characteristic wet woodland and bog habitat developed creating mosslands such as Carrington, Timperley and Hale Mosses useful to man for fish, fowl, peat and reeds. Drier clay or loam areas, were naturally wooded, useful for grazing pigs, and when cleared made good arable and pasture land. There were also spreads of sand, such as at Broadheath. Here, soils were too impoverished for early agriculture and settlement. The valleys of streams in the lowlands, liable to flood, were thickly wooded and useless for settlement, but when cleared made useful water-meadows.

(ii) *The ridge.* The broad Altrincham ridge provided a contrasting environment attractive for settlement. It dominates the landscape and the command of view from the top must have tempted many early groups to control it. The ridge consists of a mass of glacial sands, gravels and clays, over 100' thick, lying on the lower boulder clays and solid rocks. There were many springs here and wells could be dug for water. Some upland areas of sand formed moorland such as Bowdon Downs, Charlmoor (Spring Bank) and Thorley Moor, covered in light scrub and woodland useful for grazing animals. Areas of mixed sands and clays formed potentially fertile soils and were easily farmed, *e.g.* on the plateau west of Old Market Place. Cleared areas could be used as pasture for cattle. Woodland provided wood for fires and buildings.

THE ROMAN ELEMENT IN THE LANDSCAPE

A feature from the Roman period (in this area, AD70 to AD410) which seems to have affected later alignments of lands and roads in the town was a Roman road locally known as 'Watling Street' (approximately followed by the line of the A556–A56). A grid system of roads and tracks was laid off parallel and at right-angles to it over the countryside to create a system of square lands for Roman farming. It may be no coincidence that (modern names) Market Street and George Street lie parallel to 'Watling Street' and at right angles to Shaw's Road and Regent Road. They probably reflect Anglo-Saxon field boundaries which themselves may have followed pre-existing Roman land boundaries. Thus the framework for the later town may be very ancient indeed.

THE EVIDENCE FOR ANGLO-SAXON ALTRINCHAM

There are no accurate details of the creation of the settlement which gave its name to Altrincham. When the Romans left in AD410 some farming land which had been cleared from woodland and developed by them was suddenly abandoned. The land around Altrincham may have been of this nature, potentially cultivable but unused by those who remained, the native Romano-Britons (alternatively called British,

Celts or Welsh). The Angles and Saxons invaded south and east England from Europe after the Romans left in the 5th century, overcame the native inhabitants in the south and east and eventually occupied the Midlands (Mercia). Some Anglo-Saxons pressed on into north Cheshire, which is assumed to have been occupied by Welsh people at that time.

The main evidence for the date and nature of the Anglo-Saxon settlement here, derives from the meanings of place-names, rather than documentary or archaeological evidence. There have been many attempts to interpret the meaning of the name of 'Altrincham'. An interpretation by Dodgson suggested that the 'inga-ham' element, meaning the homestead ('ham') or village of an Anglo-Saxon group ('inga'), implied a very early origin, perhaps as early as the 7th century. He considered that the group which came into this area, and settled on the site of Altrincham may have been the first in the whole area.

However, the Victoria County History interpretation suggests that other places might have been earlier. One of these was Dunham, ('homestead by the curved hill') reinforced by the fact that it was subsequently the probable centre of a large Anglo-Saxon estate and, later, was the centre of a Norman barony. Another early place was Bowdon, not only because of its particular place-name meaning, (both Bowdon and Dunham possess the same 'dun' (hill) element reckoned to be early) but because it possessed a type of churchyard with a curved boundary, believed to be of an early type. Bowdon was the only church in the district for several centuries and became the centre of a huge parish. Altrincham, according to this view represents a second stage of settlement, of an 8th century date.

The Anglo-Saxon people arriving at these settlement sites may have taken over pre-existing Welsh farmsteads or hamlets but another point of view considers it possible they took over sites not farmed since they were abandoned by the Romans when they left. The incomers to the site of Altrincham were probably a family group who may have obtained the land from the local Welsh chief by negotiation in return for some service. The settlement, according to Dodgson, took the Anglo-Saxon founder's name, Aldhere. It was probably called Aldheringeham. This meant the 'ham' (homestead or village) of Aldhere's 'inga' (people), or more simply, 'Aldhere's place'. Its name subsequently developed into Aldringeham and then to its present form.

DESCRIPTION OF ALTRINCHAM IN LATE ANGLO-SAXON TIMES

It is interesting, but unfortunate for purposes of historical description, that Altrincham was not one of the places listed in Domesday Book (written later, in AD1086 by Normans) as having been in existence here in Anglo-Saxon times. Therefore, because of this, it must be made clear that any statement about its continued existence throughout the Dark Ages is pure assumption.

Domesday Book states that the vills (villages or hamlets) in Chester-shire were already organised into 10 Hundreds for purposes of justice and local government. The site of Altrincham lay in Bucklow (East) Hundred, the administrative centre of which would be a meeting place, such as a tree, perhaps on Bucklow Hill. Each Hundred theoretically contained a hundred 'hides'. Historians are adamant that a hide was a fiscal unit rather than a precise measurement of area and the number of hides reckoned to be appropriate to each vill was the basis for tax assessment. However, in order to get some idea of how Altrincham may have appeared at this time, it will be assumed that a hide was about 120 statute acres of cornland.

In this part of Britain vast acres of arable land were scarce and a mixed economy of corn cultivation and animal farming was practised and it is assumed here that a family would need about 15 acres of corn land, with extra woodland or heath as grazing for its cattle and pigs. A 1-hide vill (settlement) could therefore have a population of 8 families. Many places listed in Domesday Book, *e.g.* Dunham, were, in fact, assessed for 1 hide or less and therefore, on these assumptions, this area contained only small hamlets of a handful of families in the 11th century. In the 8th century

Altrincham had perhaps been a couple of farmsteads, notionally cultivating 30 or more acres for corn, surrounded by woods, heaths and mosslands; at the end of the Anglo-Saxon period in the 11th century, it is possible 120 statute acres (60 'Cheshire' large acres) of land had been cleared from woodland for cultivation. At this date it possibly contained about 8 households, totalling, at, say, 4-5 people to a household, perhaps 30-40 inhabitants.

An attempt has been made in Fig. 1.2 to construct a map of Altrincham at this time from field shapes identified from later maps. The location of the hamlet is considered likely to have lain near Old Market Place. It would have consisted of wattle-and-daub timber-framed single-storey thatched houses, in each of which the family would occupy one end and the animals the other. There would be no chimney, smoke finding its way up through a hole in the thatch. In a small close next to the house, vegetables would be grown and a few fowl kept. The hamlet lay in the middle of its 'township' (which meant the land round a 'tun' or farm, and did not refer to the modern word 'town'). This area would provide most of the provisions for life of the inhabitants of the farmsteads. It is assumed the township covered the same area as in later centuries

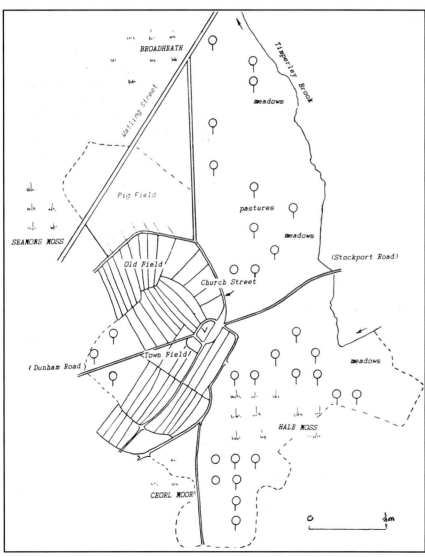

D.G.B.

Fig. 1.2. Altrincham in late Anglo-Saxon times.

An imaginary map showing 60 Cheshire-acre strips (120 statute acres) distributed between Town Field, Old Field, Pig Field and other smaller fields.

Village   V
Heath
Mossland
Woodland   ♀
– – – – – boundary of township.
Timperley Brook and Watling Street formed part of the boundary.

Source – Field names – Tithe Map.

An Anglo-Saxon Thegn

Old Ms.

and comprised 630 statute acres. Land-use would have contained communally-farmed corn, bean and barley lands, cultivated in strip-fields, of which each family might possess 15 acres (7 or 8 large 'Cheshire acre' strips), intermingled with those of other families and the lord, spread across good land and poor. There would have been large areas of pasture and meadow and there might have been a few enclosed private crofts. Woodlands would supply food in the form of animals and fowl, and honey. The mosslands and heaths would be important for animal grazing, fish, turves, and also osiers for thatch and baskets. The hamlet lay in a large estate, shown in Fig. 1.3, probably centred on Dunham, belonging to Eluuard or Alfward, an Anglo-Saxon thegn (a lesser noble).

THE ALTRINCHAM AREA FROM NORMAN TIMES TO 1290

The Normans invaded Britain in 1066 but took another four years before they violently overran Cheshire in 1070, wasting the land and killing or dispossessing Anglo-Saxon landowners, such as Alfward. William the Conqueror created the Earldom of Chester, and Hugh d'Avranches, his second Earl, gave large estates in Chester-shire (Cheshire) in 1070 to 8 loyal henchmen from Normandy, some of whom had fought at Hastings. A large estate in the Altrincham area, shown in Fig. 1.4, (in part coinciding with the former estate of Alfward) together with other manors in the south of England and north Wales, were given to Hamo de Masci, creating him a temporal baron.

Domesday Book shows the barony included the

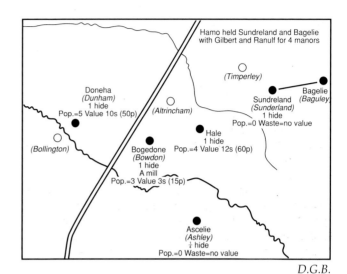

D.G.B.

Fig. 1.4. **Manors of Hamo de Masci's barony near Altrincham.**

Manors listed in Domesday Book are shown by black dots. Vills such as Altrincham, Bollington, Timperley, Sale, Ashton on Mersey, Carrington and Partington were not mentioned but were probably all in the manor of Dunham (Massey). Hamo also owned 'Alretunstall' but the whereabouts of this is unknown.

1 hide = 120 statute acres approx.

Pop = population in families.

Value = value in AD1086.

Source – Domesday Book.

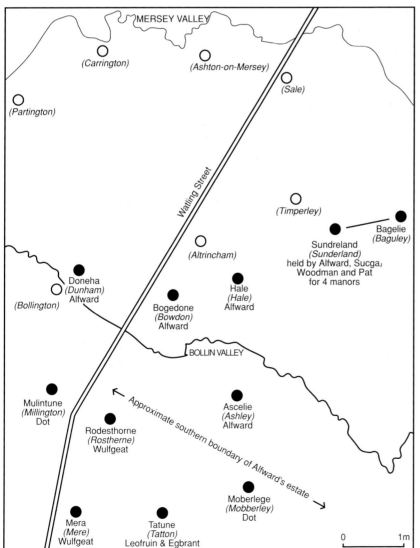

D.G.B.

Fig. 1.3. **Anglo-Saxon estates and their lords.**

Names of places shown by solid circles are from Domesday Book. Landowners' names are shown below the names of places.
There is no information for Altrincham and other places shown by open circles, they are also presumed to have lain in Alfward's estate. 'Sundreland' is assumed to be Sunderland in S.E. Timperley.

Source – Domesday Book.

11

Fig. 1.5. **Impression of Dunham Castle as a motte and bailey.**

Fig. 1.5. **Impression of Dunham Castle as a motte and bailey.**

D.G.B.

manors of Dunham, Bowdon, Hale, Ashley, Alretunstall (location unknown), parts of 'Sundreland' and Baguley and there were more distant holdings, including Bramhall, and others elsewhere (Chapter Three). The entry for Dunham makes clear this was Hamo's chief manor in Cheshire (words in parentheses have been added);

"Hamo also holds in Bucklow Hundred: Dunham. Alfward held it (previously in Anglo-Saxon times); he was a free man. 1 hide (= 120 acres) paying tax. (There is arable) land for 3 ploughs (to be at work). In (this) lordship (there is actually only) 1 (plough and there are only) 2 ploughmen; (there are also) 2 villagers and 1 smallholder. (Of) woodland (there is) 1 acre; (there is) 1 house in the City. The value (of this manor) before 1066 (was) 12s (60p); (between 1066 and 1086) it was waste; now (in 1086 it is worth) 10s (50p)".

The statement that there was 1 house in 'the City' shows that Dunham was the administrative and power centre of the barony. It informs us that its lord possessed a house in the city of Chester, the centre of the Earldom, where Hamo would sit on the Earl's Council. At Dunham there was, no doubt, a wooden motte-and-bailey castle, Fig. 1.5, later probably rebuilt in stone, in which Hamo and his family lived. Historians have different views on where the castle would have been situated but it could have stood on the mound shown in Fig. 1.6. The castle was perhaps built on the site of a

fort built by Alfward and Dunham was to be the home of six generations of de Mascis, Hamos I–VI until 1342.

Altrincham, Bollington, Carrington, Partington, Ashton-on-Mersey, Sale and Timperley were not mentioned in Domesday Book. It is most probably they were all contained in the large manor of Dunham Massey. Their details do not appear in the entry for Dunham, perhaps deliberately to exempt Hamo from full taxation.

The values of the manors which were recorded were low because there was not only a lack of economic development on this northern frontier of Mercia but also there had been devastations by armed bands during late Anglo-Saxon and subsequent Norman times. Several manors were recorded as being waste (worth nothing for taxable purposes, perhaps devastated) in the details given about late Anglo-Saxon times pre-1070. Every manor, *i.e.* Dunham, Bowdon, Hale, etc., was recorded as waste for the early Norman period between 1070 and 1086. Two were still waste in 1086. Much of the devastation had been caused during the Conqueror's march from York to Chester after a rebellion in the winter of 1069–70 and the deliberate 'Harrying of the North' which he then undertook.

Shortly after the de Mascis arrived, a 'parc' round Dunham Castle would have been enclosed as a hunting area for deer and other beasts. Meanwhile the small settlement of Altrincham no doubt continued under its new masters as a rural hamlet as before. By the beginning of the 13th century it had possibly grown into a village perhaps with a green on the site of Old Market Place. It is possible there were some small-scale industrial activities for local needs such as a smithy repairing weapons, cloth weaving, and leather being fashioned into horse trappings. There might have been a small unauthorised market. During the 13th century population rose rapidly, and a money economy developed so that villeins obtained an income and became peasants. They were taxed and had to pay tolls to attend market, use highways and bridges and had to pay tithes to the church, and pay in kind for the use of the lord's mill.

The history of Altrincham to this point was that of a small settlement essentially bound to the soil. It grew very slowly from Anglian times in the 8th century experiencing a general continuity of life in spite of changes of landlord and then grew more quickly in the 13th century. Its form and nature were to change abruptly in AD1290.

The late 13th century became a period of large scale military activity in which the de Mascis were involved in King Edward I's wars against the Welsh which ended in AD1283. In 1288 the Cheshire warlords,

perhaps relaxing after their victories, were circulated with an edict from the King reminding them of military service requirements and Hamo de Masci was no doubt jolted with the reminder that he had to continue to provide 5 mounted knights when called upon by the King. This and other commitments described in Chapter Three led to the de Masci finances being in a poor state. The general rapid growth of population meant that many people had no title to their land and we may imagine hordes of hungry peasants clamouring for food at the gates of Dunham Castle. Hence the need for Hamo V to find solutions to two problems, first a solution to his financial problems and secondly a solution to feeding the burgeoning population. If possible a solution to these two problems should also enhance the status of the de Mascis. The solution was investment in property and commercial development, the creation of a market borough. Such a development was useful in three ways: it could bring in income from tolls and dues or it could be mortgaged; it could accommodate growing numbers of people in a small area of land and it would also bring status to the de Mascis, its founder family.

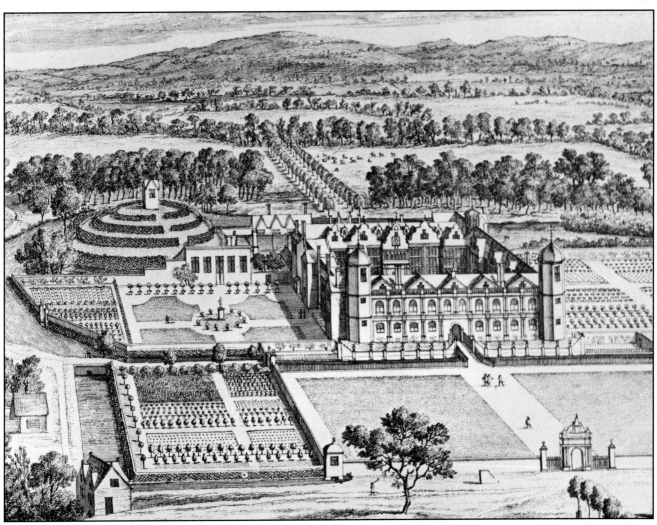

Fig. 1.6. **Dunham Massey Hall.**   *National Trust*
The possible motte of Dunham Castle, laid out as a terraced garden, can be clearly seen to the left (south west) of the Hall

Chapter Two

FOUNDATION OF THE BOROUGH

DON BAYLISS

The term 'borough' needs to be explained. In Anglo-Saxon times, in this area, a borough was a military post and a number were built in the Mersey valley, such as Eddisbury, Runcorn, Thelwall and Manchester. There is no documentary evidence that Altrincham was an Anglo-Saxon borough. The idea of a borough as a civil trading town developed in Normandy just before AD1000 and the idea spread to England. During the political duality when England and parts of France were governed together from the 11th to the 15th century over 500 boroughs were founded in England.

Mediaeval boroughs were towns where a new-fangled method of trading could be carried out. Until the Middle Ages local trade was mainly handled in small markets and by itinerant traders. A new system arose of an authorised market and fair where many of the traders dealt and resided at a fixed location. The fixed market and fair was as revolutionary then as was the hypermarket in modern times. They were sometimes operated by a self-regulating town community of tradesmen, called burgesses, who fixed the tolls and trading arrangements with the agreement of the lord of the manor. The burgesses made their profit from their deals, but the market and fair were owned by the lord who collected the dues, such as for the stalls (the stallage), and for people coming to market (the lastage) mentioned in Altrincham's Borough Charter. In small places like Altrincham, where trade did not occupy their whole existence, the burgesses had to supplement their livelihood with crafts and farming and such boroughs were partly rural in their economy.

Granting authority for a market and fair was the prerogative of the Crown. Hence a bronze plaque on Altrincham's new market cross refers to the Royal Charter to Baron Hamo de Masci granting him a market and fair. Creating a borough was a later stage and was the subsequent prerogative of the lord of the manor who could be the Crown, or the Church or the local seigneur. Altrincham borough was a seignorial borough, created by Hamo de Masci V by a second Charter, the better known Borough Charter, to house his market and fair.

The development of Altrincham Borough in the view of the writer, may have consisted of four stages. The first stage followed Hamo's consideration that the development of a market might solve his financial difficulties, and no doubt finding the people of Altrincham village also favoured this, Hamo would apply to the King for permission to hold a market and fair at Altrincham. There followed the granting by Edward 1 on July 10 AD1290 of the Royal Charter to Hamo de Masci allowing him to have these (Chapter Three). At this stage, this charter specifically refers to the fact that Altrincham was Hamo's manor, there is no mention that it was a town, and it was referred to as being administered by a Halmote, which was the ancient type of rural village court, the head of which would be a reeve, an elected villein. We can imagine that on receipt of the Charter from King Edward I, Hamo at a meeting of the Halmote, would instruct his officers to give permission to traders from surrounding places to come into the village on one day, Tuesday, each week.

The second stage was that after some initial success the traders may have pressed for permanent residence in the village. This may have been granted, and traders poured in, the place mushroomed and in this stage Altrincham grew quickly from a village into a small town, after 10 July.

Third, the incomers, in Hamo's eyes seeming to be a likely group of potential 'burgesses' confirmed his idea of the viability of establishing a borough. This led to the granting of the Borough Charter by Hamo, which would be in late 1290 or 1291. It is unlikely, but not proven there were any 'legal' burgesses already here though Hamo in the Borough Charter does refer to 'my burgesses'. Altrincham may have suddenly grown into a collection of quickly-built shacks and Hamo gave precise details of the layout appropriate for a place with the high status of a borough, detailing the size the burgages were to be, and of the corn lands the burgesses were to possess. At Oswestry, William FitzAlan's charter creating that place a borough in AD1190 actually refers to the fact he will protect the burgesses he has already invited in. It is possible something similar happened in Altrincham. The plan of the borough, its legal aspects, its administration, the social composition of the population, and their way of life were all created by Hamo's legal advisers through the Borough Charter.

The fourth stage in the creation of the borough involved the laying out of a new planned town, on agricultural ground adjacent to the old village. This followed certain principles common to many mediaeval boroughs.

CHARACTERISTICS OF BOROUGHS

Many market boroughs developed in the 13th century when 261 were founded. Each in theory was not to be within a distance of $6\frac{2}{3}$ miles (one source says 'leagues') from another to avoid competition for trade.

The inhabitants of towns were freemen called burgesses or burghers. A borough was a town distinguished by its burgesses having a particular form of tenure, called burgage tenure. This was the free holding of a plot of town land usually at a fixed money rent, and freely bequeathable, alienable and mortgageable. People moving into towns could be free or servile in their original personal status but became free burgesses by their tenure of borough land.

A wholly new town was said to be 'planted'. This was the case in Wales, where boroughs such as Conwy were militarily planted in hostile territory. A new borough could also be planted and laid out by the side of an existing town or village or planted in a virgin or sparsely-populated area. M. W. Beresford, in his book on mediaeval boroughs considers that Altrincham was possibly a planted borough. The wording in Hamo's charter 'sit liber burgus' ('to be a free borough') does not preclude this possibility and the reference in it that its burgesses were to possess some arable land outside the borough suggests it was a town with some relationship to a previous agricultural settlement on the site. The assumption is made here that Altrincham was not an Anglo-Saxon borough, nor an existing town created a borough by charter, but a planted seignorial borough, a New Town of the Middle Ages laid out on the open fields of a village of the same name.

As mentioned, the new market towns were in part a response to the general growth of trade in the 13th century because of a sudden growth in population and change in methods of the exchange of goods. In Cheshire, trade also increased because of the Welsh Wars of 1277 and 1282–83 when the King and the administration moved here from time to time. The lords of manors were sympathetic to the development of markets and could see the virtue of granting borough status, expecting returns in the form of taxes, stall rents and other monopolies.

Hamo de Masci instituted the borough by giving the settlement the following charter, Fig. 2,1.

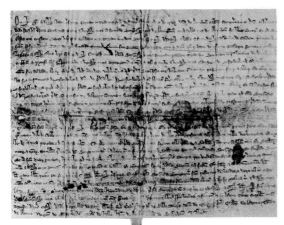

Fig. 2.1. Altrincham Borough Charter c. AD1290.

Trafford Metropolitan Borough

The lord of Dunham's name is given in Latin in the Charter as 'Hamundus' so the more familiar , 'Hamon', and 'de Massey' will now be used. For this recent translation we are indebted to Dr. P. McNiven of Rylands Library.

THE MASSEY BOROUGH CHARTER
(a glossary can be found in Appendix I)

"To all faithful people of Christ that shall see or hear this present charter, Hamon de Massey, lord of Dunham, sends greetings everlasting in the Lord. Know you that I have granted and by this my present charter, on behalf of myself and my heirs, have confirmed to my burgesses of Altrincham, that my town of Altrincham be a free borough, and that my burgesses of the same borough shall have a guild merchant in the same borough with all liberties and free customs pertaining to such manner of guild, according to the customs of the borough of Macclesfield. And that they shall be quit throughout all my lands, as well by water as by land, of toll, passage, pontage, stallage, lastage and all other servile customs. Also I have granted to my said burgesses common pasture, and turbary of the heath, within the boundaries of Dunham, Altrincham and Timperley, saving to myself and my heirs our improvements and saving to myself and my heirs the enclosure of Sinderland at our free will, without the contradiction of any person, whensoever we shall think fit to enclose the same, so that my aforesaid burgesses may have common pasture, always and everywhere for all their cattle within the bounds of Sinderland so long as the aforesaid place of Sinderland shall not be enclosed, saving to myself and my heirs the whole season of pannage in the aforesaid Sinderland, so that at that season we shall have power at our will to fence in the aforesaid Sinderland without the contradiction of any persons. And when the aforesaid Sinderland shall be enclosed, my said burgesses shall have their common up to the hedge of the aforesaid Sinderland and not beyond. It is also my will that all my burgesses who shall have pigs in the season of pannage shall pay the customary toll in my said borough either at the feast of St. James or the time of pannage when they pasture within the aforesaid commons, and they shall not go elsewhere with their pigs of the same borough at the season of pannage. Also I have granted to my aforesaid burgesses, housebote and haybote in all the woods of the aforesaid places, except my 'hays' and enclosed woods. Also I grant to my aforesaid burgesses that they shall not be impleaded outside the portmote of the aforesaid borough, nor tried in any court outside their borough, for offences committed within the borough, and if any one of them becomes liable to amercement for any offence, he shall be amerced by his peers, according to the degree of his offence. It is my will also that my burgesses shall grind all their corn growing upon the land of Altrincham or stored in the same town, at my mills, giving every eighteenth measure as multure. I grant also that my aforesaid burgesses may make for themselves reeves and bailiffs by common counsel of myself or of my bailiffs and themselves, and that no plea shall be held or determined in the said borough except before me or my bailiff. And that every burgess shall hold his own burgage of two perches of land in breadth and five in length, with one whole acre of land in the fields, for twelve pence, to be paid to myself and my heirs yearly at three times of the year by equal portions, namely at the Nativity of St. John the Baptist, at the feast of All Saints and at the Annunciation of the Blessed Virgin

Mary, freely, quit, peaceably and wholly, with all the aforesaid liberties. And that every burgess may sell, mortgage, give or bequeath his burgage to any person or persons he wishes, except to the officers of our lord the king and men in religious orders, without the contradiction of any person or persons, saving to myself and my heirs the privilege of our bakehouse in the same borough. Indeed, I the aforesaid Hamon and my heirs will guarantee for ever the aforesaid burgages and the acres of land adjoining them and all the liberties recorded above, to my aforesaid burgesses and their heirs and assigns against all people. In witness whereof I have set my seal to this present charter. Witnessed by Sir Reginald de Grey, then justice of Chester, Humphrey de Beauchamp, and Richard de Massey, knights, Gilbert de Aston, Thomas de Acton, Hugh de Baguley, Matthew de Hale, Henry de Dunham, John de Bowdon and others.."

ALTRINCHAM IN AD1290: BURGESSES AND THEIR PRIVILEGES

The charter apart from identifying a few officials and mentioning the burgesses does not give many details about them. However, there would be people of many trades such as wholesalers, retailers, brewers, bakers, butchers, and craftsmen such as leather workers and shoemakers, smiths, cloth makers, and tailors. The traders were given a merchant guild whose members had a monopoly of free buying and selling within the borough. The guild would oversee the quantity and quality of goods traded in the market and fair, and meet periodically to fix tolls and dues subject to the lord's agreement. The burgesses were freemen entitled to privileges such as to be free from servile tolls and dues which the peasants had to pay. They were free from tolls for the use of roads and bridges, and dues to rent a market stall or attend a fair or market throughout the de Massey lands. They were free from customs such as working the lord's land in the common openfield. Thus the burgesses were different in status from normal 'free' men in surrounding manors or in the town, who did not enjoy the privileges of the burgesses. There is no mention of a Court Leet in the Charter but the burgesses were given a Portmote ('trade-meet') which was a court for law and government especially designed for trading communities and probably comparable to a Leet. Here they were allowed to elect their own reeve and bailiff and there was some degree of self-government in the presence of Hamon or his bailiff. They were to be tried in this court by their peers for misdemeanours involving minor pleas, saving them the journey to the lord's manorial court (which probably sat at Dunham Castle).

One interesting feature of Hamon's Borough Charter is that it makes no mention of the granting of a market and the day on which it should be held, nor of any fair and its date. Hamon kept the tolls from the market and fair for himself.

LINKS BETWEEN THE TOWN AND THE LAND

The burgesses, although tradespeople, were also part-time farmers involved in the cultivation of corn and rearing of cattle and pigs. Access to common pasture for cattle, and freedom to cut peat (turbary) were important privileges and were freely allowed in the de Massey estates in Dunham, Altrincham, 'Sunderland' and Timperley. The translation of 'Sunderland' in the Charter might not be Sinderland near Broadheath but Sunderland in Timperley. In 'Sunderland' the baron safeguarded his family's right to make heys or enclosures at any time perhaps hinting at permanent enclosure in the future. This suggests that 'Sunderland', noted as 'waste' at Domesday was still unpopulated. Another constraint was that the burgesses could graze their pigs only in the common woods mentioned above at pannage time and had to pay a due for this. The vast extent of the grazing areas for cattle and pigs across several manors outside Altrincham suggests the burgesses were expected to develop a huge animal range. The basic purpose of this would have been to provide a resource of meat, leather and fat for military campaigning which was the prime way of life for the de Masseys. Wood for housebuilding and for hedges was available from the commons.

As well as a plot of town land, a burgage, Hamon provided for each burgess 1 acre in 'the fields'; one field was without doubt Town Field of 60 statute or 30 'Cheshire' acres. This would have been divided into narrow unhedged strips, some of which can be identified today, *e.g.* the combined house plots on either side of Sylvan Grove. Other openfields were probably Old Field, partly in Dunham Massey, and some fields north-east of the town. It is not known if the strips were communally ploughed but this was usual for the time, using large ploughs pulled by a team of oxen. It was expected grain would be grown on the plots and this had to be ground at Hamon's mills, presumably on the Bollin. 1/18 of the grain ground was exacted as a toll (one of the narrow fields existing in 1835 was called Eighteen Pennyworth which may refer to this). All the bread made had to be baked in the lord's bakehouse. The woods which then surrounded the town were useful for wood for fires, making carts and fences, and also for grazing pigs. Cattle would have grazed on open pasture and there would have been meadows along Timperley Brook.

THE BURGAGES

A burgage was not allowed to be passed on to the king, because the county was a palatinate governed separately from England; nor could it be passed on to churchmen. It could be sold, leased or otherwise passed to other persons. For the burgage and the acre strip there was an annual chief-rent of 12d paid in three instalments.

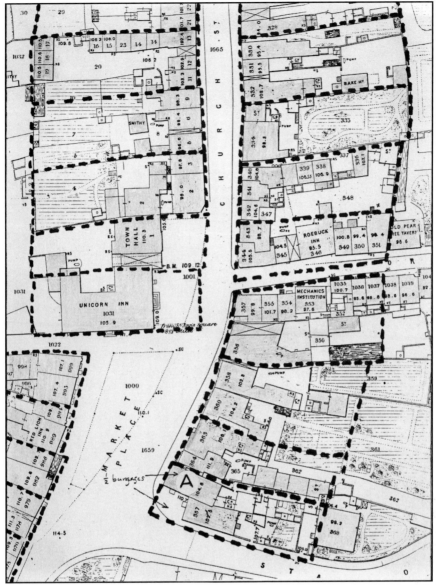

Fig 2.2. **Mediaeval burgage plots, identified from the Local Board**   D.G.B.
map of 1852, outlined in black dashed lines.

House plot A, centre bottom, is the subject of Chapter Sixteen.
Church Street is now much wider than in 1852.

Source – Local Board of Health map, Altrincham Library, with additions.

Rents of £6 from 120 holdings and all the other tolls and taxes, together with amercements (fines) from the Portmote Court, made a sound investment for the lord.

Each burgage was rectangular in shape, laid off at right-angles from a street with the narrow end fronting the street. It was 2 perches in width and 5 in length giving in Cheshire measure a plot 48 feet by 120 feet, about $\frac{1}{8}$ of a statute acre. Fig. 2.2 shows some of these plots identified from a 19th century map. On a burgage, at the street end, a wealthy burgess might have a large 2- or 3-storey timber-framed, thatched house (called a messuage or toft). The lower level would be a farmstead, and store, workshop or shop. Living quarters would be above. In the open land of the burgage vegetables would be grown and animals and fowl kept or a trade carried on such as smithing or leather-curing. Less affluent burgesses would have small properties and sub-tenants

might live in one-storey cottages with animals under the same roof.

POPULATION

The 13th century was a period of great population growth and consequently wages were low and there was land hunger. It may be the de Massey lands were overcrowded, perhaps including paid-off soldiers after the Welsh wars. A new town could absorb many people and take pressure off the land.

Some little evidence of numbers comes later than 1290. A Dunham rental of 1348/49 lists 120 burgages at that date. If there were 120 in AD1290 and if each were occupied by a few inhabitants, there could have been a basic population of 500-600 people in the original borough. The town may have been planned for 120 burgesses, the same as at Macclesfield (for comparison there were 80 at Congleton and 38 at Knutsford). Additionally there would be freemen and peasant cultivators continuing to farm the outer township lands, and there would be many people in the town other than burgesses, such as servants, artisans, labourers and petty traders.

THE FORM OF MEDIAEVAL ALTRINCHAM

A common plan for newly planted market towns involved laying out a market place with an adjacent rectangular grid of straight streets. The whole plan

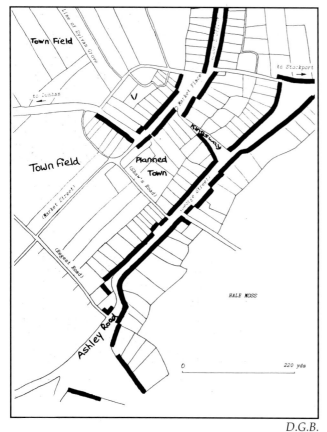

D.G.B.

Fig. 2.3. **Possible mediaeval features from a 1799 estate map, the tithe map and a map of 1852.**

V – possible site of former village.

Note the rectangular grid of the mediaeval town to the south.

could overlie, or be adjacent to, an original settlement which was often characterised by curving streets and paths. It is sometimes possible to identify these two contrasting patterns from later maps. On this basis a theoretical plan for the town as it may have been in 1290 is shown in Fig. 2.3. The area of the town would have been at least 15 acres. In the account which follows modern street names are used.

Church Street because of its curved alignment,

parallel to strips in the openfield to the west, may have pre-dated the plan. Stockport Road, and the quarter-circle curve of Albert Place and High Bank and the curved enclosure south of Dunham Road also do not appear 'planned' and may have existed as part of the original village. At the market place, the north-south road from Manchester to Ashley and Knutsford was crossed by the west-east road from Dunham Castle to Stockport Castle. Map evidence suggests 23 burgages were laid out on Church Street, 12 on one side and 11 on the other. The burgages can still be identified on the east side, and a back lane, still there in part, ran behind them from Victoria Street northwards. On the west a back lane ran north at the back of the old Unicorn along the east side of Arnold's yard. Another 7 burgages were laid out on the west side of the market place and others on its east side.

The new part of the town was a grid laid out over part of a large open field south of the market place with its axis parallel to the former arable strips. Two long and parallel streets, on the line of the present George Street and Market Street were constructed. These were crossed at right-angles by 3 cross-members of the grid, Kingsway, Shaw's Road and Regent Road. This created two boxes in which burgages were laid out. The rigidity of the plan meant that George Street was no longer in line with the ancient curving Ashley Road and had to do an S-curve (in the area of the present Graftons) to join it, Fig. 2.3.

CONCLUSION

It may be wondered why a market was created at Altrincham and not at Dunham, where it would have been protected by the castle. What mattered was the presence of roads enabling the movement of trade. Altrincham was better placed than Dunham for roads, in particular being closer to Watling Street and at cross-roads. It is most probable that Watling Street was closed between Highgate and Broadheath from the date of the charter and traffic forced to divert along the line of the present A56, Fig. 1.1. through Altrincham where travellers would have to pay tolls.

The borough was quite a large market foundation. Here 120 Cheshire arable acres could support 120 burgess households because they derived part of their livelihood from trade. The same acres could have supported fewer than a score of farming families dependent entirely on the land.

It is clear Altrincham was successful as a market borough investment because it was leased to a Chester judiciar, Sir Oliver de Ingham, in the 14th century.

The initiative was not unique. Also the clauses of Hamon's charter followed those of another town (Macclesfield), not an uncommon practice. The model must have been appropriate, however, because Hamon was able to raise a village to the importance of a successful market borough whereas some other borough speculations failed.

Chapter Three

THE DE MASCI BARONAGE

IAN SHARMAN

The family name of the baronial dynasty of the lords of Dunham Massey which lasted for over a quarter of a millenium from AD1070 to 1342 is shown as 'Masci' in many mediaeval documents and this form will be used in this chapter. All the heads of this family through six generations were given the name Hamo (later Hamon), a not uncommon Norman name. The name Hamo will be used throughout this chapter. The family had its roots in what is now a farming village of 124 people in the Manche district of western Normandy. Today the place is called Macey (Masci in early documents) and is only a few miles from Avranches, near Mt. St. Michel, Fig. 3.1.

The Norse settlement of Normandy was begun in AD911 only a century and a half before Hastings by Rollo (Ralph the Red), who was given land by Charles the Simple, King of France. The Scandinavian warrior-leaders then took the name of Dukes of Normandy and the ruler by 1066 was William the Bastard, later called Conqueror. The Goz family, the leading family at Avranches, the capital of the district called the Avranchin, were loyal to this Duke and at the time of the invasion of England, Hugh d'Avranches, nephew of William was left to support William's wife Matilda to run Normandy by council. Other loyal families seem to have included the de Masci family, the lords of Macey who were probably farmers. The men of the family were probably involved in war service for the Goz family on the frontier against Brittany when required. There is no evidence that either Hugh d'Avranches, or Hamo de Masci ever fought at Hastings (though Hamo's brother Hugh did and was listed as one of the Compagnons de Guillaume). Nevertheless they were repaid for the loyalty of their families and were given lands in Cheshire when it was taken by the Normans in 1070.

William's principle in giving land was to scatter his earls' holdings so that if they rebelled in one area he could attack their properties in another. Hugh d'Avranches had been given land in 1070 in 20 counties, including the Earldom of Chester. Hugh on his accession gave large estates in the shire of Chester, to eight followers, created temporal lords, one of whom was Hamo de Masci. For the same reasons as William, Hugh gave his barons some of the lands he had under his control in several counties. Hamo de Masci was given lands in (recent names) Flintshire, Buckinghamshire, Hampshire and Wiltshire as well as Cheshire. The tithes of Hamo's manors in Hampshire and Wiltshire were given through Hugh, Earl of Chester to the abbey of St. Sever in the Vau de Vire area of the Avranchin, which had been founded by the Earl in

Fig. 3.1. Mt. St. Michel.   *D.G.B.*

Fig. 3.2. Old Bowdon Church   *Ingham*

1070. Hamo also supported the ancient church at Bowdon, Fig. 3.2.

Hamo was given the Barony of Dunham Massey, for military reasons. The Normans first wished to stabilize their Cheshire conquest by military rule and secondly wished to press westwards into Wales. Cheshire was a marcher (boundary) earldom from which military attacks into Wales were mounted. It was also a county with palatinate status, *i.e.* the King's writ did not run in the shire, all law was made and upheld by the Earl, and Cheshire barons could not be called upon to fight outside the county by anyone but the Earl. The first four Hamos de Masci were members of the Earls' Councils and witnessed many of their charters. The Masci family had to furnish 5 knights on horseback (5 knights fees) and footsoldiers. These liabilities went on for a long time. A charter of 1288, when the King was Earl of Chester, still affirmed this service:

"Hamon de Mascy holds five knights' fees in chief of the lord King by finding for each fee an armed horse or two unarmed within the bounds of Cheshire in time of war with all his footmen holding forinsec (formerly Welsh) land within the aforesaid fees, doing their service according to the tenor of the great Common Charter of Cheshire. And if any army shall come from elsewhere into Cheshire or the castle shall be besieged then he shall come at the lord King's summons with all his force to drive it away according to the tenor of the said Common Charter".

At Domesday the family held 7 manors in Cheshire, 2 in Wales, 2 shared with other barons in Cheshire and 6 in southern counties. The value of the lands in the southern counties, totalling £17 p.a., Table 1, far surpassed the worth of the Cheshire lands £1.7s (£1·35). These figures suggest that Cheshire had suffered from William's punitive expedition, the 'Harrying of the North' following an Anglo-Saxon rebellion in the winter of 1069–70. The killing and destruction of property had obviously left its mark. At the end of the Anglo-Saxon period in 1066, in the reign of King Edward the Confessor (Tempus Regis Edwardi), the Cheshire lands had been valued at £3.2s (£3·10); at the time of Domesday, 1086, they were valued at £1.7s (£1·35). The fact that Altrincham is not mentioned by name suggests it was an insignificant place lying in a huge manor of low value land, the caput or centre of which was at Dunham. The pedigree of the de Mascis who were overlords of the barony is shown on Table 2.

Hamo de Masci I married Margaret de Sacey. Sacey is a small Normandy village in the Avranchin district, quite close to Macey. The 'lords' of Sacey were again probably also farming people. Little is known of Hamo's career. He would probably not have lived much in Cheshire, but have been away in the campaigns against the Welsh, and in Normandy with Earl Hugh in the internal Norman wars which occurred on the death of William I. Earl Hugh founded the abbey of St. Werburgh, Chester, in 1093 and Hamo is recorded in the charter for this as giving the church at Northenden for its support. Northenden, Baguley and 'Sunderland' were originally shared holdings but were probably quickly purchased by Hamo from his co-holders, Ranulf and Bigot. This was probably a strategic move consolidating the Masci holdings controlled from Dunham Castle. These now extended along the southern bank of the Mersey linking lands under the control of Stockport Castle with lands beyond Warburton and Partington in control of Halton Castle.

Hamo had two sons and when he died Hamo II received the bulk of the family lands and his other son Robert was given the manor of Puddington on the Wirral. Dunham is recorded as having been garrisoned against Henry II when the Earl of Chester of that period

TABLE 1
CONTRASTS IN THE DE MASCI DOMESDAY HOLDINGS.

	CHESHIRE	WALES	SHARED with other lords	OTHER AREAS
Value in Anglo-Saxon times	£3 2s (£3.10)	3s (15p)	£24 3s (£24.15)	£18
Value in 1086	£1 7s (£1.35)	10s (50p)	£5 12s (£5.60)	£17
Number of holdings	7	2	2	6
Number of hides (120 acres)	6½ + 2½ virgates	1½	7	10 + 1½ virgates
Ploughs	10	½	4	5
Land for ploughs	10½	2	1½	22
Ploughs in lordship				4
Ploughmen	2			
Slaves	1			13
Cottagers				3
Villeins	11	4		10
Frenchmen	2			
Smallholders	7	4		14
Riders	3	2		
Priest (Bowdon)	1			
Church	1			
Mill	1 worth 1s 4d (7p)			2
Meadow acres	1½			42 and 10 ploughs
Enclosure acres	1½			
Woodland	1 acre; 1½ leagues by 1	2 leagues by 2		10 acres & 104 pigs
Hawks eyrie (Hale)	1			
Land for	8 oxen			
House in the city (of Chester)	1			

Source – Domesday Book

TABLE 2   THE DE MASCI PEDIGREE

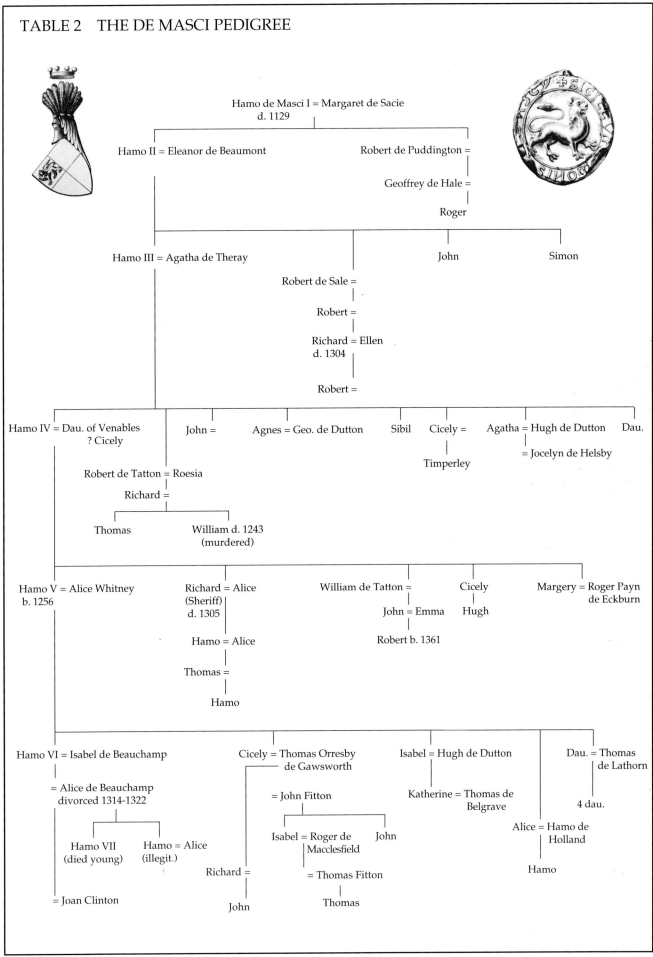

supported the claims of Prince Henry for land in France against his father during the Angevin dynastic wars. The motte-and-bailey at Watch Hill by the Bollin and another by Castle Mill are thought to have been thrown up at this time, perhaps in AD1173. When the Angevin royalty (King Henry and his family) reached a settlement, Hamo was heavily fined and it is likely the 'spurious' castles (erected without authority) were demolished by Henry.

Fig. 3.3. Birkenhead Priory   *Ormerod*

There were four sons from Hamo II's marriage, the eldest of which, Hamo III endowed Birkenhead Priory in 1150, the main Masci foundation , shown in Fig. 3.3. It is perhaps no coincidence that this followed the Battle of Lincoln. King Stephen had besieged this wealthy town. Ranulph, Earl of Chester, on the side of the besieged inhabitants called out his Cheshire barons, including Hamo, to defeat the King. This they did, and the barons would have been handsomely rewarded, so Hamo had money with which to endow the priory. But eventually the family finances gradually got into difficulty. Many Masci lands gradually became detached from the barony of the Dunham area as settlements were made on brothers, sisters, sons and daughters, and in at least one case by escheat to the Earl of Chester. From Hamo I to Hamo IV from Norman to English Plantagenet times, there were 14 divisions of land from the original Domesday block. For example in 1250 Hamon IV gave Stretford as a marriage settlement to Margery his daughter (and so to the de Traffords). The

next baron, Hamo V had 2 brothers, 2 sisters, 1 son and 4 daughters. There was a continual drain on resources.

Gradual loss of property given in dowries and expense in war had left the family in such parlous financial state by the time of Hamo V that investment in the foundation of a trading borough became essential if the family was to remain solvent. It would bring an immediate profit in rents and could be mortgaged if necessary. Richard de Masci, Hamo's brother had been Sheriff of Chester and was a deputy judge. He would have served on the semi-independent council which administered Cheshire in the absence of the King (who had become Earl of Chester after the death of the last hereditary Earl) and he would have helped in his brother's request to the King being favourably received. The grant was made at Westminster on 10 July 1290, Fig. 3.4:

"King Edward to the archbishops, (etc) . . . greetings. Know that we have granted by this our charter and have confirmed to our dear and faithful man Hamo de Masci that he and his heirs shall have in perpetuity a market each week on Tuesdays at their manor of Altrincham and a fair each year lasting for three days, namely on the eve, feastday and morrow of the feast of the Assumption of the Blessed Mary (14–16 August). Provided that the market and fair would not be to the nuisance of neighbouring markets and fairs. Wherefore we will and firmly commend, on behalf of us and our heirs, that the said Hamo and his heirs should have in perpetuity the aforesaid market and fair at their aforesaid manor with all the liberties and free customs pertaining to the halmote, market and fair. Provided however, etc., as aforesaid. With these witnesses; the venerable fathers the Bishops Robert of Bath and Wells, John of Winchester and William of Salisbury; Edmund our brother; William of Wales; Edmund Earl of Cornwall, our constable; Gilbert de Clare, Earl of Gloucester and Hereford; Gilbert de Thornton; Robert de Hertford; Walter de Beauchamp; Richard de Bosco and others".

The royal charter was followed by the baronial charter from Hamo to the new burgesses. There is no firm date for this charter granted to found the new town, however the pre-requisite for attracting burgesses would be the royal licence to hold a fair. The date of the

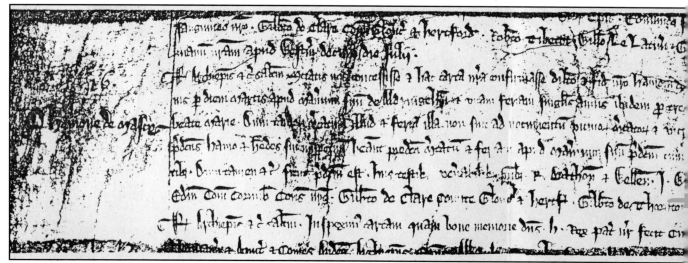

Fig. 3.4. The Royal Charter of 10 July, 1290. The word *Hamo* can be seen six lines down.

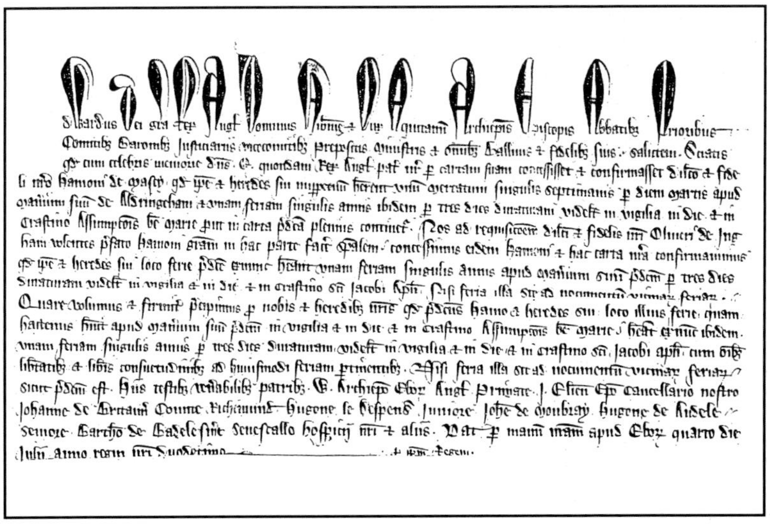

Fig. 3.5. The Royal Charter of 1319, changing the date of Altrincham's fair.

On line 4 can be seen 'Hamoni de Massy', and below this, 'Aldringeham', on line 6, 'Assumption de (St.) Mary' and at the end of line 6 'Oliveri de Ingham'. Line 9, in the middle, refers to Sti. Jacobi (St. James). The first two lines are addressed to all the nobles and clergy, and the last four lines comprise the witnesses.

National Trust – Rylands

fair was later changed to Eve, Day and Morrow of The Feast of St. James, July 24, 25 and 26, by Edward II at York, by a confirmatory charter on 4 July 1319, Fig. 3.5.

By 1290, the chief Welsh campaigns of Edward I were completed and there is no doubt that Hamo V had fought with other Cheshire knights in these wars and had incurred great expenses probably outweighing any booty won. The Mascis possessed two manors in north Wales near Hawarden from which they could assist in attacks launched by the King using Rhuddlan as the main base. There were payments to be made to support continuing ecclesiastical commitments in Cheshire and in Normandy where additions were being made to Mont St. Michel. It is just possible that the beautiful cloisters at the summit of the mount built at this time were partly paid for with Altrincham taxes, dues and rents. Certainly the de Masci lord of the manor of the village of Macey in Normandy had to find part of a knight's fee to defend the mount itself.

Hamo's war involvements continued as the King planned the invasion of Scotland and in 1297 Hamo as a 'banneret' was ordered to collect 4,000 Welsh footsoldiers, probably mercenaries, and conduct them to Durham to assist Edward. In 1301 he had to take troops to Carlisle. It was sometimes years after the recruitment of men that those charged with the task

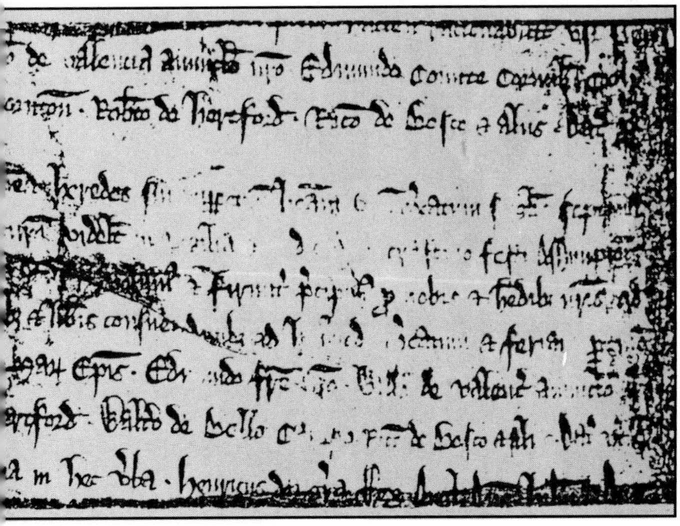

Public Record Office

(and who bore the original expense) were re-imbursed by the Exchequer. This sometimes led to the bankruptcy of baronial houses.

Of all the Masci warrior-barons the career of Hamo VI has led to much theorising. Like Hamo V his father, he left the supervision of his English estates including Altrincham borough to his bailiff. His professional career mirrored that of his contemporaries, it was in his private life that a streak of unorthodoxy is evident.

Hamo's first wife Isabel de Beauchamp died on their wedding night. Hamo next married her sister Alice by whom he had one son Hamo VII. It appears Hamo VII died in infancy or at least very young (one story is that he drowned in the moat at Dunham Castle at the age of nine). Hamo VI had no other children and it might be expected that on his death his estate would go to his 4 sisters, each of whom had married into an old-established Cheshire family. However, while her husband was in Gascony Alice bore an illegitimate son whom she named Hamo. Hamo VI divorced Alice some time between 1314 and 1322 on the grounds of her consanguinity after which, not now having a direct heir, he legitimised Alice's son to his own satisfaction for he seems to have developed a liking for the young man, the obvious cause of the divorce.

Subsequently he married a third wife, Joan de Clinton, sister of the Earl of Huntingdon. He probably met her through her brother's connection to the King, while in Gascony. Under Joan's prompting he embarked on the common baronial device of mortgaging a moiety (half) of his estates to someone outside the family, one Sir Oliver de Ingham, a Cheshire justice for a lump sum of 1,000 marks (£666) and 40 marks (£27) annual rent, whilst reserving to himself the use of the estates for his life. In other words he mortgaged his lands which were to pass to Sir Oliver on his death. Certain parts of this moiety he may have bequeathed to his sisters to be redeemed on payment of a fee to Sir Oliver de Ingham on Hamo's death. He left the other moiety to Hamo the illegitimate son.

On the death of Hamo VI in 1342 in Gascony, Sir Oliver was abroad as Steward of Gascony and unable to claim the reversion of his moiety. John Fitton of

Fig. 3.6. **Halton Castle begun by Hugh Lupus, Earl of Chester and eventually the strong Lancaster base in north Cheshire.**

Ormerod

Bollington who was the husband of Cecily, one of Hamo's sisters who believed they had a claim to the estate took it over on their behalf and a wrangle ensued. The Black Prince as Earl of Chester intervened and found for Sir Oliver. Sir Oliver then possessed the moiety but died abroad shortly after without male issue. His co-heiresses were his daughters, one of whom was married to Sir Roger Lestrange of Knockin. In 1345, Henry Duke of Lancaster bought out the claimants and kept the reversion of the moiety until his death enfeoffing the estate to Lestrange and it was to remain in Lestrange's family for a century apart from one or two periods when it was in the hands of the Crown's Lancastrian barony of Halton, Fig. 3.6.

Meanwhile the now legitimised bastard Hamo, while still in Gascony, no doubt impecunious himself, disposed of his moiety which his step-aunts deemed to be theirs, enfeoffing various Cheshire knights, though he arranged for the properties to be bequeathed to the aunts when he died. This illegal disposal was, not unnaturally, contested by the aunts and their husbands and their eldest children, bastard Hamo's step-cousins. A complicated court case resulted and the matter was taken up by the Crown. A case was made out for the legitimacy of the bastard's claim to the lands, based on his father's wishes and mentioning how well Hamo had fought at Crecy in 1346 (Fig. 3.7) where the English longbowmen under the Black Prince, including a contingent from Cheshire, cut down the French cavalry, and at Poitiers in 1356, and that he got on well with his stepfather and they had fought together in earlier battles. Hamo was successful in the case and pardoned for his actions and given certain privileges such as freedom from some taxes and jury service. He then died without issue and once again the aunts tried to press their claim. By 1377 the moiety had become directly the property of the Crown, which was also overlord of the other moiety tenanted by the Lestranges. The tenures of various temporary tenants who had obtained burgage leases in Altrincham were respected and the burgages were allowed to continue to be handed down by those who owned them. The whole shambles of the succession was not completely sorted out for almost another hundred years in which the Lestrange family and the Crown were at times together, or singly, lords of the barony of Dunham and thus of Altrincham.

Fig. 3.7. **Battle of Crecy.**

Froissart

24

Chapter Four

ESTATE AND TOWNSHIP FROM 1290 TO THE MID-19TH CENTURY

DON BAYLISS

THE ESTATE AND ITS LANDLORDS

In 1290 the Barony contained the manors of Dunham Massey, Bidston, Kelsall, Moreton, Saghall, the Borough of Altrincham and Birkenhead. After the carve-up at the end of the Massey dynasty one half of the estate passed to the Lestrange family in 1355. The other moiety, including Altrincham, passed to the Black Prince, Earl of Chester, after the death of the bastard son of Hamo VI, and eventually to the Crown and the Lestranges. An example of a lease of Altrincham from this family in 1427 states (with words inserted in parentheses to assist clarification):

"the Mann(o)rs of Dunham Massey, Hale and Altrincham (Borough . . . were to be leased by) Sir Richard Lestrange, Lord of Knockyn (who then owned a moiety of the Barony of Dunham Massey) . . . to Sir Richard de Radcliffe and others (except that Lestrange was to keep) £8 18s 3d rent, and receive (also the annual payment) of a barbed arrow, a pair of gilt Spurs and a pair of gloves and (was also to keep to himself) the rents of 39 (tenants)".

The Radcliffe syndicate was to pay *"yearlie 100 marks"* (£66·66) for the lease of the manors. The effect on the people of Altrincham of such temporary landlords, as leases were granted and expired, can be imagined. They would be taxed as much as possible.

A witness to a similar lease in 1433 was Sir Robert del Bothe (Booth) later a Sheriff of Chester. In the same year he won a claim to Lestrange's moiety through the Venables family, being husband of Douce, whose grandmother had been one of Hamon VI's sisters. By 1494 Robert's son William Booth was in possession of the whole barony, apart from the Wirral lands. It is likely Dunham had had no permanent occupant for a century and a half from the mid-14th century, as the Booths continued to live at Wilmslow until recorded at Dunham by Leland after 1500.

The number of properties owned by the estate increased over the next century and the following details about the acquisition of Warrington have been provided by Mr. R. N. Dore. Sir George Booth considered purchasing Warrington manor in 1618 and an 'advice' of William Booth, Sir George's eldest son, to the Dunham stewards, told them how to 'lean' on the tenants to get them to advance several years' rents in order to provide the money for the Booths to clinch the purchase. There was a hint that their generous landlord might make things less comfortable in the future if they didn't. Mr. Dore comments: *"Despite its borough status, I have little doubt many of those living in or about Altrincham would have been mulcted"*. Warrington was finally acquired in 1626.

Sir George Booth junior and his son Henry were actively involved in national politics. Sir George raised a revolt almost singlehanded in 1659 to restore the monarchy after the Civil War (although he had fought for Parliament). The revolt failed but he was given a peerage when the Restoration came and was made the 1st Lord Delamer. Henry spent some time in the Tower because it was suspected he was a supporter of the Earl of Monmouth who attempted to seize the Crown. He got off (although tried by Judge Jeffreys) and on release became the 2nd Lord Delamer. In 1688 he was the first nobleman in the country to openly support William of Orange. He called out his tenants, including Altrincham men, on 16 November, 1688. In 1690 in recognition of his support for William he was made Earl of Warrington.

These political activities had cost money, new lands had not been acquired since Warrington and the estate was thought to be worth not much above £2,000 a year. It is estimated Henry left debts of £50,000 when he died. His son, George Booth, the 2nd Earl, 1694–1758, Fig. 4.1, decided he must, Mr. Dore wrily notes, *"eschew politics and devote himself to rebuilding the family fortunes. He started on this by marrying Mary Oldbury, heiress to a London merchant, whom he did not know!"*. He tightened up the administration of his estates and became wealthy enough to convert the Elizabethan mansion to its present fine structure and create Dunham Park as we know it today. During his lifetime the estate contained about 60 properties in Cheshire, Lancashire, Derbyshire, Leicestershire and Staffordshire. The estates then passed at the death of George into the hands of Harry Grey, the 4th Earl of Stamford by his marriage with Lady Mary Booth. The Grey family had 3 family seats and for the next 40 years the 4th and 5th Earls preferred their Leicestershire and Staffordshire residences to Dunham. In contrast the 6th Earl of Stamford (1765–1845) took a great interest in Altrincham's civic affairs, and made alterations to the Hall. He became Baron Delamer and Earl of Warrington in 1796. From the time of George Harry, his son, the 7th Earl (1827–83) the Greys, although living at Enville were noted for their civic responsibilities to Altrincham including establishing high standards for buildings erected on their lands and St. Margaret's was built in this period (Chapter Nine). The family was not in residence again

Fig. 4.1. **George Booth, 2nd Earl of Warrington, 1675 – 1758.**
Also the Booth's armorial bearings and those of the Greys who followed.

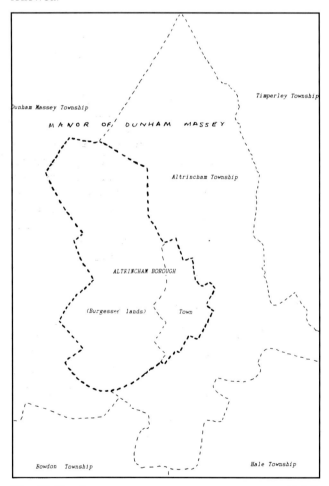

Fig. 4.2. **Court areas.** *D.G.B.*

1. Altrincham Borough. Inhabitants were responsible to the borough court.

2. Manor of Dunham Massey. Inhabitants of all the townships shown here (Including Altrincham Township outside the borough and others towards the Mersey) did suit and service at the Manor Court of Dunham Massey. Altrincham Borough and the Manor of Dunham Massey were two manors in the Barony of Dunham Masssey.

until the 9th Earl's return to Dunham in 1906. The 10th and last Earl died in 1976 and bequeathed the Dunham estates to the National Trust, not only the hall and park but properties over a wide area including parts of Altrincham and 24 farms.

LOCAL LAW, ORDER AND ADMINISTRATION

National Trust

From Anglo-Saxon times the landlords in this area had organised the tasks of law and government under a system of local courts called Halmotes which selected officials to carry out administrative tasks and also settled minor criminal and civil actions, major cases being dealt with at the Hundred Court or the County Court. Common verdicts in local courts included fines up to a maximum of 39s, restitution of stolen property, committal to a higher court, a number of hours in the stocks or a number of lashes by the whip.

The Halmote was still in existence in the Barony of Dunham Massey in the 14th century. No records are available to illustrate its proceedings. In the late mediaeval period it may have continued as the Court Leet. Court rolls show that from the 16th century such a court met once or twice a year. There was a court of this nature for the small townships of the Barony of Dunham Massey called the Barony Court; and similar courts for each of the large manors of the estate such as the Manor of Dunham Massey, the Manor of Ashton-under-Lyne and the Borough of Altrincham. Details of the Borough Court Leet can be found in Chapter Six. The areas under the jurisdiction of the courts of the Manor of Dunham Massey and Altrincham Borough (both in the Barony) can be seen in Fig. 4.2.

ALTRINCHAM AS A COURT CENTRE

In the 17th century Henry Booth, 2nd Lord Delamer, signalled the development of Altrincham as a local court centre by building a new courthouse in Altrincham market place in 1684. In the 18th century it was the location for three separate Court Leets—for the Barony of Dunham Massey, The Manor of Dunham Massey, and the Borough of Altrincham; also for the subsequent Court Barons for each of these three bodies which met every 3 weeks; and in the first half of the 18th century a Court of Record (a magistrates' court) was also held on a three-weekly basis. These brought regular trade to the town; no doubt the alehouses were busy on court days!

THE CHANGING NUMBERS AND CHARACTER OF THE POPULATION

For convenience the populations of both the borough and the outer township will be considered together, Fig. 4.3. In the borough the population probably rose as more traders were attracted to the town at the beginning of the 14th century. This was probably the high point of population and importance for the next 4 centuries. In the outer township a number of peasants and free men lived near the town.

A major catastrophe occurred between 1328 and 1377, when population fell perhaps to half or two thirds by fatalities due to onsets of bubonic plague, the worst of which, the Black Death, occurred in 1349. A Dunham rental names only 45 burgesses with their holdings and rents which may indeed record the tragic results of the Plague in that year. They held 120 burgages between them. The same rental also lists 21 tenants of agricultural lands, who were not called villeins but tenants-at-will. Eleven of these had the same names as some of the burgage-holders in the town, which shows that some burgesses did not object to being customary tenants to obtain more land. No doubt they had to do servile, manorial day-work on the lord's demesne as tenants-at-will while retaining free rights in the town. The 10 tenants-at-will who were not burgesses, would make the 'rural' township population about 40-50, at 4 or 5 persons per household.

There is no evidence of rural numbers immediately after the Plague. Sir Peter Leycester in his book of 1673 about Cheshire noted that by 1402 there were only *"about forty freeholders or charterers in Altrincham, the rest of the tenants of Altrincham, then not above eighteen in number, were tenants-at-will"*. The charterers were perhaps not all burgesses but freeholders holding land by individual charters, forerunners of yeomen. A document of 1414 mentions 110 burgesses and a rental of 1500 lists only 13 tenants-at-will. The impression of the figures suggests there was population decline by the end of the 15th century.

Leycester reported the number of 'charterers' had fallen to 20 families in 1673 but the number of tenants had risen to 65. In total 85 households seems a low total for the town. It is probable his 'charterers' were a special type of free tenant, rather than burgesses. The rural population seems to remain steady but low during the 16th century but began to rise during the 17th so that the number of Altrincham people on the estate lands by 1701-4, numbered 61 tenants and 47 freeholders. Several of the freeholders of some properties were also listed as tenants of other properties, and some appear to have been burgesses.

Fig 4.3 shows how small the population in the town and township together seems to have been until 1700 after which it 'took off' perhaps initiated by increased productivity arising from the excellent estate management of the 2nd Earl of Warrington. Population probably more than doubled by 1801 by which date it was 1,692. Numbers continued to rise and almost trebled again to 4,488 persons in 1851. The population was growing rapidly by natural causes and in-migration

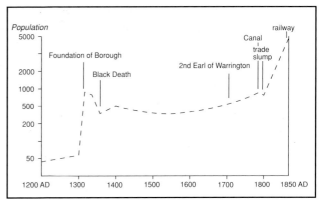

***Fig. 4.3.* Population graph**　　　　　　　　*D.G.B.*
Population number – – – –
Sources :– mediaeval: estimates; later: Leycester and Aiken; 19th Century: censuses.

before the coming of the railway in 1849 (Chapter Eight), a form of transport which was to attract even more people to live in the town.

THE CHANGING RURAL LAND-USE AND TENURES OF ALTRINCHAM TOWNSHIP OUTSIDE THE BOROUGH

After 1290 the free and customary agricultural tenants of that rural part of Altrincham Township in the Manor of Dunham Massey probably enclosed new fields from the woods and wastes, with the baron's permission, to replace openfields abstracted for the burgesses of the new borough. Enclosures were called 'hey' meaning 'clearing', such as Oonlant Hey Field, 'almond tree clearing', and Bradleyhey, 'broad lea clearing'. Intakes were made from poor land as shown by the names of Gorsey Field, Briery Field and Charlmoor Field shown on Fig. 4.4. These represented a progressive clearance of woodland and heath around the original core of openfields. A concentric pattern developed of peasant and burgesses' strip openfields near the town with enclosed patch-shaped arable fields, pastures and meadows, and common grazings farther out. The chief animals continued to be cattle and pigs. The arable land would be sown with wheat, barley, rye and beans. There was no clear 2- or 3-field system but a multiple-field system perhaps like that indicated by Dr. N. J. Higham at Tatton.

There were periods when men were strongly bound to the lord, *e.g.* in the land-hungry times of the 13th century when there was a large population willing to carry out onerous tasks as the lord's tenants-at-will to obtain land. When population was low in the 14th century, land left untenanted through the pestilence would be returned to the lord as demesne, but he would have to pay such high wages to get the land cultivated that he would be glad to lease it. This would lead to a period when there would be more free men and less requirement of feudal service.

With a lower population less arable land was required. A hamlet developed in Oldfield perhaps when part of the former openfield was taken out of communal production and enclosed. In 1348 John and Thomas de Oldefelde who took their name from this hamlet were named as holding burgages in the town and in 1616 part of Oldfield became the site of Oldfield Hall and its park.

Crofts were another type of privately-owned, or leased, enclosed land, such as the 'patches' on Dunham Lane (between Groby Road and Dunham Road) perhaps created out of the waste or a former openfield between the town and Dunham Park. Robin de Aldecroft took his name from his croft (and also held a burgage in 1348). Crofts were very suitable for animal farming and vegetable cultivation, being small and enclosed.

As well as farming, other activities would include bee-keeping, growing fruit trees, trapping birds, keeping doves and fishing. Pastimes included coursing, hawking (a hawk's eyrie was mentioned at Hale in Domesday Book), archery practice on the butts (land where the communally-owned plough turned), and gaming.

Men generally sought to become free and acquire land because this was the chief means of social betterment. Some peasants acquired leaseholds as copyhold tenants (*i.e.* they were given a copy of their lease from the manorial rolls). Wealthier free farmers acquired freeholds or long leases by charter and became yeomen farmers. However, when labour was cheap as in the 15th century or in poor times for agriculture, *e.g.* caused by bad weather in the 1580's, holdings of some small proprietors were bought out and these men reverted to becoming manorial tenants. When Leycester stated in 1669 there were about 20 charterers whereas the number of tenants had grown to 58, this again may have referred to fewer free farmers and more people dependent on the will of the landlord. Many tenancies-at-will involved day-work and other services for the

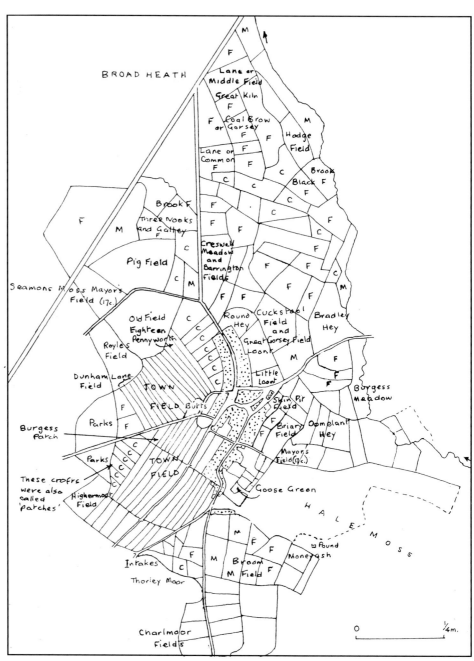

Fig. 4.4. **Possible field system of late-mediaeval times.**
F = (arable) field, with examples of names.
M = meadow.
C = croft.
Town area dotted.
It is not known if fields other than Town Fields and the fields called Loonts were in strips.
Source – tithe map with additions.

D.G.B.

lord as well as money rents, and an increased number of tenants implied a return to manorialism. Leycester amplified the parlous situation of freeholding at this time when he stated: *"Robert Parker's (holding) of Oldfield Hall, Gentm, is of greatest value, next to which is that of Wm Leycester of Hale Low, Gentm. Most of the rest are very small parcels not worth the reckoning up"*.

Following this, the end of the 17th century was a time when manorialism weakened and there were more freeholders. This was a time of enclosure of the commons used formerly for grazing and turbary. When men were allowed to carve out new holdings, an increase of freeholding and yeomanry occurred. The resulting increase in private land holding led to innumerable cases in the Altrincham courts for trespass, overstocking the shrinking area of commons with animals and taking too many turves from the reduced wastes. George Booth the 2nd Earl of Warrington made enclosures in 1699 and in that year was able to grant land to the mayor of Altrincham. It was all poor quality heath or mossland.

This particular phase of widespread freeholding was not to last long. The evidence of the Earl of Warrington's estate Survey of 1701 and Rental of 1704, transcribed by Mrs. Joyce Littler, suggest on the one hand this period was a turning point, leading to a better-run estate and an improvement in Altrincham's fortunes, but on the other hand to a return to manorial semi-feudalism as the Earl turned the screws on his tenants, as he strove to recoup the family's lost fortunes. The Earl owned three quarters of Altrincham, managed the estate himself and even wrote the rentals of 1709-43 in his own hand. The estate corn lands in Altrincham covered 151 (presumably Cheshire-) acres, half the area of the township. 61 tenants were named, of whom 42 must have been urban tenants, or cottagers, as they had less than 1 acre each. Tenants paid rent calculated on the number of 'bays' (timber-framed sections) of their buildings, Fig. 4.5, and the quantity of ground they farmed. The rents varied from 6d ($2\frac{1}{2}$p) a year to £2 17s 6d (£2·88) paid by George Birch for 36 acres of land opposite St. Margaret's; a George Birch was mayor of Altrincham in 1701.

There was a remarkable system of 'boons', perhaps vestiges of mediaeval services which had to be performed as well as paying rent. The range included

1701 Estate Survey
National Trust - Rylands

Mrs J. Littler

Fig. 4.5. **Bowdon farm building cruck**   *Pat Faulkner* **construction used in the area showing timber frames.** This would divide a building into bays.

requiring the tenant ('yearlie') to: provide a specified number of *'henns'* or capons, bring a number of *'loads of Coale to ye Mannor House'* (Dunham Hall), carry out agricultural services, and *'serve in the Warre'* and provide a *'muskett'* or *'halberd'* (only 13 years earlier the 2nd Lord Delamer had supported William of Orange's invasion). George Birch, though apparently a burgess had to supply 4 capons, 2 hens, take 1 load of coal and load 16 carts with turves, muck out for a day and be ready with a musket! There were also 47 freeholders paying chief-rents, no doubt many were town-dwellers, probably burgesses, and, like George Birch, also renters.

The land of copyhold tenants on their death was assessed for a duty called a heriot which was really a fee for the next tenant to acquire the land. One type of heriot was to give the 'Best B or G' *i.e.* the best beast or other valuable 'good' to the Earl. Another type of heriot was *'to plant 4 oaks and 2 ash trees until 100 are planted'*.

Guide books inform us that this Earl is the one we should thank for planting Dunham Park with trees. The probable truth is his tenants did much of the work through the device of the heriot and we should thank tenants of Altrincham (and other manors) for their labours, which, together with their other services, they must have found very irksome. They created a prospect which we enjoy today in its maturity, Fig. 4.6.

In the late 18th century, Altrincham lay in Bowdon parish and registers show two thirds of the workers were husbandmen, farmers or gardeners, and only one third tradesmen. Altrincham had become noted for market gardening, developed to satisfy the growing demand in industrial Manchester. Night soil from the town was used for manure and more came by barge from Manchester.

The schedule of the 1835 tithe map (excluding the 70 acres of built-up area) shows:

Arable	165 (statute) acres	(26%)
Meadow	308 (statute) acres	(49%)
Garden ground	46 (statute) acres	($7\frac{1}{2}$%)
Commonland	38 (statute) acres	(6%)

The market gardens were arranged in a pattern of square enclosures east of George Street and on some of the burgesses' strips. It is likely that half the built-up area, amounting to 35 acres would have also grown vegetables for market, bringing the area to about 13% of the total area of Altrincham. Dairying was now dominant and the area of arable had been halved since the early 18th century. From the late 18th century the proportion of people mainly concerned with agriculture had fallen from three fifths to one fifth. From the mid-19th century the town was to spread out and eventually engulf the whole of the rural township.

Fig. 4.6. **Dunham Massey Park.**

Chapter Five

THE BOROUGH FROM 1290 TO THE MID-19th CENTURY

DON BAYLISS

THE TOWN PLAN IN EARLY TIMES

The population of a few hundred in 1290 probably rose over the next few years as people were attracted to the town with its new buildings and trade. With probably only one farmstead on each burgage plot, the town had a spacious air.

During the 14th century, partly through plagues when population declined, a few burgages may have been abandoned and reverted to farmland. (Some were still empty in the late 18th century at the top end of Church Street). Where industrial activities developed some burgages lost their residential and food-producing function and became work yards.

When a concentration of population began to develop round Old Market Place a number of burgages were divided longitudinally. The division resulted in the street end of a half burgage being 24 feet, so two houses could be built where there had been one (see Fig. 2.2). Some shop fronts today are approximately of this size. Cottages, stores and workshops were built down the length of some burgages, resulting in more congested conditions.

MEDIAEVAL TOWN ACTIVITIES

The chief functions of the burgesses were to engage in trade and crafts and to farm. The weekly market would be heralded by a town-crier, opened by the mayor and constables and presided over by the lord's bailiff or steward whose duty it was to see all dues and court fines for market offences reached the baron. Disputes between traders would be settled at the Portmote Court. There would be stalls for basic foods, grocery and honey, meat, fish, metal wares, dairy products, drink, shoes, clothes and hose, leather, salt, pottery, cloth etc., which would be set out around a market cross. The fronts of burgage houses would also have been opened to show wares. At this time wine and furs were being imported and skins exported through Chester and no doubt would augment the wide range of local products for sale or exchange. At first the annual fair was held in the market place on 14, 15, 16 August, changed in 1319 to 24, 25 and 26 July. From the early 14th century there was a second fair on the 10, 11 and 12 November. The fairs were probably for trading in animals for local needs and also for the de Massey military campaigns. The dues from the fairs went into the baron's coffers. Miscreants at the fairs were summarily dealt with on the spot by the Court of Pye Powder (Chapter Six) and general trading arrangements were controlled by the town's merchant guild. The guild, the Halmote and the Portmote would meet in a courthouse in the market place. A rental of 1348/49, Fig 5.1, noted that a burgess must be prepared to become mayor or bailiff if elected. This is the first mention of the office of mayor which must have developed between AD1290 and 1348. The rental also includes people whose Christian names were 'Hamo' and others whose surnames were 'de Massey'. Fig 5.1 shows a 'Hamo le massy'; who he was is not known.

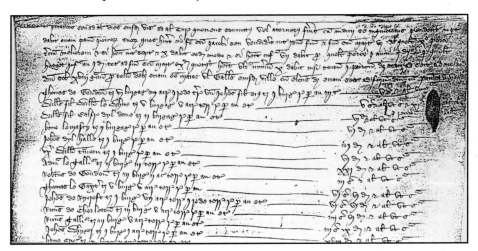

Fig. 5.1. **Part of a rental of 1348 listing 45 burgesses.**
The 4th entry (9th line) reads:
"Hamo le massy holds ii burgages at a rent per year of _____ vid (6 pence).

National Trust – Rylands

The agricultural pursuits of the burgesses continued. The rental distinguished between their burgages and their farmlands. In a preamble to the rental the burgesses were warned to make sure to pay their pannage (pig-grazing) dues at the Feast of St. James or in pannage times, even though they might be summoned for jury service 'at other courts', presumably the Hundred, Barony and County Courts. This calculation of dues was highly complex, related to the number and age of the pigs, and the impression is given that Altrincham was a prime source of pigs!

An iron-making 'bloomery' is known to have existed near Dunham in the 14th century and in 1405 there was a 'smethyburgage' or smithy in the town. A woollen cloth domestic industry was in existence in the later Middle Ages. Its existence is recorded in a court roll of 1503, quoted by Ormerod. This refers to *"three burgages of land, of which one was situated between the burgage of Edward Massey and the late Richard Chaddurton of Timpyrly called Flaxyorde and the two burgages called Tayntrcrofts in the same town"*. The two tentering crofts would have been covered with wooden frames on which wool cloth was stretched on tenterhooks and bleached. In the flax yard, linen fibre would be steeped and processed. The fact that all three burgages were together and there is no mention of houses suggests there was an area which had suffered population decline, and also that there was already a small industrial area in the town. This was perhaps on the east side where there was plenty of water for textile processing. Additionally in the town there would be tailors, curriers, stonemasons, wainwrights and wheelwrights, shoemakers, and other tradesmen and possibly a professional man or two such as a physician and lawyer. It is not known if separate guilds developed for some of these activities.

A burgage in the market place was more valuable, being on the spot for trade, than one in the (present) George Street area and a social and economic distinction probably emerged quite early between the commercial Higher Town and the less attractive more industrial locations in Lower Town.

Another duty for the townsmen was to provide a contingent for war. No doubt Altrincham men were archers for which Cheshire was famous. They took part in the Welsh, Scottish and Hundred Years War and other campaigns of the period. One of the fields outside the town, in the modern Groby Place area was called Short Butts where archery practice would take place. Sir Oliver de Ingham, tenant-in-chief of Altrincham, using Altrincham men, smashed a revolt against the Crown by Thomas, Earl of Lancaster at the Battle of Boroughbridge in 1322 . In later times Altrincham men mustered for the politico-military involvements of the Booths.

LANDHOLDING

Land holdings were not static. Burgage, messuage and field holdings were increased by more prosperous burgesses buying from others. The rental of 1348/49 shows 45 burgage-holders who between them held 120 burgages and 120 acres of land. Not all were resident burgesses. Only 14 had 1 burgage each, 31 held between 1 and 9 each. In 1290 a burgage was probably linked to one acre in the openfield but in 1348 this occurred in only 7 cases, *e.g.* Alicia fils Ball held 1 burgage and 1 acre. Several burgage-holders possessed no field acres, *e.g.* Hamo le Massy 2 burgages, no lands, Fig. 5.1; William le Carpenter, 3 burgages no lands.

During the chaotic period following the death of Hamon VI outsiders are listed as owning burgages. In 1361 Robert le Baxter from Warrington possessed some 'tenements' in the town. In 1423, Henry 'le Massy' of Dunham, had a huge holding. He held (i) 100 acres of land in Dunham and Altrincham of the King (who owned a moiety of Altrincham at this time); (ii) 3 acres in Whytemoor, and 4 other acres of Richard Lestrange (lord of the other moiety of Altrincham) 'by burgage'; (iii) 6 other burgages, and a parcel of land in 'Brondurthfyld'. People like Baxter, and Massey had probably moved into the town. In later centuries county gentry held many town properties, and representatives of the Breretons, Savages and others, knights and squires, were called as burgage-owners to do suit at the borough court. It is doubtful if they actually attended, preferring to pay their 'ession' or fine for absence.

The sequence of change in burgage holding is clear. i. at the outset most burgesses probably possessed 1 burgage and 1 acre in the fields; ii. there was subsequently accumulation of several burgages in a few residents' hands e.g. during the plague; iii finally wealthy external landlords bought properties as investments.

LIVING CONDITIONS

There were contrasts in housing conditions from the outset. Wealthy incoming traders would have built better houses than villeins who had been made up to burgesses. A handful of wealthy merchants may have built houses so large they filled the 48' frontage of a burgage, perhaps splendid town houses with elaborately carved wooden frames. Because of the ample width of a burgage plot in Altrincham it is likely most houses were built parallel to the street (in some towns with narrower plots, the gable end faced the street). Roofs were thatched, walls were wattle and daub and floors of better houses stone-flagged, otherwise earthen and covered with rushes. Few people could afford glass for windows and there were few chimneys. Smoke often found its way up through a hole in the thatch of the roof. Living conditions were primitive by modern standards. There were no sewers and liquid waste ran in channels down the middle of the streets. Upper Altrincham fared better than the lower part of the town into which the drainage ran. Solid human and animal waste accumulated in people's pits ('sloughs' or 'slutches') or in middens behind the houses or in heaps on the roads. Several noxious trades were carried on in the burgage plots. In some, urine was used for bleaching cloth and smiths had furnaces in others; leather curing was carried on in pits such as in Skin Pit Field (under the present railway near the Sports Centre) in Lower Town.

Historians generally agree that most urban populations were lower in 1500 than in 1300. This seems true of Altrincham. Just after 1500, with no doubt many of the original but now 200-year old houses still standing and some burgages empty, the place looked run down and the traveller Leland described the town as a *"pore thing with a mayre"* (*i.e.* it was in bad shape but had preserved its attribute of mayoralty). In the middle of the 16th century, in Tudor times, trade increased and there were improvements in the condition of life, which might have resulted in housing improvement. Smith in the late 1580's or early 1590's stated that the inhabitants of Cheshire had had a *"fire in the middle of the house against a hob of clay and their oxen under the same roof, but within these forty years it is altogether altered so they have builded chimneys and furnished other parts of their houses accordingly"*. This 'Great Rebuilding' went on into the 18th century.

TUDOR TIMES TO MID-19TH CENTURY

The Tudors protected the woollen cloth industry and this probably encouraged local trade. In the early 17th century flax production increased and there were numerous court cases prohibiting the cultivation of unauthorised quantities of flax and hemp. Marketing prospered and population grew slowly. Webb in his travels a few decades later than Smith, in 1621 noted Altrincham's *"fine little market"* in a town of *"no meaner government than the mayor of an ancient institution"*.

In the same year, 1621, a channel was cut from Hale Moss to bring water to drive a water-powered mill. George Birch, a freeholder and mayor in 1622, granted *"to Sir George Boothe for ever free liberty for a watercourse from Hale Mosse through a close called Little Poolefield to the Pecke Milne of Dunham"*. The use of the Pecke Mill is unknown. It was probably built for grinding corn but might also have doubled as a fulling mill for processing woollens. It was outside the borough on land of the Manor of Dunham Massey, Fig. 5.2, opposite Kennedy's on Grosvenor Road and was demolished before 1835.

During the Civil War the town was not disturbed except when Prince Rupert of the Rhine moved his army from Shrewsbury to York and stopped on the Downs. The middle 17th century does not appear to have been prosperous because in 1673 Leycester complained of the number of small cottages erected in the town with the permission of the lords at Dunham and referred contemptuously to Altrincham as a *"nest of beggars"*. This might have been partly true, but Leycester was a Royalist and was opposed to the politics of the Booths and used his writing to criticise the property of his adversaries. It is true that men without work and home roamed the area and terrorised the inhabitants, and the courts were full of cases of assault and battery. Many people were tried for harbouring vagrants, some of whom were probably aspiring yeomen fallen on hard times.

The rest of the century was more prosperous as dairy farming grew in importance. In 1684 Lord Delamer acknowledged this trend by building a buttermarket with courthouse over, in the market place near the market cross (Fig. 5.3). It is likely there had been a stone cross since AD1290 marking the centre of

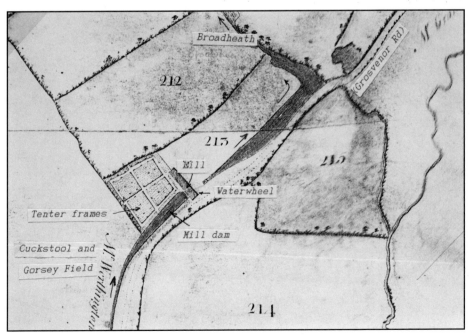

Fig. 5.2. Site of water powered mill of 1621 (approximately opposite Kennedy's) demolished before 1838.

National Trust – Rylands

Fig. 5.3. **Buttermarket with courtroom over and cross, Old Market Place.**

Trafford Leisure Services

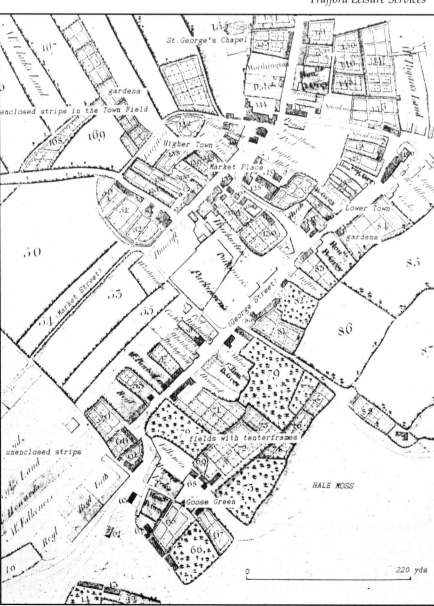

Fig. 5.4. **Estate map of the Earl of Stamford and Warrington, 1799.**

The Earl's properties are numbered (plots of land held by other landowners are not numbered). By this time some buildings had encroached on the market place.

National Trust – Rylands

trading activity. It symbolised the close relationships of all economic activity to the Christian way of life. Rents and other dues were paid on Saints' days and the agricultural year revolved round the church calendar. In the 18th century, records show that intending brides and grooms had to declare their wishes three times at Altrincham cross. It was therefore important to keep it in existence and the cross was rebuilt by the 2nd Earl of Warrington in 1730. A third fair for cattle sales, was granted in 1734. These three features, new buttermarket-courthouse, cross and fair, affirmed the change of emphasis from corn growing to dairying and the increasing importance of the town for its market, fairs and courts. Population grew steadily through the century.

An exciting occasion occurred in 1745 when a troop of the Pretender's kilted cavalry rode through the town as a feint to draw the Hanoverian forces westward. The ruse worked, allowing the Prince and the main Scottish army to proceed from Manchester to Derby via Stockport. Description of another colourful occasion was recorded by the young ex-Manchester Grammar Schoolboy, Thomas de Quincey in his 'Confessions of an English Opium Eater' when he described the genial scene of Altrincham market in 1814: *"Fruits and flowers were scattered about in profusion; even the stalls of the butchers from their brilliant cleanliness appeared attractive; and the bonny young women of Altrincham were all tripping about in caps and aprons coquettishly disposed"*.

Until the mid-18th century, houses had remained wood-framed buildings from mediaeval times with thatched roofs, and in the courts many people were fined for allowing their chimneys to get on fire. A new prosperity followed the opening of the Bridgewater Canal in 1765 and the success of textiles, particularly worsteds. Fast boats were used by a few wealthy commuters living in Altrincham and travelling to Manchester each day. Other new residents were concerned with operating the canal trade. The canal was used for the importation of slates (which prevented fire risk) and other constructional materials, and a second 'Great Rebuilding' of part of the town took place in the late 18th century. Wattle-and-daub walling in timber frames was replaced by brickwork within the same frames. Some wood-framed houses were given new shells of brick and with new windows were given a 'Georgian' appearance; there was also demolition and new building. Merchants, attorneys and other affluent people built fine houses in Higher Town. Fig. 5.4 shows that 5 houses were owned by the Hon. B. Grey. One on the east side of Church Street has an imposing rear shown in Fig. 5.5. The former houses at the north end of Market Street are particularly fine. The Stamford Estates Office of c.1780, Fig. 5.6, was originally the home of the Worthingtons, stewards to the Earls. Market Street is still a small 'professional' area today.

However, many thatched cottages remained the homes of poor people and the numbers of the poor and of vagrants continued to be a problem. Following the

Fig. 5.5. **Rear of a Georgian house owned by Hon. B. Gray in 1799.**   *D.G.B.*

Fig. 5.6. **Stamford Estates Office.**   *D.G.B.*

General Workhouse Act of 1723 a small workhouse was built in 1756 at Broadheath, forcing labour on the able-bodied poor.

The estate map for the Earl of Stamford drawn in 1799, part of which is reproduced in Fig. 5.4 shows he owned three quarters of the town and township property. Higher Town was more compact than in 1400 because the urban area had shrunk from the north towards Old Market Place, and some burgages which in earlier times would have had houses on, had been replaced by open crofts. St. George's Chapel was built in that year behind such an open croft and marked the northern edge of the built-up area. Higher Town stretched from St. George's to where the present town hall lies. At this point the Dunham Road joined High Street (now Market Street) by a junction at the Stamford Estates Office (the present course of Dunham Road was not cut through to Old Market Place until the early 1860's). Higher Town was separated from Lower Town by a steep hill called Hollow Bank (Kingsway).

Lower Town extended from the Malt Shovels area to cottages at Goose Green on the edge of Hale Moss. Houses, workshops and shops lined George Street. There were more cottages round a green on Pinfold Brow (Lloyd Street). Here, the town animal pound or pinfold was situated on the edge of Hale Moss. From St. George's Chapel across the fields to the north of the town were two small hamlets of Sandiway and Broadheath, the latter had developed since the 1760's. East of Broadheath bridge, a warehouse had been built on the north side of the Bridgewater Canal and on the south side are the remains of a boathouse of the period (now a tool-hire firm), built for the popular and frequent packet boats to Manchester and Runcorn; also the Packet House, a canal pub, and the (since rebuilt) Navigation Inn.

Gardens lay behind many houses and there were also rectangular enclosures along the east side of the town which were market gardens, flax yards or tenteryards. Most of the former burgesses' strips were hedged and most were in the Earl of Stamford's hands. A patch of unenclosed strips lay in part of Town Field south of Regent Road and these were privately-owned. There were a few villas and farms outside the town but the main place of residence for rich and poor, was still the town.

Altrincham was described in 1791 as *"the seat of a considerable manufactory in the worsted branch"*. This suggests there might have been a waterpowered mill, perhaps the one of 1621 adapted to machine spinning. Aiken in 1795 described a late-18th century flourishing domestic industry in jersey-combing, linens and woollens which had declined due to Irish competition. Leech, a late-19th century writer mentions that Altrincham had had a hundred handloom weavers in the early part of the century. At the same time town directories describe a subsequent phase when Altrincham had factory industries, perhaps two mills using steam power near the original waterpower site. Between 1813 and 1852 there was cotton and velvet manufacture, fustian cutting, worsted making, wool combing, woollen yarn making, bobbin-turning and corn milling. Only the corn mill remained in 1852. No traces remain today of Altrincham's early factory industry.

Following the Municipal Corporations Act of 1832 government inspectors visited towns and provided reports on their attributes. That for Altrincham was derogatory pointing out that it was *"a mere appendage to the barony"*, stressing its subservience to the Dunham landlords, and underestimating its degree of self-government by the Court Leet. There were now markets twice weekly and three fairs per year. In other activities the town was stated to be almost wholly agricultural except for some handloom weavers (the local factory work was not noted). The poorer class were *"principally employed in the cultivation of small plots of garden ground"*—highlighting the vegetable industry. The report finished on the sour note that there was a *"redundancy of beer shops and . . . deficiency of a local magistracy"*.

The Court Leet was now supported by the Vestry and Town's Meetings in maintaining law and order, administration and public health. Court cases indicated the insanitary conditions of life for the population which grew from 1,692 in 1801 to 4,488 in 1851. There was no organised sewerage system nor waste disposal. Animal and human excrement lay about in heaps called 'nuisances' in the courts. People were accused of not emptying their privies called 'necessary houses' and of piling their dung against the side of their neighbour's house so that it seeped indoors. Refuse was piled against the side of the public wells contaminating the supply. Conditions were the same in other urban areas and following the Public Health Act of 1848 inspectors were asked by towns to assess their problems. Sir Robert Rawlinson's observations on Altrincham are described in Chapters Six, Seven and Fourteen.

The main built-up area by 1835 consisted of three parts, Fig. 5.7; Higher Town, Lower Town and a separate

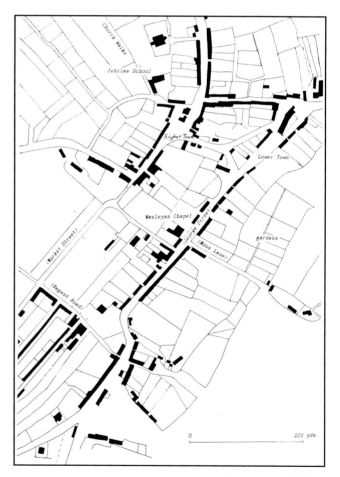

Chester Record Office

Fig. 5.7. **Tithe map of 1835 (part), with additions.**

Trafford Leisure Services

Fig. 5.8. **Old scene in 19th century Altrincham.**

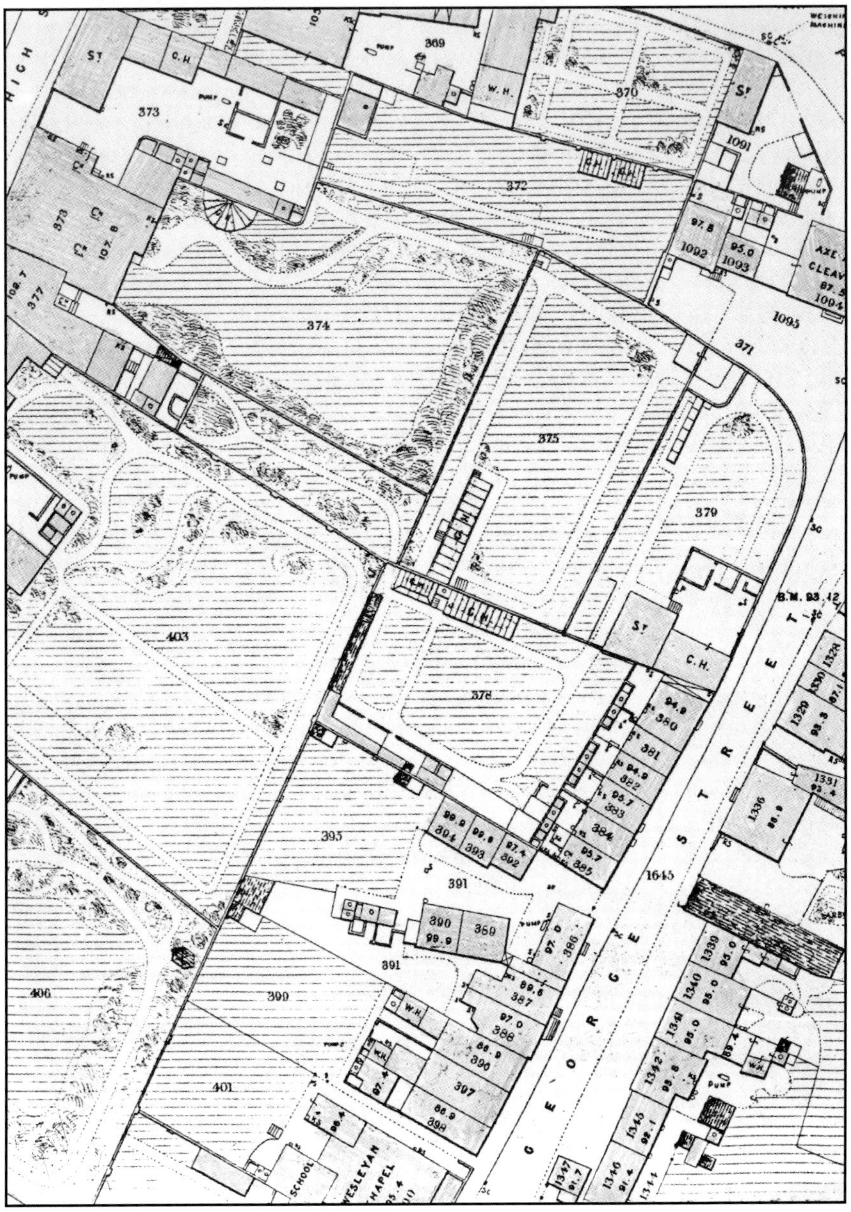

Fig. 5.9. **George Street, 1852. Top left, High Street (now Market Street).**

G.H. Glasshouse. Note the privies at the back of the houses. Plots around the Wesleyan Chapel (bottom centre) are now occupied by Marks and Spencer.

Source – Local Board Map of 1852

Trafford Leisure Services

area beyond Regent Road between The Downs and The Narrows. The last area was the southern part of the former Town Field which had been acquired by speculators and was not subject to the rigour of the Earl's design standards. It was laid out in parallel streets, with mainly working class terraces and cottages. By this date central Atrincham was not as built-up between the George and Dragon and Regent Road as it had been in mediaeval times as can be seen by comparing Fig. 5.7. with Fig. 2.3., though its population was probably twice as large.

By the 1850's the town's residential and commuting function was reflected in the start of the building of many large villas on the western part of the former Town Field. Many of the former burgages were still owned individually though sub-divided and densely occupied by tenants' cottages, workshops, stables and wash-houses. The buttermarket had been demolished which may have signified the end of two centuries of dairying as a prime function of the town. There were now eight inns or public houses including the Unicorn, Red Lion, Waggon and Horses and a temperance hotel.

The chief new landscape feature by mid-century was the railway built in 1849 in Lower Town. Altrincham Station lay where the Stockport Road crossed the line over a level-crossing, and the line had been extended to Bowdon Station next to Lloyd Street. There were still many old and thatched cottages in the town, as in Fig. 5.8. Following the complaints of lack of magistrates in 1832, a county court office in George Street had been established by 1852. Also on that street was an office of the gas company established in 1846, and a post office on Post Office Place. The Earl provided the first town hall in 1849 adjacent to the Unicorn. This building anticipated the change from seignorial control to a new form of more democratic local government in 1851. Fig. 5.9 gives an idea of the open nature of the central part of the town at this date.

In conclusion, one viewpoint is that of the inhabitants over the whole period 1290–mid-19th century. The burgesses had been given land and other perquisites making them freemen where they had previously been servile. They had some degree of self-government through their courts but not total control and there were many dues to pay and duties to perform. Though the main population in 1290 consisted of burgesses the town eventually developed a mixed society ranging from gentry to mendicants. Whereas there were many resident burgesses at the outset the number of these gradually diminished as burgages were

acquired by outsiders. The fall in the effective number of burgesses available to govern the town by the 19th century created a crisis. However, influential men were eventually invited to take part in local government through the device of the supportive 'Town's Meetings' and Vestry in the late 18th and early 19th centuries. By mid-19th century manorial government could not cope and central government stepped in to widen the franchise under an elected Board of Health.

Over the period the inhabitants must have been proud of the military exploits of the Masseys, the political forays of the Booths and the civic awareness of the Greys, but relationships with the landlords alternated between periods of irksome manorialism, when there was tight control from Dunham and other periods when there was more freedom. Manorial duties seem to have ended when the Grey family took over in the mid-18th century.

Another viewpoint was that of the landlords at Dunham who in early times regarded Altrincham only as a source of men for military service, as a source of animals and their by-products for military activities and as a source of rents, agricultural dues and duties, market dues and court fines. The monetary income was used by the Anglo-Norman lords for military adventures and to the benefit of ecclesiastical foundations in Cheshire and Normandy. When the continental connection ceased, income from the town contributed to the upkeep of the Booth family estate and residence, and the cost of political forays. In return, paternalism from Dunham preserved Altrincham's urban status, fostered local trade, and developed the borough as a court centre. In the middle 18th century the Greys supported the building of the Bridgewater Canal, and in the middle 19th, the railway. At this time, Dunham control provided a more orderly existence than in the burgeoning industrial towns elsewhere. Though administrative and financial control by Dunham came to an end in mid-19th century, the influence of the Earls of Stamford as major landowners continued through the following century, in the form of civic duties, in fostering the development of the Broadheath industrial area, as benefactors in providing parks and other land for the public to enjoy, and in regulating land-use. Today the National Trust carries on this last role. One result, through the Earls' stringent building standards, was the excellent design and appearance of many of Altrincham's buildings, now a valued element of Altrincham's heritage.

Chapter Six

THE COURT LEET

RON HIGGINBOTTOM

The Court Leet or Halmote was introduced by the Anglo-Saxons and was the method of carrying out local government, law and order. One was established in every substantial manor, and when the Normans conquered the land they allowed the system to continue. Before AD1290 Altrincham was probably beholden to the Halmote of the Manor of Dunham Massey. A Halmote Court in the Barony was mentioned in a document of 1361. The procedures of this local court were probably the same as those carried out by the Court Leet; (i) the Suit Roll and View of Frankpledge (elsewhere than in Cheshire, the View was a system of maintaining order by making men responsible for the behaviour of their neighbours; in Cheshire it was simply a roll call of all the inhabitants); (ii) the appointment of Court officers and selection of a jury (after AD1166 when the jury system started); and (iii) the holding of a Court session at which offenders were tried for minor civil and criminal cases.

In the Charter of 1290 the only court mentioned was the Portmote in which the burgesses were empowered to elect their own reeve or bailiff. The precise scope and nature of this court are unknown as no court rolls are available at present. From the 14th century the office of Mayor in Altrincham is known and a list of mayors from 1452 can be found in Appendix 2. It is possible that the Halmote or Court Leet took over the functions of the Portmote, though this is not certain. Court rolls of Altrincham's 16th century View of Frankpledge court and 17th century (and later) Court Leet are available and these show little difference of scope and ceremony between the two, suggesting the Borough court could have had different names at different times.

The Court Leet met once a year, in October, and at some periods again in April or May. It had at its disposal the selection of many officials necessary for the administration of the town's bye-laws. The court was held before the lord's steward accompanied by the mayor of the borough. The mayor whose office lasted a year was chosen by the lord's steward from 3 burgesses elected by the court. Another officer was the borough bailiff also chosen by the burgesses. He began the proceedings, summoned a jury, Fig. 6.1, and carried out the collection of any essions (fines for absence). The steward's office was salaried by the lord; in addition both he and the bailiff were entitled to a proportion of the fines collected, though the bulk went into the baronial coffers.

The burgesses were originally men who held land inside the borough on payment of a chief rent. Eventually, in the 19th century, as the number of traditional residential burgesses dwindled due to absentee landowners possessing land, 'men of substance' were accepted as 'burgesses'. Aldermen were burgesses who had served a term as mayor. Any of these men could be appointed to the unpaid offices needed to run the town, undertaking the tasks themselves or employing others to do the work for them.

It should be remembered that these men were, for the most part, men of little learning. We are reminded of this when we read that in 1709 Alderman John Higginson (Mayor in 1706) on the 20 October in a parish meeting at Bowdon Church *"made his mark . . . resembling the figure 4"*.

Some practices continued for a long time. In 1290 Hamon de Massey had instructed his burgesses to use the borough bakehouse and as late as 1696 the Court pronounced *"We do make an order that no-one do make a common practice to allow others to bake in his oven to the hindrance of the common bakehouse of the Town on pain (i.e. a fine) of sixpence"*.

Fig. 6.1. Part of the Court Leet 'Directions' issued in the 19th century.

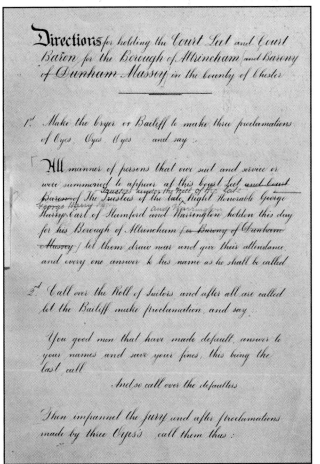

Trafford Leisure Services

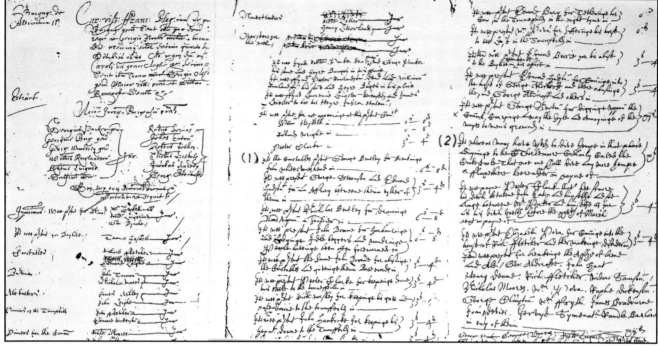

National Trust – Rylands

Fig. 6.2. **Extract from a court roll of the Borough View of Frankpledge (Court Leet) for 4 October, 1640.**

The top left section describes the court. Middle left – the 12 jurors. Bottom left – the officials selected: mayor (from three proposed), bailiff, constables, burleymen, aletasters, pinders of the Town fields, pinders of the commons, market lookers and overseers of the poor. The second and third columns detail the offenders and offences presented and their fines or sentences.

Extract (i)

Item, the Constables p'sent George Bentley for Breakinge John Whitestone's head, in (= a fine of)	6s 8d
Item, wee present George Steenton and Edward Hudson for an Affray betweene theim, eyther of theim	3s 4d
Item, wee p'sent Nicholas Bentley for Drawinge Blood upon a Souldier, in	6s 8d
Item, wee present John Broome for harbouringe and lodging Idle beggars and Wanderinge People havvinge been often forewarned	6s 8d

Extract (ii) – a bylaw:

Item, whereas many have (used?) to dibe hempe in that place adioninge to the Thorlemoore Comonly Caled the Cookstoole that noe one shall dibe any more hempe or fflaxe there hereafter in payne of	10s 0d

There are examples of the court taking action against the harbouring of inmates or vagrants. In 1709 four aldermen were ordered to *"go through the town and review what inmates are come into the town and give a full account to the Overseers"*. The poor of the town were in the care of these officers who were salaried and appointed by the Court, which in Altrincham had taken over the power of Bowdon Parish Vestry. Thus the poor were supervised and all those who received relief were 'badged' by order of the Court. It directed which children were to be put into apprenticeship and it also contracted for the feeding of the inmates of the workhouse in Broadheath.

Municipal services were provided such as the paving of some streets, the provision of public water pumps and in 1762, a fire engine.

By the close of the 18th century the Court Leet was the all-important civic government of a rapidly growing town. It was a tribunal of burgesses called regularly, or whenever the need arose, to discuss the problems of the town and attempt to resolve them.

COURT LEET OFFICERS

These were selected by the burgesses, approved by the lord's steward and appointed by the new mayor at Michaelmas:

Constables were to keep the peace, arrest offenders and present them for trial, Fig. 6.2. The Constables were on active duty until 1856 when the county created a police force.

Ale tasters tasted the ale brewed in the town, and the bread baked, to ensure they were good and wholesome, of correct measure or fair weight and "wholesome for men's bodies".

Market lookers controlled the market until December 1878 when the Local Board of Health bought from the Earl of Stamford the right to collect market tolls. The market lookers were the last of the Court Leet officers "on active service". They would test the weight of butter on sale to see that the long pound had been given (*i.e.* 18 ounces instead of the usual 16). Unfair trading would have been reported to the Court Leet.

The three cardinal sins in trading were:

(a) Forestalling *i.e.* obtaining the goods before they even reached the market, by buying them outside market hours or outside the market place.

(b) Regrating *i.e.* buying in bulk in order to sell retail.

(c) Engrossing *i.e.* 'cornering' the market.

All three offences were forbidden until as late as 1844.

Common lookers were responsible for the common and waste lands used by the townspeople. They guarded against the theft of soil or peat and illegal building. Common lands were not to be used by diseased animals. The common lookers made certain that no fishing or hunting took place without permission. In brief, the common lookers' duty was to ensure that nobody exceeded his rights in the use of common and waste lands.

Pump and well lookers had to see to the cleanliness of Altrincham's pumps and wells. They were supposed to ensure that the surroundings were free from refuse and litter.

Burleymen (or Bye-law men) enforced all byelaws throughout the town.

Cattle lookers (and Swine lookers) oversaw the selling of all animals. They had to see they were good enough to be sold and that they had not been stolen. They reported any diseased beasts found in the town whether they were cattle, swine, goats, sheep or horses.

Chimney lookers guarded against fire by attempting to prevent the deliberate firing of chimneys. Accidental firing was also punishable, as was the carrying of fire from one place to another. In an age of thatched roofs fire was a constant danger. The chimney lookers had to ensure that fuel was properly and safely stored.

Surveyors ensured that all roads, footpaths, bridges, hedges and fences were kept in a safe condition.

Scavengers had to report all offenders found depositing rubbish and other offensive matter in the streets of the town. *"If any person lay any wood, muck, carrion or the like in the streets or highway whereby the passage is straightened or persons otherwise annoyed by the filth and stench of it, this is a common nuisance and here enquirable and if any soil be cast into the street or highway and suffered to remain there, this offender forfeits 12 pence for every load."*

Overseers of the Poor dealt with all vagrants, beggars, and all who could give no good account of themselves, having no visible means of support. They carried out the law laid down in the Poor Law Relief Acts of 1597 and 1601.

Dog Muzzlers were responsible for muzzling all stray dogs (or dangerous dogs whether they had an owner or not). They had the right to destroy such animals if they wished.

Pounders or pinders 'impounded' all stray livestock in the town pound or pinfold on Pinfold Brow (Lloyd Street). It was important that cattle should not stray into unfenced open arable fields. The pounders were also empowered to impound goods and chattels on the orders of the Court Bailiffs.

Court Bailiffs enforced the court judgements, collected debts and saw that a felon's property was confiscated.

The Afferer collected all monies, including tolls and market fees.

Assessors valued property to assess rates and dues. *"You shall fairly and impartially ley and assess all leys, taxes, aids, impositions and assessments to be laid, taxed, imposed and assessed on the several inhabitants within this borough for the year ensuing or until others shall be sworn in your room"* (*i.e.* place).

Leather Sealers ensured that leather was properly tanned, of good quality and fit to sell.

The Town Crier (or Bellman) made all public announcements and led the Court in procession. His job was important in an age of illiteracy and when few people had a good timepiece. This can be gauged by the following extract: *"1st March, 1796, Meeting at the Court House. It has been found by experience to be inconvenient to hold the Town's Meetings without notice by the bellman-therefore, in future, it is ordered that notice by the bell shall be given"*. Not using the bell resulted in poor attendance.

BEATING THE BOUNDS

A Court Leet responsibility each year was to 'beat the bounds' of the township lands to re-affirm their precise location. The bounds in question are shown on the map in the Introduction to this book.

THE COURT'S JUDICIAL ROLE

Officials presented plaintiffs and defendants before a jury of 12 burgesses. This part of the proceedings was called a Court Baron and continued at 3 weekly intervals throughout the year.

EXAMPLES OF CASES

The Chimney Looker once had to present George Twyford, Mayor in 1750, and Edward Cook for failing to sweep their chimneys. Mr. Cook's chimney caught fire becoming a danger to his neighbours' property. They were fined 5s (25p) each.

The Dog Muzzler presented Alderman Creswell (Mayor in 1716) for failing to muzzle his dog. He was fined 6s 8d (33p) for the first offence, but for a further offence, 10s.

The Leather Sealers had John Worthington (Junior) fined 3s 4d and William Ellam of Lymm fined 6s 8d for *"selling leather insufficiently tanned"* (13s 4d = 1 mark; 6s 8d = ½ mark).

The Ale Taster brought a brewer to court for not brewing *"good and wholesome"* ale or beer. He was fined £1. Yet another alehouse keeper was said to have allowed a townsman to sit for 6 hours drinking with a stranger, when the limit was only 1 hour. He was fined 10s. The Ale Taster also had a Mr. Tipping, the baker, fined for giving short measure. Moreover Mr. Tipping had not made *"good, wholesome bread for man's body, of sweet corn and not corrupted"*. His punishment was twofold:

1. for giving short measure he was sentenced to be immersed in 'stercore' (*i.e.* stinking water) by the cucking (ducking) stool, in one of the town's ponds in Cuckstool Field, off the road to Stockport, probably the mill pool.

2. For using poor corn he was fined 10s.

There were also floggings. In 1847 William Walton the watchman remembered that early in the century three men were flogged in the Old Market Place for stealing clothes drying on a hedge in Sale. This could have been in April, 1801, when Thomas Owen was whipped in public. His friends tried to prevent it, damaging the horse mounting block at the Unicorn. It cost 15s to repair the damage.

In 1823 a man auctioned his wife for 1s 6d (7½p). Auctions like this were a punishment for infidelity. There was no divorce in those days for ordinary people, so the unfaithful wife was usually sold to her lover. The Court Leet seems to have turned a blind eye to this.

The scold's bridle (or branck) was used not only for scolds, but for bakers who gave short weight and other petty offenders—often after being immersed in stinking water on the cucking stool. John Mort (Mayor for 1858–59) saw this used in 1815.

The lock-up was attached to the court house built by the lord of the manor in 1684 in the market place. It was his personal property. A new one was built in 1838.

THE COURT OF PYE POWDER

This was a corruption of the Norman French 'pied poudré' *i.e.* the Court of Dusty Foot which was intended to deal with travellers and visitors to the town fairs. The court was to change its function over the years.

Traditionally, at the time of the fairs in July and November this court was held before the steward of the lord of the manor, the town's mayor and a jury of leaseholders. The mayor and steward walked round the fair and then proceeded to the Old Market Place, where the crier of the court read the proclamation to the public. This stated:

1. All had to keep the peace or face a severe fine of £5.

2. No buying, selling or exchanging could take place except in the open fair.

3. All goods over 4½d in value must carry the 'usual toll' or the goods would be forfeited.

4. Nobody should keep 'in or about' their houses any goods with the intention of denying the lord of the manor his toll. Failure to comply resulted in a fine of 6s 8d.

5. The public must carry no weapons. Any weapons found would be confiscated.

6. All rogues, vagabonds and unwelcome strangers were warned to depart or suffer the legal consequences.

The court dispensed justice on the spot to buyer and seller.

In time, this court became a tribunal for the presentation of tenants to the lord of the manor. It appeared to have lost its more commercial functions, becoming instead a court before which rack tenants were called to do 'suit and service'. For example, in the "Suit Roll for the Borough of Altrincham" for the years 1786–1792, there is a list of freeholders and subtenants, of the Earl of Stamford, beginning with the name of *"The Most Noble Francis—Duke of Bridgewater"* i.e. he held some land along the recently built canal.

By 1834, the ceremony of walking the fairs had been discontinued 'though within living memory'.

THE MAYOR'S LANDS

In 1699 the Right Hon. George Harry, Earl of Warrington, conveyed a certain *"parcel of waste land"* and in 1716 another parcel to the Mayor for a term of 5,000 years at an annual rent of 12d. The mayor on the last occasion was John Eccles, a shoemaker. The transaction was subject to certain conditions, but the presumed intention was to help to provide the mayor of the town with an income.

The Mayor's Lands as they came to be called comprised a total of 6 Cheshire acres, *i.e.* 13 English acres. They included Further Moss Mayor Field and Nearer Moss Mayor Field down Moss Lane, and Thorley Moor and Higher Thorley Moor between the Lower Downs and Ashley Road. There was also the Mayor's Field at Seamon's Moss.

In the Report of 1834, we are told that the lands were let by auction to the highest bidder and *"have produced as much as £70 a year"*. In fact, most of it was being spent on two Court Leet dinners a year and often there was no balance left to spend on the general good of the town. Eventually, in 1827, Lord Stamford's steward wrote to express His Lordship's displeasure and suggested that the Court Leet should only spend money on one dinner a year and use the balance to employ a deputy constable. The letter (Fig. 6.3) was

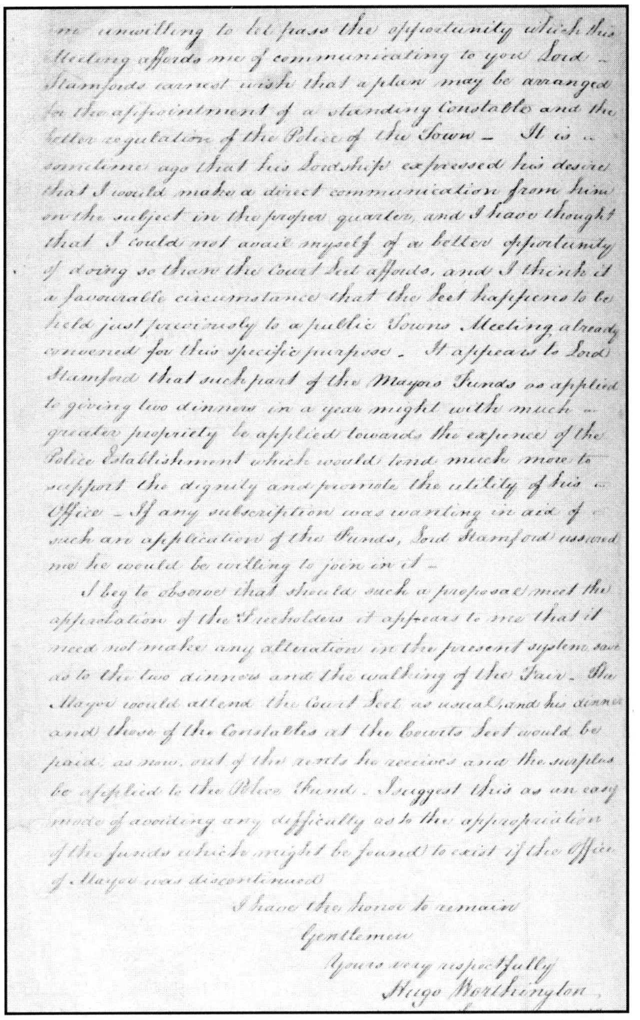

me unwilling to let pass the opportunity which this Meeting affords me of communicating to you Lord Stamfords earnest wish that a plan may be arranged for the appointment of a standing Constable and the better regulation of the Police of the Town – It is sometime ago that his Lordship expressed his desire that I would make a direct communication from him on the subject in the proper quarter, and I have thought that I could not avail myself of a better opportunity of doing so than the Court Leet affords, and I think it a favourable circumstance that the Leet happens to be held just previously to a public Towns Meeting already convened for this specific purpose. It appears to Lord Stamford that such part of the Mayors Funds as applied to giving two dinners in a year might with much greater propriety be applied towards the expence of the Police Establishment which would tend much more to support the dignity and promote the utility of his Office – If any subscription was wanting in aid of such an application of the Funds, Lord Stamford assured me he would be willing to join in it –

I beg to observe that should such a proposal meet the approbation of the Freeholders it appears to me that it need not make any alteration in the present system save as to the two dinners and the walking of the Fair. The Mayor would attend the Court Leet as usual, and his dinner and those of the Constables at the Courts Leet would be paid as now, out of the rents he receives and the surplus be applied to the Police Fund. I suggest this as an easy mode of avoiding any difficulty as to the appropriation of the funds which might be found to exist if the Office of Mayor was discontinued

I have the honor to remain
Gentlemen
Yours very respectfully
Hugo Worthington

Trafford Leisure Services.

Fig. 6.3. **A copy of a letter from Lord Stamford's Steward, April 1827.**

worded very politely, but its meaning was clear. The point was taken and a promise was made to be more responsible.

Mr. W. Devereux Nicholls (Mayor 1856–57) had the monies made into a Trust, with the consent of the lord of the manor and the Charity Commission, forming the "Mayor's Land Charity".

THE REPORT OF 1834 FOLLOWING THE MUNICIPAL REFORM ACT OF 1832

The contents of this Central Government report about Altrincham made it quite clear that the Court Leet, Select Vestry and other bodies such as the Town's Meeting, could not meet the demands of this time of dramatic change and growth.

The Report is scathing about the office of mayor, describing it as purely honorary. However, a short time spent looking through the Town's Meeting minute books will show that the mayor and his officers were very active in the life of the town and many had to carry out several roles. In a Town's Meeting of 17 April 1827 called by the constables to consider the appointment of a standing constable, the Chairman was Isaac Harrop (Mayor in 1835–36). Also present were eleven previous mayors.

These men were community leaders of wide experience, but there only seems to have been a few of them. In fact, the 1834 Report mentioned there were only 20–25 burgesses resident within the limits of the borough, though there were others who were non-resident. This may explain why the same names appeared repeatedly in different capacities.

The 1834 Report stated that the steward had to ensure that two Court Leet meetings were held each year. The steward was reported to receive no salary at this time but could keep all the fees and profits belonging to his office. The bailiff, appointed by the steward with the approval of the lord of the manor, summoned juries and collected fines. By courtesy, 1s 3d (6p) out of every fine could be kept by him.

The term given in the Report for making a new burgess is "The Mode of Becoming Free", already an archaic concept. The new burgess was expected to be a freeholder of land within the borough. He was known as a 'colt'. He would be recommended by the lord's steward as a fit person for the burgesses to summon. The jury invariably returned that person as a new burgess. If no freeholder could be found to "warn" (recruit) as a burgess, the return was kept blank for a year. The 'colt' gave a guinea (£1 1s) towards the cost of the Court Leet dinner and the lord of the manor gave £3. We are told that the dinner *"assisted in getting the jury together"*.

At the same time health problems in Altrincham led to a report in the Town's Minute Book (7 February, 1832) which complained about the large number of vagrants and lodging-house keepers who harboured them. The vagrants, it was reported *"have a tendency to bring infections and disorders into the townships and . . . it is extremely probable, if the spasmodic cholera should make its awful visitation in this district that they (the vagrants) would be the means of introducing it into the township whence it might spread . . . to the great injury of the inhabitants and the distruction of their best interest"*.

The detailed minutes of The Sanitary Committee for 25 July 1849 show that its members were aware of Altrincham's problems. These problems were really defined in Sir Robert Rawlinson's Report in July 1850. This report said that Altrincham was *"dirty, with pigs wandering at will"*, and water was polluted. The result was that the death rate in the town was higher than it should have been.

Consequently in 1851 a new method of local administration was formed, a Local Board of Health, which lasted until 1895 when the Urban District Council was formed. This in turn operated until 1937 when a Municipal Borough was created. The surprising thing is that the ancient Court Leet seemed to exist in apparent harmony alongside the other bodies. Altrincham U.D.C. until 1937 had a Chairman of the Council as well as a Mayor appointed by the Court Leet. After 1937 the

Altrincham Guardian

D.G.B.

R.G.H.

Fig. 6.5. (Above) Beating the Bounds
Lt. Col. Pollard who revived the Court Leet strikes the gound with a willow twig.

Fig. 6.6. (Top left) Leading the Altrincham Carnival procession 1989.

Fig. 6.7. (Left) Rewarding Community Service
Mr Norman Bickers, Headmaster of Altrincham Grammar School for Boys is presented with an award in recognition of his service to the community

R.G.H.
Fig. 6.4. The modern badge used by the Court Leet.

Court Leet was discontinued until it was revived in 1977, in modified form, to preserve old customs.

THE COURT LEET TODAY

It was the wish of the last Earl of Stamford that the Court Leet be revived for reasons of tradition. Colonel W. Leslie Pollard was appointed as Lord Stamford's steward. The first meeting was held in September 1977 in the Court Room in the old Town Hall adjoining the Unicorn. The Traditional Charges (or Duties) were read to the assembled company of townsfolk and the ceremony of appointing the officers (the Ale Taster etc.) was recreated as near as possible to the old pattern. A livery representing dress in mediaeval times was chosen. A coat-of-arms formerly used by the de Masseys was also selected, Fig. 6.4.

Each year since 1977, members have 'beaten the bounds' of the old borough limits—a circuit of over 8 miles, Fig. 6.5. This ceremony was to establish clearly Altrincham's boundaries when accurate maps were not available. Attractive cast aluminium plaques have been placed at some 14 points on the circuit to identify the perimeter. The bounds are beaten physically with a willow branch and a short ceremony is held at several points. Court sessions are held during the year at which the officers are appointed. The Court Leet leads Altrincham carnival each year, Fig. 6.6. Ale is solemnly tested periodically in public houses by the Ale Taster with members of the Court and a certificate awarded, attesting to the fact that the beer is 'fit for men's stomachs'. Very successful Fellowship Carol Services are organised each Christmas to which the Mayor of the Metropolitan Borough of Trafford is invited together with many of the municipal officers, councillors, police, firemen, members of many local voluntary organisations and Freemen from Chester, York, Newcastle and Coventry. The Court Leet is affiliated to the Freemen of England.

It is a busy organisation, trying to fulfil the new role given to it by Roger, the last Lord Stamford. The motto chosen by Trafford MBC is "Hold fast that which is good". Members of the modern Court Leet believe they are doing that in trying to maintain old customs and traditions and fostering community service, Fig. 6.7. In 1990 the Court co-ordinated arrangements for activities to celebrate the 700th anniversary of the granting of the town's borough charter.

Chapter Seven

LOCAL GOVERNMENT SINCE 1851

JOAN FRENCH

Altrincham has been fortunate in its administrators. They have generally been progressive and mindful of the public good. Evidence of this is in their choice of mottos 'A ma puissance' (To the best of my ability) for the Altrincham Court Leet, and, later, 'Altrincham en avant' (Altrincham leads the way) for Altrincham Municipal Borough, 1937–74. The first town hall was small and erected in 1849 next to the Unicorn Hotel. The present town hall is large and freestanding, built in Market Street in 1900 and opened in 1901 at a cost of £6,500. It was extended in 1930 and again, by the addition of St. Margaret's Institute, in the 1960's.

THE LOCAL BOARD OF HEALTH 1851–95

By mid-19th century local government was facing severe strain, especially in respect of health as houses had been erected without proper supervision, water supply or drainage. The Public Health Act of 1848 laid down that on the petition of one-tenth of the inhabitants who were rated to the relief of the poor, not being less than 30 persons they might ask for a Superintending Inspector to visit and make public inquiry as to the sewerage, drainage, supply of water and state of the burial grounds, paving, lighting and cleansing of the streets.

The request for an Inquiry was granted and in July Sir Robert Rawlinson attended at the Unicorn Hotel for this purpose. In his subsequent Report to the General Board of Health in 1851 it was stated that the borough was governed by constables and though a mayor was annually appointed he had no magisterial jurisdiction and his duties were chiefly opening the fairs and expending a yearly sum at his discretion. There was no local power to pave or cleanse the town except under the General Act for Watching and Lighting adopted in 1832 and no power with regard to new streets as the Act had extended only over a specified existing area. Reference was made to the greater facilities for transport by horse-bus, boats and the railway to Manchester and because more people might be expected to come to the town it was important that the inhabitants should possess a proper form of local government which had the power to pave the streets and provide sewerage.

Evidence was given to the Inquiry by Mr. Broadbent and Mr. Robinson, surgeons, who believed that the town might be improved by a system of public drainage since typhus prevailed more or less every year. They referred to the presence of sewage near the houses; the fact that pigs were often kept in the lower storeys; that larger drains were required and that paving of the streets would ease travel.

After consideration of the Report by the General Board of Health the following recommendations were made:–

1. That the Public Health Act, 1848 except Section 50 should be applied to the town and chapelry of Altrincham.

2. That the Local Board of Health to be elected under the said Public Health Act shall consist of 9 persons and that the entire number shall be elected for the whole of the said district, *i.e.* the township.

3. That one-third in the number of the said Local Board shall go out of office on the 25th day of March in each year subsequently to that in which the said first election takes place.

4. That every person at the time of his election as a member of the said Local Board shall be resident as in the said Public Health Act, 1848, and is required to be seised and possessed of real or personal estate or both to the value of not less than £1,000 or shall be so resident and rated to the relief of the poor in the said parish upon an annual value of not less than £25.

Fig. 7.1. **Local Board of Health Offices, High Street, now Market Street** *D. Rendell*

As a result of the recommendations Altrincham was given powers to set up a Local Board of Health in 1851 consisting of 9 elected members to be responsible for the repair and improvement of highways. The Board of Health offices were in Market Street (Fig. 7.1). An efficient drainage scheme was adopted, and ultimately in 1869 sewage was diverted from Timperley Brook to Woodcote Farm at Sinderland, which had been purchased for the purpose of building a sewerage works at a cost of £11,000.

In 1850 the widow of Jeremiah Lloyd of Oldfield Hall gave £300 towards the erection of a new hospital named Lloyd's Hospital on land on Pinfold Brow (later named Lloyd Street) given by the Earl of Stamford for this purpose. In 1877 the hospital was leased to the Local Board of Health.

In 1880 the Earl of Stamford gave 16 acres of land on Hale Moss to the town to create Stamford Park and the Borough took responsibility for this. This gift involved some problems because of the loss of commoning rights by the burgesses. The Earl also allowed free access for walking in both parks adjacent to Dunham Hall. In 1894 a cemetery in Hale Road was constructed by the Local Board at a cost of £9,189.

URBAN DISTRICT COUNCIL 1895–1937

Under the Local Government Act of 1894 the Urban District Council was constituted as successor to the Local Board of Health and came into being in 1895. It was provided with a new town hall, Fig. 7.2 Behind this, premises were provided for the fire brigade. An extension to the police station on Dunham Road was built for the county Police Force in 1903.

The town was divided into 5 wards each with 3 elected representatives. The council was presided over by a Chairman who was the First Citizen of the town. In addition Mayors continued to be elected by the Court Leet but the office was merely ceremonial and social and did not have any executive powers. This dual arrangement continued till 1936–7. The officers at the beginning and end of the period are shown below.

	Mayors of the Court Leet	Chairmen of the Council
1895	David Morrison	Councillor G. Bowen
1896	F.R.B. Lindsell	Councillor J. Newton, C.E.
ending with:–		
1936	William Waterhouse	Councillor J. Robinson
1937	Charter Mayor of the Municipal Borough, the Earl of Stamford	Councillor Edgar Webb

By 1895 legislation had permitted the improvement of highways, the provision of an adequate sewerage system, a police force and fire brigade. Public health was administered by a part-time Medical Officer of Health and Sanitary Inspectors who undertook the control of infectious diseases, protection of food supplies, supervision of slaughter-houses, markets and food establishments together with the supervision of housing conditions.

Altrincham Bridge (or Broadheath Bridge) had been originally commissioned by the Duke of Bridgewater in 1765 and had been widened in 1830 but needed widening again for tram operation in 1907, and it was widened again in 1935 and 1988.

Education in 1903 became the responsibility of the County Council and the local authority was represented on the area sub-committee. With increasing demand for leisure as working hours were gradually reduced there was an increase of provision funded by the rates. In 1901 the Jubilee Baths were built (demolished 1975), Fig. 7.3, and named to commemorate the Diamond

Trafford M.B.C.
Altrincham Regalia.

Fig. 7.2. Altrincham Town Hall in 1937.

Trafford Leisure Services

Fig. 7.3. **Jubilee Baths.**   *Trafford Leisure Services*

Fig. 7.4. **Stamford Hall.**   *Trafford Leisure Services*

Jubilee of Queen Victoria's reign. Parks and recreation grounds totalling some 111 acres were maintained. In 1917 Oldfield Hall and grounds were purchased by Sir John Leigh M.P. and given to Altrincham Urban District Council, creating John Leigh Park. Land was purchased by the council from the Earl of Stamford in 1929 to create St. Margaret's Rest Garden at the corner of Dunham Road and St. Margaret's Road. (In the early 1970's the Earl of Stamford paid for the war memorial cenotaph to be moved from its site on the highway into the present Rest Garden.) In memory of their father, John Beech Wilson who had been a trader in the town and actively engaged in philanthropic and educational interests, his two sons, Albert and John gave a small area of land at the corner of Hale Road and Ashley Road for the Wilson Memorial Garden. In 1934 an 18-hole public golf course of 98 acres with another 30 acres of open land around was established in the grounds of Timperley Old Hall, and in the same year an art gallery and museum were established in the library premises.

The following statistics show the population and rateable value 1891–1937:

Year	Population	Rateable Value £
1891	12,424	59,660
1901	16,831	88,311
1911	17,813	101,301
1921a	20,450	126,277
1931	21,356	149,436
1933	21,360	153,182
1937b	36,133	283,150

a. Following the Altrincham Extension Order, 1920, a new ward was added when parts of Dunham Massey and Carrington were brought within the boundary.

b. Timperley was added in 1936.

MUNICIPAL BOROUGH OF ALTRINCHAM 1937–74

In 1937, following a petition, King George VI granted a Charter of Incorporation to the Urban District Council creating a Municipal Borough. Timperley and part of Dunham Massey had been added to the area in consequence of the County Review of Districts and this took effect from 1 April 1936. This increased the population by 14,000 to 36,133 in 1937, adding an extra 1,638 acres and a rateable value of £85,000. The number of wards was increased to 8 with 24 councillors and 8 aldermen. One of the clauses of the charter stated that the Court Leet had unanimously assented to the fusion of the mayoralty of that body with the mayoralty of the Borough. A list of mayors from 1937 can be seen in Appendix 2. In the same year the Earl of Stamford donated a pool and landscaped surroundings, formerly known as Dean's Pond, on land north of Urban Road off Moss Lane, to be named King George V Pool. Mention should be made of the gift by Lt. Col. Charles E. Newton of 5 acres of land and the house at Watling Gate in 1936. In 1937 Mr. J. Buckley gave an additional 2 acres here, and Newton Park was created a children's playground.

The services at the old Altrincham library were extended with reference sections and a picture-lending service. In 1940 the old public hall was extended to seat 500 persons and renamed Stamford Hall, Fig. 7.4 (it was demolished in 1975). New baths were built on Oakfield Road, provision being made for a leisure centre to be built alongside later. Shaftesbury Avenue, (the Timperley by-pass), and Thorley Lane–Delahays Road, (the Wood Lane by-pass) were built. The flyover from Church Street via Woodlands Road to the Stockport Road was built, eliminating the use of the level-crossings. It was opened by the Rt. Hon. Anthony Barber, T.D., M.P. on 17 November, 1972. Atlantic Street, formerly a cul-de-sac was opened to the Bay Malton

Fig. 7.5. Altrincham Cemetery, Hale Road.   *D.G.B.*

Fig. 7.6. Altrincham Crematorium, Sinderland.   *D.G.B.*

Fig. 7.7. Broadheath Incinerator.   *D.G.B.*

Hotel and a trading estate built.

The parks and open spaces maintained by the Municipal Borough (some outside 'old' Altrincham) included: Stamford Park, John Leigh Park, Broadheath and Timperley recreation grounds, Newton Park and Watling Gate, King George V pool and King George VI Playing Fields, Pickering Lodge, Woodheys Clough, Coronation Field, Grange Estate, Oldfield Brow, St. Margaret's Rest Garden, the Wilson Memorial Garden, Spring Bank Park, Riddings Acre, Larkhill, Broomwood, 12 acres of allotments, and the 18-hole golf course.

CEMETERY AND CREMATORIUM

Reference has been made to the cemetery on Hale Road opened in November 1894, Fig. 7.5. On 1 July, 1946 the Altrincham, Bowdon, Hale and District Joint Cemetery Board was constituted by Order of the Minister of Health and from that date the administration of Altrincham Cemetery was transferred from the Municipal Borough to this Board.

A new crematorium, Fig. 7.6, was opened on 18 April 1959, situated in Whitehouse Lane, Dunham Massey. In May 1963 the Bishop of Chester consecrated a Lawn Cemetery adjoining.

REFUSE COLLECTION AND DISPOSAL

By 1937 the Council was operating an efficient method for the collection and disposal of domestic and trade refuse ensuring that rubbish was removed from every house in the district at least once a week. By 1949 refuse amounted to 14,700 tons annually.

In 1968 a Joint Committee was set up consisting of representatives of the Boroughs of Altrincham and Sale, the Urban Districts of Hale and Bowdon and Bucklow Rural District to consider the implementation of a joint incineration plant. Due to the need to operate the Clean Air Act, 1956 and the creation of Smoke Control areas, the Committee decided to opt for a joint plant.

Work commenced in March 1971 and the plant was completed in 1973 and opened by the Rt. Hon. Anthony Barber, T.D., M.P. on 2 February, 1973. It was handed over to the Greater Manchester Council in April 1974.

The plant, Fig. 7.7, was built on land off Sinderland Road, adjoining the Altrincham Sewage Treatment Works. In addition to crude domestic refuse the plant will burn limited amounts of industrial and trade refuse and approximately 24,000 gallons per day of raw primary and humus sewage sludge. Facilities were also provided at the plant for bulky waste reduction to enable pianos, trees, refrigerators, beds etc., to be broken down into small pieces so that they could be fed through the furnaces.

TOWN CENTRE REDEVELOPMENT

In 1968 a report was submitted to the Council by the County Planning Officer outlining a policy for the redevelopment, improvement and conservation of the town centre. It mentioned the necessity for further car parks, service roads and the pedestrianisation of the shopping areas. A scheme was approved and subsequently carried out by the Petros Development Co. Ltd., which involved the demolition of property in Stamford New Road, Stamford Street, Lower George Street, George Street and Kingsway including the original Jubilee Baths and the Stamford Hall. George Street was to be closed to vehicles and service roads were to be formed at the rear of shops in George Street and Stamford New Road. At the same time Goose Green was improved, Fig. 7.8, and restored into a quiet backwater with a few small shops. New firms, such as Rackhams, were brought into the town and with Marks & Spencers already established on George Street greatly enhanced the shopping potential. The Town Centre scheme has been particularly welcomed for the pedestrianisation of George Street enabling shoppers to move with ease, and for the removal of the large delivery vans into the service roads. It has however, had the effect of denuding Stamford New Road of numerous shops which have been replaced by banks, estate agents and insurance companies.

METROPOLITAN BOROUGH OF TRAFFORD 1974 ONWARDS

Under the provisions of the Local Government Act of 1972 the structure and functions of local government authorities in England and Wales were reorganised. Some 1,390 authorities were replaced by a 2-tier system of county councils and district councils and 6 new metropolitan counties were created. The number of authorities was reduced by two thirds.

Locally it had long been thought superfluous for there to be 3 authorities each within a mile of each other—Altrincham, Hale and Bowdon—and that it might have been beneficial for the areas to be amalgamated. Many services provided by Altrincham were already extensively used by the residents of Hale and Bowdon but despite numerous meetings over a period of 80 years, this had been repeatedly turned down.

Later thoughts were expressed about the desirability of the addition of Knutsford, Lymm and even Sale which would have taken the boundary up to the Mersey. The ultimate decision was taken by central government to extend the Altrincham area to include Stretford. This decision, which took Altrincham out of rural Cheshire into industrial Lancashire and made it part of Greater Manchester as part of Trafford Borough, was far from popular.

Altrincham Town Hall subsequently ceased to be the administrative centre for the Altrincham area and is now a sub-office of the main town hall of Trafford Metropolitan Borough Council situated at Stretford. Altrincham Town Hall only contains a cashier's office, building control office, area careers office, social service and housing offices.

The functions of Trafford Metropolitan Borough which affect Altrincham are carried out in various places. The main centre is at Trafford Town Hall, Stretford, with other departments at Sale Town Hall, Warbrick House (Sale), and at Altrincham Town Hall.

The formerly large Altrincham Municipal Borough area now contains Altrincham, Broadheath, Timperley and Village Wards, and is represented by 12 councillors, whereas as a Municipal Borough Altrincham had 32 councillors of its own. 'Ancient' Altrincham is represented by only 3 councillors out of 63 in Trafford Metropolitan Borough.

Some recent schemes carried out by Trafford Metropolitan Borough in Altrincham are as follows:

There have been sewer works on Manchester Road and Wellington Road in 1984 and Peter Street in 1986, and a new sewer outfall at Seamons Moss in 1984. A new traffic scheme was formulated in 1984–86 ready for the re-development of the Denmark Street area. Road traffic along Peter Street ended in 1986. Traffic between Shaw's Road and Cross Street was ended in 1989, completing the pedestrianisation of George Street. A roundabout at the junction of Hale Road and Ashley Road in 1989, which admittedly has taken part of the Wilson Memorial Garden, has nevertheless been a great improvement for traffic.

The Broadheath and Sinderland Local Plan of 1984 proposed the building of 1,130 houses and flats, housing improvement of older property near the ice-rink, encouragement of light industry and warehousing, better roads and footpaths, landscaping,

Fig. 7.8. **Goose Green overshadowed by the Graftons office block.**   *D.G.B.*

49

Fig. 7.9. **Play area elephant in Stamford Park.**

D.G.B.

Fig. 7.10 **Manor Road, Housing Action Area.**

D.G.B.

Fig. 7.11 **White Moss area housing,**

D.G.B.

recreation spaces, shops, a pub and a community centre. The Timperley Brook Plan included many schemes of environmental improvement such as tree-planting in the King George V area and surrounding open spaces. Recent planning policies have led to the building of large office blocks in north Altrincham, such as Tabley Court and Valley Court, 1984. These have changed the character of former residential and shopping areas. Acceptance of many proposals for flats and residential homes has raised protests about extra traffic generation, and also change of the townscape when impressive Victorian villas are demolished.

An environmental improvement scheme has been undertaken on the west side of Old Market Place to include the erection of a replica market cross. This scheme has replaced a parking plot. The recent Stag industrial estate at Broadheath and the Oakfield estate have been successes with every unit let. A scheme of the G.M. Waste Disposal Authority for a second incinerator for clinical waste at Broadheath was still under discussion after a great deal of local concern about health dangers from the emission. Plans for the new town centre development east of the railway were

Altrincham Municipal Borough

Trafford Metropolitan Borough

Chief Executive W. Allen Lewis, 1987 –

received from five developers in 1988. By 1991 only one developer remained interested.

In 1984 Stamford Park facilities for youngsters were made more attractive by provision of brightly-coloured full-size animals such as a white elephant with internal slide, provided by Marks & Spencer (Fig. 7.9). Playing field facilities for football have been improved *e.g.* at King George VI field and a new pavilion at the golf club. In 1986 a substantial grant was given for repairs to St. Margaret's Church and in 1987 £150,000 was spent on Albert Place Day Centre for the mentally handicapped, providing 20 places with bathing and toilet facilities. A new tourism office was established next to the library in the same year.

In 1982 a large-scale General Improvement Area scheme for 100 houses started in Oakfield Street and this was followed in 1983 by Housing Action Area work starting on 300 houses in the Manor Road area (Fig.7.10). The houses now look vastly better. The whole of the west side of Manor Road is under Compulsory Purchase Order for demolition for the new town development scheme. York Street back-yards and front walls have been rebuilt and 54 new flats for old people on Manor Road also look very attractive. There have been modernisation schemes at Oldfield Brow in 1984–85 and at elderly people's homes on Seamon's Moss Road. A scheme at White Moss for 121 excellent brick council homes with gas central heating and fitted kitchens is almost complete, Fig. 7.11.

Trafford also distributes each year over £60,000 to societies and worthy causes. Many in Altrincham benefit in this way and local groups also receive disbursements from Trafford Lottery. There is generally an increasing co-operation between the authority and the populace and this is welcomed.

Chapter Eight

POPULATION GROWTH AND CHARACTER

ADAM DABER

During the 19th century Altrincham experienced a period of sustained growth which built upon that of the previous century. Table 1 shows that the town's population nearly trebled between 1801 and 1851, doubled in the period between 1851 and 1871, and doubled again by 1901. In the early years of the 19th century, Altrincham's main function was as an agricultural market town, selling its produce to Manchester, although a few small factories had appeared, and the town profited from being on the canal and turnpike routes to the metropolis. The middle years of the 19th century were to witness a transformation when middle-class people, with a desire to distance their residences from their workplaces in the city, were able to do this, following the opening of the railway in 1849. The scale upon which this occurred made Altrincham one of the pioneer commuting suburbs of Victorian Britain, with decennial population increases of 32% between 1841 and 1851, and 48% between 1851 and 1861. The remainder of the century continued to be marked by growth but of a more variable scale. In the 20th century growth has been by a combination of 'artificial' increase by boundary changes (which brought in population formerly outside Altrincham) and by natural change and in-migration. For example, 14,000 were added in 1936 by enlarging the town's boundaries to include Timperley. Altrincham reached a population high of 41,122 in 1961.

The high growth rates between 1841 and 1871 seem to the writer to be of crucial significance to the history of Altrincham because they led to a fundamental transformation in the later character of the population

TABLE 1   GROWTH OF POPULATION

Year	Population	Decennial Increase (Decrease)	% Increase (Decrease)
1750	c. 1,000		
1772	1,029		
1801	1,692		
1811	2,032	340	20.09
1821	2,302	270	13.29
1831	2,708	406	17.64
1841	3,399	691	25.52
1851	4,488	1,089	32.04
1861	6,628	2,140	47.68
1871	8,478	1,850	27.91
1881	11,249	2,771	32.68
1891	12,424	1,175	10.45
1901	16,831	4,407	35.47
1911	19,092	2,261	13.43
1921	a) 20,450 b) 25,513	a) 1,358 b) 6,421	a) 7.11 b) 33.63
1931	a) 21,356 b) 29,353	a) 906 b) 3,840	a) 4.43 b) 15.05
1951	39,789	10,436 (* 20 years)	35.55
1961	41,122	1,333	3.35
1971	40,787	(–335)	(–0.81)
1981	39,650	(–1,137)	(–2.79)
1987	40,070	420 (6 years)	1.06
1990	c. 41,000		

In 1920 and again in 1936, the census boundaries for Altrincham were increased.
a) represents the enumeration at the time of the census.
b) represents the adjusted figure taking into account the changes.
The increase for 1951 is derived from the 1931 figures. * There was no census in 1941.
Sources – 1750 and 1772 from the Public Health Act – Report to the General Board of Health, 1851.
All subsequent data from census reports and enumerators' books.

and this period will be examined in greater detail in the following pages.

It was only from the end of the 18th century that writers began to look upon the effects of the growth of industrial Manchester as anything other than a fine example of an expanding and increasingly industrial town, and to comment upon its noise and filth and the effect these had on the health of its inhabitants. At the end of the 18th century all social classes lived together in the city but as environmental conditions deteriorated the wealthier professionals and merchants began moving out to better suburbs in Manchester. However, as Thompson explains in his book on suburbia *"there were simply not enough comfortably-off middle class families in Manchester to populate an exclusive residential district as distinct from the occasional square or crescent, or individual mansions scattered in the surrounding country"*.

This initial outward movement was on a small scale, and commuting occurred by private carriage, but it gained momentum in the city from the early 1830's when the horse omnibus began serving the suburbs within four miles of the city centre, enabling outmigration by lower middle-class traders, school teachers, clerks and the like. Once the omnibus had opened up the inner suburbs to the less wealthy middle-classes (social class III), the appeal of these areas to the social elite was lost and they sought residence elsewhere in order to distance themselves from their social inferiors. The Altrincham area became a location for their settlement as its attractions on health grounds had been known prior to the turn of the century. Discussing the presence of the turnpike roads and the Duke of Bridgewater's canal, on which a small commuter traffic to the city had already begun, R. N. Dore states *"this comparatively plentiful transport is the probable explanation for the undoubted fact that something very like commuting did exist on a minor scale before the coming of the railway"*. The initial incomers to Altrincham were those who had made enormous wealth in the Manchester commercial world (social class I). It is probable that this movement had begun as early as the close of the 18th century and once underway, it became self-sustaining as gradually more and more people had the wealth and desire to move from the city and its inner suburbs.

Ormerod, the Cheshire historian writing in 1819, noted that *"the town of Altrincham is considerably increased of late years in extent in consequence of the vicinity of the Duke of Bridgewater's canal and the short distance from Manchester. It contains many houses of very respectable appearance and has a general air of neatness and cleanliness"*. By 1834, Pigot's Directory notes the existence of *"the Navigation Inn and Packet House, where passengers receive every accommodation while waiting for the packets"* to Manchester. An examination of the directories reveals that in 1834 Altrincham had only 4 merchants and/or manufacturers, rising to 8 in 1848. By 1860 the number had risen to 28, a clear indication not only of the town's increasing social status but of the facilities which made commuting possible. In 1860 White's Directory comments upon the increased prosperity the town had

enjoyed in the previous 20 years *"by causing numbers of merchants and manufacturers of Manchester to fix their abode in this pleasant and salubrious locality"*.

Proof that these newcomers were wealthy can be seen in the reference to their dwellings, and this was reinforced by the exacting building conditions imposed by the Earl of Stamford and Warrington, the principal landowner. From the 1840's he allowed areas of his estate to be built on, the purchaser being obliged to fulfil extensive and, for the time, advanced conditions, designed to maintain the prestige of the area. Demand was such that, by the late 1870's, little estate land was left for further development, a result of the impact of the railway. The Directors of the Manchester South Junction and Altrincham Railway, uniquely for the time, promoted the line for commuter traffic from its inception, providing a great impetus for suburban development. The Earl insisted upon every home being insured against loss or damage by fire, and that the properties should be well maintained. *"Sufficient and proper drains, sewers and watercourses"* must be laid and maintained at the owner's expense. Building materials should be of good quality and plots should be paved as appropriate. Certain trades were also prohibited on the estate, although generally the conditions were less stringent in Altrincham than in Bowdon. Despite the cost involved this did not worry the purchasers because such conditions guaranteed the social exclusivity of the neighbourhood, keeping it beyond the means of the less affluent.

In the early 1840's horse omnibus services and canal passenger boats were serving Altrincham, and the railway did so by the end of that decade. By the middle of the 19th century a large but less affluent middle-class group (social classes II and III) could also afford to distance their homes from their work in the city leading to a substantial period of growth for Altrincham. However, a consequence of this was the out-migration from Altrincham of the former socially elite in-migrants choosing the exclusivity which their wealth made possible by establishing residences farther afield in townships such as Bowdon. Evidence of their brief period of stay can be found in some of the fine domiciles built in Altrincham in the form of Georgian and early Victorian period town houses and villas.

By the time the railway opened in 1849 Altrincham's population had already reached a point where its growth was self-sustaining. It can be said that the subsequent transport development of the mid-19th century merely enabled suburbs such as Altrincham to grow more rapidly than before, but had not actually created them.

ALTRINCHAM BETWEEN 1841 AND 1871

A detailed study has been made of the changes in the character of the population between 1841 and 1871. Information has been obtained from the local census enumerators' books in which data was collected for every resident and any visitors on the night of the census. As it was not possible to study the whole population, which in 1841 was 3,399 and in 1871 was 8,478, a sample group was studied of 104 families in 1841 rising to 211 in 1871, selected from across the town to give a representative cross-section. The characteristics examined were social class, family size, marital status, non-immediate family living with a household, and employment of servants.

SOCIAL CLASS

People were classified according to Victorian perceptions of their occupations, with a 5-tier model being adopted:

Upper class (social class I):
    landed proprietor, gentleman, J.P., annuitant.
Upper middle-class (social class II):
    attorney, merchant, surgeon.
Lower middle-class (social class III):
    clerk, innkeeper, schoolmaster/mistress.
Upper working class (social class IV):
    blacksmith, police sergeant, butler, skilled worker.
Lower working class (social class V):
    labourer, servant, laundress.

Fig. 8.1 shows that between 1841 and 1871 the proportion of class I residents in Altrincham fell from 25% to 2%. This was due to the out-migration of members of the upper class to townships such as Bowdon. Class II percentages remained fairly stable throughout the period. Class III and V increased slightly whereas class IV rose to a peak in 1851 and then declined. The general pattern was a decline in the

proportion of upper class people and a rise in that of the lower classes.

FAMILY SIZE

During the period 1841 to 1871, the average family size (parents and children) for all classes was 3·36 in 1841, 2·74 in 1851, 3·10 in 1861 and 3·07 in 1871. This is surprisingly low but, of course, conceals variations from single-person households to those with large families. Table 2, p.57, shows that family size for class I households was generally smaller than that of the other groups and declined further through the period. Class II family size was variable, but for the other classes was fairly constant.

MARITAL STATUS

Returning to the question of why social class I families were so much smaller than those of classes II to V, Fig. 8.2 shows that class I stands out from the rest because of the low percentage of married heads and high percentage of single persons, with the exception of 1871 when the widowed comprised the largest percentage group. For this class, marriage became an increasingly rare phenomenon. From 1841 to 1861, the percentage of single people outnumbered the combined percentage of the married and widowed, which did not rise above 37% of the total. Of the remaining classes, only rarely did the number of married heads fall below 60%. The next lowest proportion of married people was in class III. For whatever reason, being single was not a popular state among classes II to V, particularly so for class V. In all probability, survival at the lowest

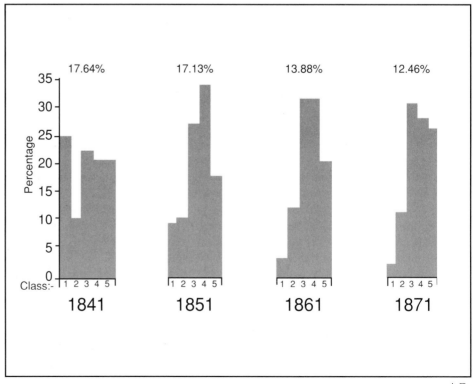

Fig. 8.1. **Sample of size of households by social class of head of household.**

A.D.

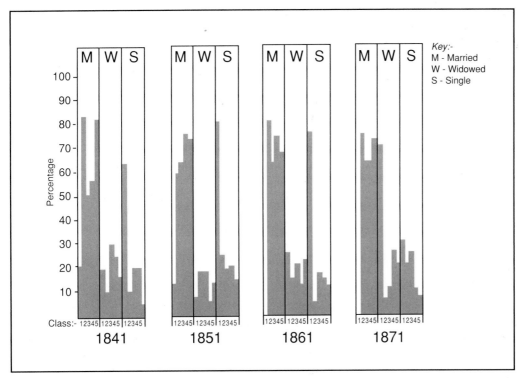

Fig. 8.2. **Marital status by social class of head of household.**   *A.D.*

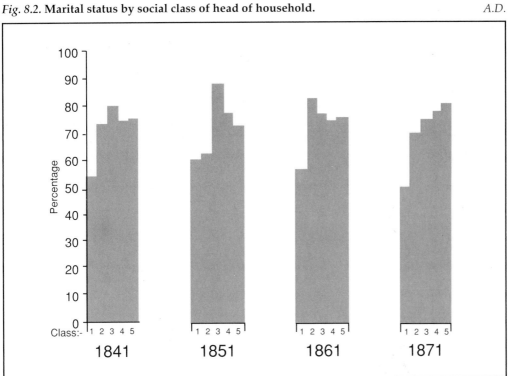

Fig. 8.3. **Incidence of kin living with a household by social class of head of household.**   *A.D.*

level of subsistence required more than one wage-earner per household, thus making it an economic necessity for the lowest class to marry.

NON-IMMEDIATE FAMILY LIVING IN A HOUSEHOLD

The incidence of this (kin co-residence) by social class is shown in Fig. 8.3, a mean figure for each year showing 71% to 73% of all households containing such relatives. In all cases class I households were considerably less likely to contain distant family than classes II to V, suggesting that they alone had the financial means to remain independent of family and to use servants to perform household duties. Clearly for so many households in classes II to V to contain kin the benefits must have outweighed the disadvantages, whether it be another wage coming into the household or help with domestic chores.

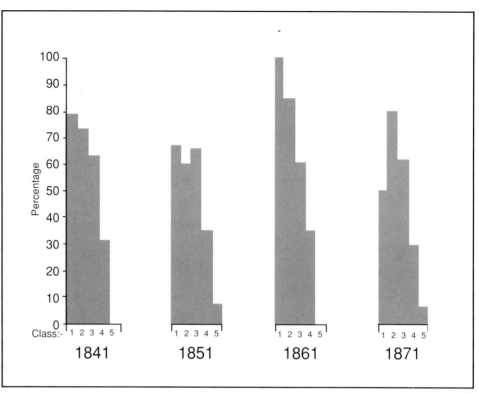

Fig. 8.4. **Distribution of domestic servants by social class of head of household.**

A.D.

SERVANTS

Social class I households, with fewer married heads, children and non-immediate family living with them, had a greater need for domestic servants than other classes, Fig. 8.4, but by 1871 employed fewer in total number than other classes due to the shrinking number of households in this class. Of classes II to V, although class II employed the greatest percentage of servants, class III employed the greatest number and included a majority of households containing four or more domestics. The majority of class III households employing servants were in the service industries and the servants were likely to have been assistants in shops or trades, and thus were different from the servants employed by the socially superior classes.

TWO CONTRASTING AREAS

Tables 3 and 4 show the development of a 'respectable' area, The Downs, contrasted with a 'working class area', Goose Green, over the period. In household size they were similar, but in social composition quite different. Numbers in the family in The Downs fell from 3·0 to 2·7 between 1841 and 1871, with a low point of 2·1 in 1851, whereas in Goose Green the figures steadily increased from 3·2 to 4·5. Generally, other members of the households consisted of servants and kin in The Downs, but only kin in Goose Green. Whereas The Downs was transformed from a rural area into a street of smart terrace- and villa residences for commuters, Goose Green retained its cottage-style appearance.

LATER POPULATION CHANGES

The population of the town doubled between 1871 and 1901 to 16,831. The development of a larger railway system, gas and electric power, coupled with the presence of the canal for transporting coal led to the growth of Broadheath as an industrial area (Chapter Nineteen) and to a large associated labour force. Similarly the improved transport facilities of the 20th century, trams, electric trains, buses and cars enabled more in-migration to take place and growth to continue to a greater figure though at a lesser rate than that in the mid-19th century. The population doubled in the 50 years from 1911 to 1961, growing both by natural change and in-migration. One stimulus was the provision of local authority housing in the inter-war and subsequent period to house some of the overspill population of Manchester and another was the building of private homes. Eventually Altrincham became largely built-up with little room for any new estates. Population grew to a maximum of 41,122 in 1961 after which it began to decrease. In fact, in the period after 1961 it seemed the town's growth had drawn to an end. Population declined between 1961 and 1971 to 40,707 and to 39,650 in 1981. During these decades while there was still a slight surplus of births over deaths, net out-migration was sufficient to cause a loss of population. It could be that two factors have recently been operating: a low birth rate and the increasing impact of high car ownership enabling people to move farther out into Cheshire and commute to Manchester and other workplaces over much greater distances.

TABLE 2 MEAN FAMILY SIZE
Mean Family Size by Social Class of Household Head

Year	I	II	III	IV	V	Household Sample Size
1841	2.04	4.00	3.63	3.62	3.52	104
1851	1.82	1.71	3.39	3.55	3.23	155
1861	1.00	3.74	3.34	3.42	4.00	165
1871	1.33	3.46	2.93	3.95	3.69	211

(Refer to Tables 3&4 showing examples of high and low class areas.)
NOTE: These figures refer to parents, children and their spouses, and grandchildren. All other relatives are dealt with when discussing kin. When compiling the table, problems arose due to the relationship to the household head not being stated on the 1841 Census: it was assumed that the first listed female beneath the head was his wife, providing their ages differed by less than 15 years. Subsequent listing showing the same surname, were considered to be their children. From 1851, such assumptions are no longer necessary due to relationships being recorded in the enumerators' books.

TABLE 3 HIGH CLASS ROAD THE DOWNS

Year	No. of Households	No. of Residents (Inc. Kin and Servants)	Mean Persons/ Household
1841	29	172	5.93
1851	43	194	4.51
1861	43	230	5.34
1871	48	247	5.15

Throughout these years The Downs was mainly occupied by class I and II householders. As time passed, class I began to move further afield to be replaced by a small but growing number of class III householders. Although the street remained exclusive, members of the lower classes (IV and V) were present, as it was these classes which provided the domestic services essential to the maintenance of the household. The movement away by those in class I was a result of an influx of commuter households caused by the opening of the railway in 1849, the Bowdon terminus being at the foot of the road.

TABLE 4 A WORKING CLASS AREA GOOSE GREEN

Year	No of Households	No. of Residents (Inc. Kin and Servants)	Mean Persons/ Household
1841	16	64	4.00
1851	22	108	4.91
1861	17	96	5.65
1871	17	89	5.24

Throughout, it was an exclusively working class area, fairly evenly split between classes IV and V, but perhaps with a slight tendency to become more lower working class (V) from the opening of the railway and development of Altrincham as a commuter suburb. The area was close to the Bowdon terminus, explaining the greater numbers per household after 1849.

However, after 1981 there was a slight upturn to 40,070 in 1987 and to about 41,000 in 1990 which may imply there will now be a period of slight growth with minor variations for a little time to come. This may be the result of the modern trend of building multiple-occupancy units such as blocks of retirement flats. This will mean more pedestrians on the streets, more cars and yet another shift of population character for Altrincham, in age-, household- and marital structure.

Without doubt Altrincham is still a high-class residential suburb, though perhaps not as exclusive as it was prior to the opening of the railway, nor even for a short time thereafter. In this respect Bowdon and parts of Hale have taken its place. If these areas are included as 'greater Altrincham' today, the first two social classes comprise nearly one-third of the population.

Chapter Nine

PLACES OF WORSHIP

Until the late-18th century Altrincham township had no church and lay in the huge parish of Bowdon Church. Bowdon church and parish were probably created in Anglo-Saxon times and the church was mentioned in Domesday Book. From the mediaeval period onwards the populous borough of Altrincham and townships over a wide area relied on Bowdon as their ecclesiastic centre, but important though it is, Bowdon Church is not described in this chapter because it lies outside the geographical area covered in this book, namely the ancient bounds of Altrincham borough and township. Similarly descriptions of several other well-known and loved churches and chapels of the district round Altrincham centre have been omitted because of this constraint, (except St. Margaret's because of its proximity to the Altrincham boundary). Many readers will no doubt be disappointed to find their favourite places of worship omitted but it is hoped that the reason for this will be understood.

ST. GEORGE'S CHURCH, CHURCH STREET, ALTRINCHAM
GEORGE FAIRLEY

On 20 August 1799, the chapel of St. George, Fig. 9.1, was consecrated by the Bishop of Chester as a chapel-of-ease to Bowdon Parish Church which was the parish church for the area.

The first incumbent, Oswald Leicester was the son of a well-to-do shopkeeper in the town. He had been much influenced by the teaching of Mr. Samuel Bradburn, the Wesleyan minister stationed in Altrincham. In 1783 he had started the first Sunday school in the county, in a cottage, in Thorley Moor Lane (Ashley Road where Byroe House now stands), then in his house (The Poplars) in the fields now Norman's Place, and finally in a cottage near the entrance to the present church. In 1810 he founded the first Jubilee School to commemorate the Jubilee of George III and remained the incumbent until 1832 when he was succeeded by George Ranking who served for two years.

In 1834 Wilmot Cave Brown Cave took over the incumbency, and the following year the Female Jubilee School of Industry was founded. During 1837 the vicarage was built and a new organ was installed in the west gallery. Dr. Orton succeeded to the incumbency in 1843 and served for 13 years. During his ministry mission services at Broadheath were commenced in a boat chapel on the canal. In his early days the church was filled with square pews—a three-decker pulpit held the place of honour in the centre of the east end, whilst the school children, in a large pen-like structure at the west end, were disciplined by means of a long pole wielded by the officer in charge.

During the short stay of John Honeywell from 1856 to 1859 a new infant school was opened and the church was enlarged by taking down the west wall and enlarging the building at that end, necessary because the population of the parish was growing rapidly.

George London was incumbent from 1859 to 1893 during which time the population served by the church doubled from 2,800 to 5,600. During George London's long incumbency several schools were built, and in 1868 the district was converted into a parish, with St. George's as its church.

From 1893 to 1902 W. M. B. Lutener occupied the incumbency. Re-building of the church became necessary. Work commenced in July 1896 and was completed in 1897, the dedication service being held on 17 November. At about the same time the whole of the church yard was relaid and the west end approach greatly improved.

The centenary was celebrated on 20 August 1899. In honour of the occasion Church Street was decorated. The pathway to the church was bordered by a series of shields upon each of which was recorded some particular event in the history of the church.

Fig. 9.1. **St. George's Church before the repairs of 1896** *G.F.*

There are few records of the first quarter of the twentieth century; E. R. Tarbuck was the incumbent until 1914 when he was succeeded by Canon E. S. Oliver who in turn was succeeded in 1925 by Canon Palin.

Oscar Littler, appointed incumbent in 1944, introduced many changes in the form of worship. The present vicarage was built on the bowling green of the parish hall and he started the negotiations with the neighbouring parishes of St. John's and St. Margaret's to build a joint church school on the site of the old vicarage.

Oscar Littler was succeeded in 1963 by Michael Henshall, later Bishop of Warrington, who continued his predecessor's changes. The new Church of England school was built at the end of Townfield Road and was opened by the Duchess of Kent on 15 June 1968.

In 1976 Bishop Michael was succeeded by Canon Roger Faulkner. Shortly after his arrival a new organ was installed at the west end of the nave. Built in 1857 by William Holt the organ was acquired from a Congregational church in Brighouse. The lady chapel was moved in 1984 to the site of the old organ chamber north of the choir stalls. A Garden of Remembrance was consecrated on St. George's Day 1989 and plans are now being considered for rebuilding the church hall.

ST. MARGARET'S CHURCH, DUNHAM MASSEY, ALTRINCHAM
C. KENNETH LEWIS

Some time before 1851 the seventh Earl of Stamford expressed a desire to erect a church in Dunham Massey. Building was started but for some reason unknown did not proceed further than foundation level. After the elapse of some months the project was revived and a competition among six architects, three from London and three from Manchester, took place to design a church utilising the existing foundations. William Hayley of Manchester was the successful architect. By the time the church was completed in 1855 the Earl's sister, Margaret Henrietta Maria Milbank, to whom he was very much attached, had died (1852) and the church was dedicated to her memory.

The church was cruciform in design with a central tower surmounted by an imposing spire rising to a height of 210 feet, supported by flying buttresses and terminating in a cross, Fig. 9.2. Within twenty years the spire was causing problems and by the turn of the century the bells were silenced to prevent damage to the structure. In 1927 the spire, now in a dangerous condition due to vibration caused by traffic was thought likely to fall into the road and so was hurriedly dismantled.

From time to time the stonework facing of the church had given problems and in the early 1950's that on the tower was found to be unsafe. Extensive repairs were carried out and the appearance of the tower simplified.

Fig. 9.2. **St. Margaret's Church when it had a spire.**   *C.K.L.*

The tower contains a peal of ten bells cast by Taylors of Loughborough in 1854. They are reputedly one of the finest peals of that era. Towards the end of World War II an inspection of the tower was made and it was decided that it was safe to ring the bells. They were rung for the first time for nearly fifty years in March 1944. In 1974 they were completely overhauled and rehung in an iron frame with new fittings.

On 12 July 1985 an inspection of the building was undertaken. As a result the gutters have been renewed and altered and the parapets rebuilt and new stonework introduced where necessary between January and July 1988.

The beauty of the interior of the church with its very fine carved roof has been enhanced from time to time by gifts of screens and entrance doors and memorials to departed worshippers. When All Saints Church was demolished the stained-glass windows were brought to St. Margaret's and installed in the former Stamford Chapel, which also contains the funeral hatchment of the seventh Earl of Stamford. The Chapel was handed over to the Parochial Church Council in 1945 by the Earl of Stamford and today it is used for small services.

The best known incumbent was the Rev. Hewlett Johnson. His period of office is often spoken of as the palmy days of St. Margaret's as Hewlett Johnson was an influential person. He had a great pastoral care for the under-privileged and this led to his involvement in the social gospel and though many disagreed with his views none doubted his sincerity. In 1924 he left to become Dean of Manchester and the Rev. Charles C. Potts succeeded him. He had had boxing experience and it is related that coming upon one of the typical Saturday night disputes in the town he dealt with one of the participants in a salutary manner. The Rev. John Heywood during a long incumbency from 1953 saw through, among other things, the conversion of the Stamford Chapel; the building of the Church Hall, and All Saints Church; the sale of the old Vicarage and the building of the new; the rehanging of the bells; and the closure of St. Margaret's School and its replacement by Altrincham Church of England Aided Primary School. Since 1980 the recent incumbent has been the Rev. J. Arthur Roberts who addressed himself vigorously to the work of revitalising the parish, until he left in 1991.

ALL SAINTS CHURCH, ALTRINCHAM

The original All Saints Church, located in Regent Road next to the Grapes Hotel, was previously a Wesleyan Chapel opened in 1788. John Wesley preached there on 5 April 1790. Subsequently it became a Congregational Chapel and in 1896 it was presented to St. Margaret's parish as a daughter church by Mr. John H. Grafton. A new church was built on a site in New Street in the early 1960's as part of a Church Hall complex. The new church is unusual in shape, being six sided, and furnished with pews, lectern and candlesticks from the famous workshops of Robert ('Mousey') Thompson of Kilburn whose trademark is a little mouse.

ST. VINCENT DE PAUL ROMAN CATHOLIC CHURCH
Details extracted from a history of Shrewsbury Diocese

In 1847 Rev. O'Reilly was appointed as parish priest and became so popular that when he left in 1853 the people 'went wild' and barricaded the chapel against the new priest. During these first six years Mass was said in the house of Mr. McDermott in George Street. After a few months Mass began to be said in a cottage in higher New Street. A little later a house was purchased lower down the street (now Nos. 71 and 73). This served a double purpose of chapel and presbytery.

In 1856, Father Alcock came to the town. Soon after his arrival the foundation stone of a new church was laid. While the church was being built Mass was sometimes said in a tent when the weather permitted. The new church was opened in 1860 and remained in use until the present church was opened in 1905. In 1858 Father Alcock found among his parishioners some exiled members of the family of Louis Philippe who had been King of France from 1830 to 1848. Father

Fig. 9.3. **St. Vincent de Paul's Church**   D.G.B.

Alcock retired in 1876.

In the time of Fr. C. Ryder, Bishop Allen laid the foundation stone of a new church on 18 June 1904 in the presence of the mayor and Court Leet. On Rosary Sunday the following year the Bishop opened the new church, Fig. 9.3. The presbytery was completed a little later.

During the long rectorship of Canon H. F. Welch (1907–31) many improvements were made in the church and school. In 1908 a new classroom was erected and the school enlarged. The outlay for this was £1,000. Two years later the high altar and communion rails, of marble and alabaster, were erected. 1911 is notable for the opening of the new pulpit and the election of a Catholic mayor, Mr. G. Whitwham. In 1912 a magnificent organ costing £2,000 was installed.

Canon Welch's successors were Canons Kirby and Donnelly, Rev. John Lyons and Provost Burgon. Provost Burgon in 1985 set about the re-ordering of the sanctuary which was rather cramped. This was made more serviceable, and a permanent altar was built and many other alterations were made in the main body of the church.

The Convent of Our Lady of the Vale, a nursing home accommodating 30 patients in a delightful setting near the Bollin is conducted by the Sisters of St. Joseph of the Apparition. It opened on 8 September 1930 and a fine extension costing £10,000 was opened in 1938. St. Philomena's Convent, Bonneville Road was created on 9 December 1933 when the novitiate of the Franciscan Missionary Sisters of St. Joseph was transferred from Freshfield near Southport. The house, The Woodlands was purchased from Lady Veno. The top room in the turret of the hall was used as a chapel, and Mass was offered there from time to time on the occasion of the Bishop's visits. The Sisters gave up the house in 1966. In its later years it was known as St. Joseph's.

In September 1909 four sisters came from Loreto Convent, Manchester to start a school in Altrincham. Their success was immediate and in 1913 a house called Bellfield was acquired in Dunham Road. The fine greenhouses were converted into classrooms, the old coach-house became a science room and even a hayloft was brought into use! The grammar school now caters for 850 girls. It has a science block built in 1955, a teaching block built in 1965 (extended in 1982), a specialist block built in 1976, and a new Hall built in 1987.

ST. JOHN THE EVANGELIST, ALTRINCHAM
REV. W. J. MOXON

The church was built in 1865 on land provided by Lord Stamford and opened on 14 December 1866. It is built in the Early English (13th century Gothic) style of architecture, Fig. 9.4. The architect was Medland Taylor and his particular style is evident in the design of the font and pulpit. The seating capacity was 920 and the building cost £7,000. The school, parish hall and

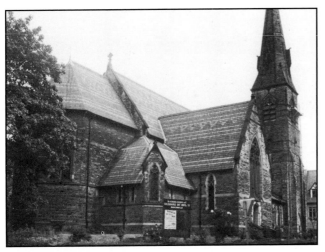

Fig. 9.4 **St. John's Church.**   *D.G.B.*

vicarage, which adjoined the church were built in a style which blended with the church.

An increase in the population of part of the parish area known as Newtown led to the building of a mission church, St. Elizabeth's, in 1890. The architect was J. McNamara. The church was brick built at a cost of £2,000 with a seating capacity of 150. St. John's school had its infant department at St. Elizabeth's and junior department at St. John's. The schools were closed in 1968 and pupils transferred to Townfield Road, where a new Church of England Aided Primary School had been built to serve the parishes of St. George's, St. Margaret's and St. John's. The school building at St. John's was sold and is now St. John's Medical Centre housing local doctors. St. Elizabeth's church was closed and purchased by the local authority, demolished, and the land used to build the Pownall Road Day Care Centre.

St. John's parish hall was sold to a property developer in December 1987 and has subsequently been converted into three town houses. The proceeds of the sale were used to enable the church to be divided by a floor to ceiling wall at the west end so as to provide a lower and upper hall with kitchen, toilets etc. There are some notable stained-glass windows in the church, particularly the east window rising above the altar. The two central panels depict the Annunciation—Archangel Gabriel on the left, Our Lady on the right with the Dove, symbol of the Holy Spirit.

ALTRINCHAM METHODIST CHURCH
CATHERINE M. MERRELL

John Wesley the founder of Methodism first visited Altrincham in 1738. On subsequent visits he preached at Oldfield Brow, probably in the open air, and in the town itself.

The first Wesleyan Chapel to be built within the borough was at Chapel Walk (now Regent Road). Wesley preached there on Easter Monday 1790. The Altrincham Church was associated with various Manchester Circuits until 1850 when it became part of the newly formed Altrincham and Sale Circuit.

An off-shoot of Wesleyan Methodism, the

Methodist New Connexion opened their own sanctuary in George Street in 1821 (where Marks & Spencers store is today) Fig. 9.5. The Bank Street Church was built by the Wesleyan Methodists in 1866 to replace the original building in Chapel Walk.

The Primitive Methodists' Church on Oxford Road (now the Club Theatre) was opened in 1875. Five years later the Wesleyans opened a magnificent building in Enville Road, Bowdon, which was affectionately known as "The Dome Chapel".

There were sixteen Methodist Societies in the Altrincham area but in 1932 the terms 'Wesleyan', 'Primitive' and 'New Connexion' disappeared and nationally, a United Methodist Church was established.

By January 1965 the Societies of Borough Road, Broadheath and George Street were working together as closely as possible. On 28 August 1966, closing services were held in these three churches and the congregations moved to Bank Street Church, renamed The Altrincham Methodist Church, Woodlands Road. Work on a new Church and Community Centre at Barrington Road began in April 1967, when prominent personalities in the civic and religious life of the town combined to ask God's Blessing on the venture.

The new Altrincham Methodist Church was opened and dedicated in September 1968.

Fig. 9.5. **The old Methodist Church in George St.,**   *C.M.M.*
1821-1966, and the modern Church in Barrington Road

ALTRINCHAM BAPTIST CHURCH
JEAN MORGAN

The first recorded meeting of Baptists in the area was in September 1872, and the first Baptist 'church', comprising 25 members, was formed in January 1873.

By 1878 the community numbered 100 and had outgrown its meeting-place: a small chapel on The Downs. The present Hale Road site (then semi-rural) was obtained from the Stamford Estate at an annual chief rent of £25. William Owen, a Manchester architect, designed the church in the Italian style, and it was built by local contractors, Penningtons, at a cost of £3,000, Fig. 9.6.

Fig. 9.6. Altrincham Baptist Church. *D.G.B.*

Additional rooms were provided by an extension in 1908–9, and an organ installed in 1909. Electric lighting took the place of gas in 1925–6. A church office started to function in 1961. The 'tower' was demolished in 1971. A major refurbishment in 1988 included carpeting and complete redecoration of the main church, removal of the organ and the replacement of pews by chairs.

The church 'schoolroom' has been put to a variety of uses over the years. In 1904 it was let to the Education Committee for up to 2 years, pending the completion of local schools. During the Second World War it provided emergency shelter for local people made homeless by bombing. It has been used regularly by numerous church organisations, particularly groups for children and young people, and was refurbished in 1989.

DEVONSHIRE ROAD EVANGELICAL CHURCH, BROADHEATH

MR. R. C. EVANS

The church recently celebrated the fiftieth anniversary of its use of the building at Broadheath from 1934, Fig. 9.7, but its history goes back before that date.

The church was first formed early this century and met in a number of hired premises including, in 1910, a room over the stable of the Bowdon Bread Company in Lloyd Street. In 1920 a move was made to Newtown Night School until the present building was acquired from Primitive Methodists in 1934. Until 1970 it was known as Hebron Hall.

The Sunday School at one time was held in the cellar of Morrison's Sale Rooms, before moving to the Devonshire Road chapel. Sunday School outings were

Fig. 9.7. Devonshire Road Evangelical Church. *D.G.B.*

quite an event going as far afield as Ashley or Delamere Forest. Food had to be taken, bread sliced and buttered, and milk obtained from a farm. The means of transport was by train or by lorry with wooden forms tied on for seats.

DUNHAM ROAD UNITARIAN CHAPEL

JOHN MIDGLEY

In September 1816 the Unitarians of Altrincham opened their first building. This was a daughter congregation of Hale Chapel and for 62 years the congregations shared their minister. By 1869 the building on Shaws Lane was found to be too small and in 1872 the fine chapel on Dunham Road, Fig. 9.8, was opened by Rev. William Gaskell, husband of the famous novelist Elizabeth. The cause in Altrincham had been supported by eminent families including the Worthingtons. It was Manchester architect Thomas Worthington who designed the chapel, built at a cost of £3,054. The Shaws Lane building stood until the 1960's.

In 1875 the need for a Sunday School was met by the building of a small school room with chapel keeper's house attached, on Sylvan Grove. In 1883 an organ was presented by Mr. James Worthington, and in 1890 a series of beautiful stained-glass windows was inserted. In 1884 the large schoolroom was built and in 1899 The Parsonage was constructed, giving a suite of premises all on one campus.

Fig. 9.8. Dunham Road Unitarian Chapel. *M.M.K.*
Drawing by local artist, Thomas Pitfield.

The congregation has been served by ministers with their own special talents and interests. Rev. Dendy Agate (1898–1916) developed Sunday school and youth work. Later came Edgar Innes Fripp, a Shakespearean scholar, Arthur Holland Biggs who was awarded the MBE, Arthur Vallance, a scouting enthusiast, Peter Godfrey who also ministered to the congregation in Urmston, and Rev. John Midgley who also taught at the Unitarian College in Manchester. He was succeeded by his wife, Rev. Celia Midgley, in 1989.

THE WELSH PRESBYTERIAN CHAPEL
MRS. M. M. KETTLE

Worship in the Welsh language in Altrincham has been traced back to 1850. However, the first recorded meetings were in 1869 in a room in George Street owned by the Water Company and occupied by a Mr. William Jones who was employed by them. In the course of his duties, Mr. Jones discovered that a number of Welsh girls in service in the area were homesick for a Sunday Service in their native language. The meetings outgrew the room in George Street and at the beginning of 1870 with a membership of 28 they moved to a room in the British Schools in Oxford Road.

In the 1890's there was a desire among the members for a chapel of their own, and in 1899 it was decided that steps should be taken to acquire a permanent building.

In 1902 a site for the new chapel was obtained in Willowtree Road and with a nucleus of £150 and an appeal launched locally, plans were drawn up and the work entrusted to Thomas Williams & Sons for the sum of £716 10s (£716·50), Fig. 9.9. The chapel was officially opened on 19 December 1903.

The chapel is the focus of the spiritual and cultural life of Welsh people in this area, and it is with regret that we view the passing of the well-known drama and concert groups and choir, the Eisteddfod in Broadheath and the St. David's Day concerts. There is a St. David's Day dinner each year.

Fig. 9.9. Appeal for the Welsh Presbyterian Chapel, 1902.

M.M.K.

Fig. 9.10 First Church of Christ Scientist
D.G.B.

Fig. 9.11. Altrincham National Spiritualist Church
D.G.B.

FIRST CHURCH OF CHRIST, SCIENTIST, ALTRINCHAM
RAYMOND GENTLE AND MARJORIE JAQUES

A group of Christian Scientists held services in a private house on Dunham Road in 1907 before taking rooms in the old Post Office at 1, Market Street and later in the British Schools, Oxford Road. Services continued there until the present site at 55, Ashley Road was purchased in 1920 where services started in 1926, Fig. 9.10. It was soon found necessary to take rooms in the old Y.W.C.A. building for the growing Sunday School. By 1957 the church auditorium had been enlarged and an extension provided for use as the Sunday School.

From 1924 the Church has been a branch of The Mother Church, The First Church of Christ, Scientist, in Boston, U.S.A., founded by Mary Baker Eddy between 1879 and 1892 to reinstate Christian healing.

A Reading Room offering ready access to the Bible and Christian Science publications has always been a vital function of the church. Housed over the years in various premises in the town centre, the present premises at 1, Peter Street, Oxford Road, were purchased in 1967.

ALTRINCHAM NATIONAL SPIRITUALIST CHURCH
JOAN BAVERSTOCK–BOSLEY

The first Spiritualist Church in Altrincham was opened at the beginning of this century, under the Presidency of Mr. Bell. It was housed in a wooden hut, which was later moved piecemeal to a site in the Clarendon Avenue area. By this time, the church had a new President, Mrs. Bowden. Eventually the wooden hut had to make way for the new flyover. For several years the Church was given temporary accommodation in St. Anne's Church, Altrincham, and later in the Altrincham Unitarian Church. Finally, in September 1976, under the Presidency of Mr. Garraway, the present Church was built in Clarendon Avenue, Fig. 9.11. It was re-dedicated and affiliated to the Spiritualist National Union. Today, its President is Joan Baverstock–Bosley.

Chapter Ten

SOME SERVICES

HILDA BAYLISS AND LESLIE POLLARD

Before the 19th century the Court Leet organised basic services. As population increased, though some services remained in the public sector, others were developed by private companies. This chapter gives a short history of some of the public services the town enjoys today. No mention is made of the many valuable voluntary social and care organisations which are so necessary to modern life.

POLICE

Law and order in the borough had been regulated for many centuries by the borough court. Cheshire obtained authority in 1829 to appoint a special High Constable and an Assistant Petty Constable for each of the 9 Hundreds into which the county was divided at that time. The constables for Bucklow Division worked alongside the constables of the Altrincham Court Leet. In 1856 the County and Borough Police Act obliged the Justices to establish a paid police force for each county. The Committee of Justices in Chester decided that for law and order purposes the county force should continue to operate through the 9 Hundreds of the county. The colour of the uniform was to be blue and superintendents were to be issued with 1 frock coat with braid and 1 pair of trousers; they were also to receive £60 per annum horse allowance. Inspectors were to have the same uniform without braid and no horse allowance. Sergeants and constables were issued with

2 frock coats, 2 pairs of trousers, hat, 1 stock (truncheon) and they received 6d. (2½p) a week boot allowance. White metal badges carrying 'Prince of Wales Feathers' and the words "Cheshire Constabulary" were adopted. The Bucklow Division continued to use the stations at Knutsford and Lymm as well as the George Street Lock-Up which had been built in 1838, Fig. 10.1. It had living accommodation for the constable as well as 3 cells. In 1866 new premises on Dunham Road were opened.

The only transport was the Divisional Superintendent's horse and cart which he had to maintain on his horse allowance. In 1868 the Bucklow Division was divided; the western part was named Runcorn Division and the rest of the Bucklow Division became Altrincham Division. The post of High Constable disappeared in 1869.

Superintendent Steen in Altrincham was so popular that his posting in 1876 to Eddisbury was contested by prominent inhabitants signing a roll (4 feet long) petitioning that he be allowed to remain in the town. It must have been successful because his name appears in Kelly's Directory for 1878 where he is entered as Superintendent of Police and Superintendent of the Fire Engine House.

In 1878 Captain Arrowsmith, the head of Cheshire Constabulary introduced helmets to smarten the uniform. The new helmets had removeable spikes which were only worn on special occasions, orders always specified helmets to be worn "with spikes" or "without spikes". Spikes had always to be worn when the wearer attended Divine Service. The Altrincham force used 'shako' hats until the 1930's.

Police Museum - Crewe
Pre-War II Police Car

Fig. 10.1 **Police lock ups in George Street, 1975, now demolished.**
The words over the door read "Police Lock Ups 1838". The shop on the far corner is Walton's Model shop. The lintels to the lock-up have been incorporated into a seat by the replica stocks in the Old Market Place.

W. Wilson

Fig. 10.2. Police Force, back of Town Hall, 1920. *Police Museum - Crewe*

Officers' jackets were closed to the throat and fastened by 'frogging' (button-and-loop braiding) across the front. A badge depicting their rank was worn on the stand-up collar, a crown for a superintendent and a crown and star for a chief superintendent. Inspectors' jackets were similar to superintendents' but shorter with rank badges of 1 star for inspector and 2 stars for chief inspector.

In 1903 the premises on Dunham Road were enlarged and contained the Magistrates Court, sessions of which were held there until 1985–86. A small building housed the mortuary trolley which was pushed by hand to bear corpses, *e.g.* from accidents, to the mortuary on High Street. The Altrincham Force numbered 22 officers and men in 1904. During World War I special constables were enlisted to help the force depleted by men joining the armed forces. By 1920 the division had reached 65 officers and men, Fig. 10.2.

During the '30's the force became mechanised and used Rover patrol cars with wirelesses. The cars were painted in forest-green livery, constables used bicycles. Inspectors' uniforms were changed to include open necked jackets and Sam Browne belts similar to army officers with rank badges on the lapels. After the war ordinary ranks changed to open-necked jackets with cloth belts, their numbers mounted on the shoulder straps.

During World War II special police were enlisted to provide assistance when emergencies occurred and this voluntary force continues to the present day.

After the war the force adopted the helmet recommended by the Home Office with a 'comb' of reinforcement along the crown. The use of Panda cars with 2-way radios speeded the detection of crimes. Because helmets proved awkward when using the Panda cars, flat caps were issued, these are now worn by all ranks.

In 1974 Altrincham severed its links with Chester after 145 years. It is now part of M Division of the Greater Manchester Police force and since 1981 has been administered from offices on Barrington Road. The communications for the whole of M Division are controlled by a computer centre in Stretford. The Division controls an area where there is a population of 227,400 inhabitants. The force consists of 1 Chief Superintendent, 3 Superintendents, 3 Chief Inspectors, 15 Inspectors, 49 Sergeants and 273 Constables, a total of 344 officers and men. In 1987 M Division recorded 19,133 crimes of which 5,220 were solved.

FIRE SERVICE

The Court Leet was responsible for trying to prevent fires but had little equipment to deal with them. In 1798 when the township purchased a new fire engine, no regular brigade was employed, and men were paid 5s (25p) to work the machine whenever required. Although it was a horse-drawn vehicle no horse was kept to pull it, and when required a horse had to be hired. This had dire consequences on 11 August 1855, when a fire started at the Orange Tree public house. A newspaper report stated . . . *"several men had to drag the engine along the streets while one man was running about from one public house to another trying to get a horse"*. Water was also a problem . . . *"the water that could be got was from pumps, cisterns and wells. The fire was only extinguished after several people had died"*. The fire engine, called 'Neptune', was also present on 10 March 1863 at the celebrations on the occasion of the wedding of H.R.H. the Prince of Wales. The celebrations ended with a firework display. In case of fire, Neptune was stationed nearby, each fireman was to receive 3s 6d (17½p) danger money but nothing untoward was reported.

The wage bill in 1871 included the Superintendent's salary £10 10s (£10·50), £22 for the Volunteer firemen, Fig. 10.3, and £5 for the hire of the horse. The previous year the force needed a new hose and reel which cost £29 10s (£29·50), almost three times the Superintendent's yearly salary. After the formation of the U.D.C. a fire appliance house was built in High Street. Here the brigade kept a horse-drawn wagonette appliance which needed 11 men each side to work the pump, men volunteering were given free beer and many Insurance companies complained about the high cost of this refreshment. In 1903 it was replaced by a horse-drawn Merryweather Fire Appliance which had a pump powered by steam.

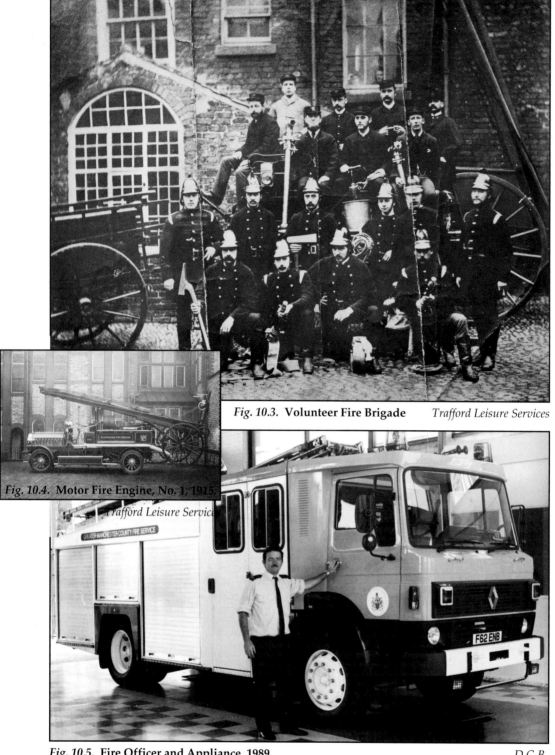

Fig. 10.3. **Volunteer Fire Brigade**   *Trafford Leisure Services*

Fig. 10.4. **Motor Fire Engine, No. 1, 1915.**
Trafford Leisure Service

Fig. 10.5. **Fire Officer and Appliance, 1989.**   *D.G.B.*

The first motorised fire engine in the town was a John Morris Belsize model with wheeled escape ladder, Fig. 10.4, purchased in 1915. Inspections of fire precautions at public places were undertaken and recommendations made and as a result of an unfavourable report in 1933 the Central Theatre had to close. In 1947 the Fire Service Act made it obligatory for councils to provide a full-time Fire Service.

In 1962 the Brigade moved to new premises on Princes Road near Manchester Road, Broadheath. It provides fire cover for Altrincham and its environs as far as Knutsford. Fire appliances included two water tenders, each with a pump, one carrying 400 gallons of water and equipped with a 45 foot extension ladder, the other carrying 300 gallons of water. A further appliance was a Foam Tender which carried 560 gallons of foam compound and foam-making equipment suitable for dealing with fires resulting from aeroplane crashes or oil installations. In the 12 months to 31 March 1962 Altrincham appliances answered nearly 500 calls. In 1989 the Brigade operated under Station Officer Smethurst with 28 officers and men arranged on a four-watch system; it is on call 24 hours a day, 365 days a year. It has a fire appliance, Fig. 10.5, and an Operational Support Unit which is fully equipped to deal with any large-scale disaster. The station's communications are automatically controlled and response to calls occurs within 10–30 seconds. The records for 1987/1988 show that the Brigade answered 1,200 calls, 600 of which were in the Altrincham area.

AMBULANCE SERVICE

The fire station in High Street also housed a horse-drawn ambulance. This was replaced by a solid-tyred motorised vehicle in 1916. A charge was made for use of the U.D.C's ambulances until 1930 after which date the service was free for residents day or night, for journeys within a radius of 10 miles.

The association with the fire service continued and the premises on Princes Road (1962) were built to accommodate both services. After this date the divisions for Sale and Lymm were also administered from Altrincham. The premises contained 6 ambulances and 7 sitting cars and had its own repair bay. In 1989 the station staff complement was a First Officer, 5 Leading Ambulance men, 13 Qualified Ambulance men and 7 Auxiliary Ambulance persons. The station has 1 ambulance operating 24 hours per day, 7 days per week; 2 ambulances operating 10-hour weekdays; 1 weekend ambulance; and 3 auxiliary ambulances (Monday to Friday) carrying day cases to clinics. Each month ambulances travel 8,500 miles and carry about 210 '999' cases, 100 urgent cases, 800 'out-patient' and 'day' cases.

GAS

Gas was first introduced to Altrincham by George Massey who lit the first gas lamp in 1844 outside the Unicorn Hotel, powered by his small gas generator plant near the bowling green. As well as being the publican he was involved with a gas works in Ashton-

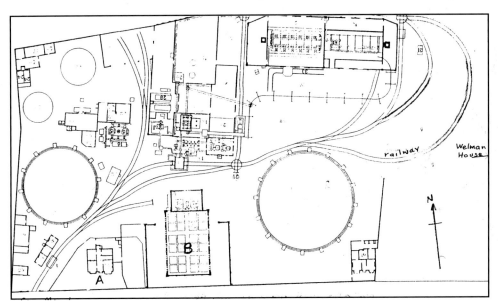

Fig. 10.6. **Plan of Gas Works.**   *N.W. Gas Archive*
Moss Lane runs across the bottom of the map.

Fig. 10.7. **Old photo of Gas Works taken from Moss Lane. Manager's**   *N.W. Gas Archive*
house in foreground.
Building A – Manager's house. B – Purifier building.

under-Lyne which had been built in 1825. After this demonstration, Altrincham Gas Company was formed in 1846 but had difficulty obtaining land for a works near the canal or railway. The manager of Ashton-under-Lyne Gas Works advised the company to buy Mr. Massey's plant which was used until a field off Moss Lane was purchased at a chief rent of £15 per annum and a gas works built. There was difficulty with the unstable ground which was a filled clay pit formerly used for brickmaking. In 1847 production started and gas was sold at 10s (50p) per 1,000 cu.feet and this was reduced in 1850 to 8s 4d (42p). The gas was used to light houses, factories, schools and highways and its 'quality' was deemed to be 16 candlepower. The first school to request gas was the Jubilee School in 1857 next to the original plant in Albert Place.

Coal to make the gas was brought to Broadheath by canal and railway and by road to the Moss Lane works. By 1872 sales had risen to 17 million cu.feet per annum requiring the movement of large quantities of coal to the works and coke and other products from there. Permission was granted to construct a tramway from the railway sidings to the works along which coal wagons were pulled by horses.

Mention must be made of Ellis Lever, one of Altrincham's most controversial inhabitants. He was a wealthy coal merchant who lived first at Spring Bank on Ashley Road, Fig. 15.8, and then at neighbouring Culcheth Hall (before it became a girls' school in 1891, Fig. 11.2). Altrincham municipality did not own its own gas supply and the ratepayers had tried to buy the Company, but the latter had friends on the Local Board and the purchases were blocked. In 1881 when Lever's low tender for coal was rejected by the Company he took the Company to court and obtained some redress for the town being overcharged for gas. He was treated like a hero. He then got involved in the Great Gas Scandal in Salford in 1887. Gas there was made by the local authority. Lever exposed much corruption in Salford especially bribes for coal contracts paid to Samuel Hunter, the Salford Gas Manager. Hunter sued Lever for libel but Lever was acquitted and returned to Altrincham to be fêted. In 1888 Hunter was tried and gaoled for five years for corruption. The following year Hunter agreed to name those who had bribed him. One of those named was Lever who was fined £2300 and left the district in disgrace.

The gas works was a huge industrial undertaking, Figs. 10.6 and 10.7. In 1919 showrooms adjoining the company's offices in Moss Lane were opened to display a large range of goods available to be powered by gas. In 1926, 25,000 tons of coal were carbonised at Moss Lane, and 9,750 customers used 3,557 million cu.feet of gas. 13,500 tons of coke, 1,200 tons of tar and 2,000 tons of ammoniacal liquor were sold, by-products of the gas-making process, all having to be moved along Moss Lane. In 1925 the Board of Trade gave permission to replace horse-power by a steam locomotive and a Peckett saddle tank steam engine was acquired to haul the wagons to and from the Altrincham line.

In 1948 the Gas Company became part of North West Gas and continued to produce gas until 1957 when grid-fed gas became available and production ceased. A new complex of offices called Welman House was built on the site and a compressor added to the 2 gas holders in 1964. The buildings were constructed on piles for stability as computers were to be used there. The gas holders were demolished in 1986. Gas is stored in caverns in salt deposits under the Cheshire plain and is piped under pressure along 8 inch (20cm) mains. Welman House is the head office for the whole North West area, Fig. 10.8. Gas cost 7·75d (3p) for 1 therm in 1936; in 1989 it cost 38·5p.

ELECTRICITY

In 1882 Manchester Edison Swan Company acquired premises in Broadheath producing dynamos and switchgear. From this company the Altrincham Electric Supply Ltd. company was formed in 1894 by Mr. W. P. J. Fawcus and was registered to operate the rights originally granted to the Altrincham and Bowdon Councils to supply electricity. A generating station was built on a site between the Bridgewater canal and the L.N.W.R. line ensuring transport for the thousands of tons of coal necessary to make steam to drive the dynamos. The station was one of the first 50 in the country and production of

Fig. 10.8. **Welman House, Gas Offices, Moss Lane.** *D.G.B.*

Fig. 10.9. **Broadheath** *D.G.B.* **Electricity Sub-Station** – site of former Altrincham Electric Supply Ltd., Davenport Lane.

D.G.B.

Fig. 10.10. **Altrincham Sewage Works, Carrington Moss.**

electricity for the Altrincham area began in 1895.

The local Guardian of 6 February 1897 printed a letter from Mr. Fawcus to the U.D.C. offering to supply electricity to light the 430 street lights for £416 per annum which was £140 less than the cost of gas then being used, but the Council deferred making a decision. At this time there was no standard 240 voltage 50 cycle a.c. system; within some towns there were different voltages. Broadheath at first provided power at 2,000 volts at 83 cycles a.c. and though this was eventually changed mainly to 240v there are in fact still some supplies to older houses and other premises at 2,000 volts. The voltage is stepped down at such houses by a transformer about the size of a dustbin.

In 1935 Altrincham Electric Supply Ltd. became part of the National Grid and three years later the company introduced a two-part tariff with a cheaper rate for 'power' to encourage the sale of appliances which were on display at their showrooms at 60 Stamford New Road. Electricity was generated at the Broadheath works until 1940 after which the company supplied electricity wholly provided by the Central Electricity Generating Board. In 1947 the Labour government nationalised the electricity industry and the Altrincham area became part of NORWEB.

Altrincham's supply at 132,000 volts comes from Carrington by overhead pylon to Broadheath, Fig. 10.9, where there is a substation on the site of the original company. Here the voltage is reduced to 33,000 and again to 11,000. It is then distributed underground to smaller sub-stations where it is reduced to 1,000 volts and then again to 415/240 volts. Electricity now costs 5·79p per unit and 2·07p per unit for 'Economy 7' compared with 1939 when a unit for lighting cost $4\frac{1}{4}$d (2p) and for power $1\frac{1}{4}$d ($\frac{1}{2}$p).

laid to Altrincham in 1857 at a cost of £2,500. Water was sold to the company at a little under 5d (2p) for the first 1,000 gallons and 3d ($1\frac{1}{2}$p) per 1,000 gallons thereafter. Users were charged 5% of the value of the rack rent of their property with a minimum of 5s (25p) per annum. For properties with a rack rent under £30 per annum the use of a water closet incurred a further charge of 6s (30p), and the use of a bath 12s (60p) per annum.

In 1870 an underground brick reservoir was built at Devisdale. It could hold 1,000,000 gallons and was used until 1965 when the site was filled in and the land returned to its owner, Lord Stamford. NCWC's entitlement was for 500,000 gallons per day but this was proving insufficient, the Company also felt threatened as their brief allowed MCWW to end the supply at a year's notice. It was also noted that MCWW was selling water at a lower rate elsewhere. Consequently in 1917 NCWC took a case to the House of Lords to obtain a longer contract and one was granted for 21 years for the supply of 2,000,000 gallons per day. A charge of $7\frac{1}{2}$% of the ordinary rateable value was suggested. At the same date of the hearing, MCWW tried to take over the NCWC but this was refused. However, two years later, its request was successful and MCWW took over NCWC which had supplied Sale, Northenden, Baguley, Northern Etchells, Dunham Massey, Bowdon, Hale, Ringway and Ashley as well as Altrincham. A Standby Booster Station was completed in Altrincham in 1928 and in 1965 another was completed in Dunham Park. In 1972 Altrincham was linked to Davyhulme with a 914mm main.

In 1973 the North West Water Authority (NWWA) was formed and took over 24 companies including Manchester Corporation. The NWWA now supplies Altrincham's water and is responsible for supplying clean water and disposing of dirty water which it does at the sewage works on Carrington Moss, Fig. 10.10. Little renewal of plant had taken place since 1939 but Trafford MBC as agent for the NWWA undertook five major sewerage schemes between 1975 and 1989 which have virtually replaced the original Victorian sewers, and the Carrington works are being improved.

When water was obtained from wells in 1852 it would have to be carried, each gallon weighed 10lbs ($4\frac{1}{2}$Kg) and even 2 gallons per head for each member of the family each day would involve carrying a heavy weight to the house. After piped water arrived the estimated use was 25 gallons per person per day. Nowadays the figure is 71 gallons. Both these last figures include water used by industry.

WATER AND SEWERAGE

Prior to the formation of the North Cheshire Water Company (NCWC) in 1857 Altrincham's water came from wells and springs but its well water was very hard. The NCWC had premises at 114, George Street and purchased water in bulk from the Manchester Corporation Waterworks, MCWW. A mains pipe was

HOSPITAL SERVICES

In 1840 a fever hospital was built near the junction of the present Beech Road and Stamford Road. It was maintained by the town authorities but proved too small so a larger hospital was built in Lloyd Street on land given by the Earl of Stamford and Warrington in 1853. The main benefactress was the widow of Jeremiah

Fig. 10.11. **Altrincham General Hospital.** *D.G.B.*

Lloyd of Oldfield Hall after whom the hospital was named. In 1860 a dispensary was added where children could be treated on payment of 1d per week if over 14 years and ½d per week if under 14 years. One of the rules stated that *"patients must provide their own bottles, bandages &c"*. During the first year 109 cases were treated and the scheme was enlarged to include treatment for adult subscribers in 1861. There were 4 visiting surgeons. Patients with a broken limb could find themselves in the next bed to a patient with fever as there was no separation of cases. This building also proved inadequate and the Altrincham Provident Dispensary and Hospital (APDH) was built in 1870, Fig. 10.11, on the old drilling ground of the Rifle Volunteers on what was called Bowdon Road (Market Street). The hospital also catered for patients needing treatment for eyes and teeth. Lloyd's Hospital was managed by the governors of the APDH. Both hospitals shared the same medical staff but the new hospital had its own domestic staff and dispenser. When an epidemic occurred in 1877 the scheme became unmanageable and the administration for Lloyds was transferred to the control of the Local Board of Health. Lloyd's Hospital continued to be used until 1911 when an Isolation Hospital was built in Sinderland Lane. As it is not now needed as a hospital it is used as a home for elderly patients and is called Gibson House, after a former mayor of Altrincham.

The hospital did not welcome the National Health Act of 1913 because employers who had previously generously supported the hospital were no longer able to do so as they had to contribute towards the national scheme for their employees. At the outbreak of the 1914–1918 war two wards were reserved for war wounded. In 1915 an X-ray operator was appointed but a department was not created until 1924.

One private patient paid £7 7s (£7·35) for a general anaesthetic in 1934. Her stay in hospital cost £7 17s 6d (£7·87). By 1937 there were 100 beds, and clinics for X-ray, massage, ultra-violet ray, rheumatic and orthopaedic treatment. During World War II accommodation was again reserved for injured of the armed services. In 1940 the average number of beds occupied was 85. 1,342 major operations were performed and 11,867 out-patients were treated. Escalating costs were making the running of the hospital difficult. However, in 1948 when the National Health Service took responsibility it was not welcomed by management nor staff.

The statistics for 1986–87 show that it was a busy hospital.

Inpatients	Long stay	2315
	Day cases	623
	Average length of stay	7·2 days

(In 1912 the average length of stay had been 36 days.)

937 clinics were held at which 5,622 people were treated on a first visit and 11,784 on subsequent visits. The Casualty Department treated 9,916 patients on a first visit and 6,400 on subsequent visits. Problems of ear, nose and throat are dealt with at St. Anne's Hospital in Woodville Road.

Since April 1988 the main hospital has ceased to be an Acute Hospital. The Casualty Department is not open at the weekend and any patient needing residential care has to be referred elsewhere. Altrincham General still has outpatient clinics but is mainly an Assessment and Rehabilitation Centre for elderly patients.

CONCLUSION

The police, fire service and care of water supplies were once under the control of the Court Leet. Gas, electricity, piped water and hospital services originated privately within the township. Today most services are organised by bodies outside Altrincham.

Chapter Eleven

EDUCATION

HILDA BAYLISS

There are no records of any formal education for children in the Altrincham area until the 16th century. The first known person to be concerned that children went untaught was Edward Janny who left money in 1553 with instructions to *"kepe a ffre scole at Bowdon to instruct youthe in vertue and lerninge"*. As Altrincham lay within the parish of Bowdon it is possible that some Altrincham children would have attended this school. It was rebuilt by the parish in 1670 and 1806 and was used until 1968 when the site was sold realising enough money to build a school in Bowdon Vale.

In 1759 a school was founded at what is now called Oldfield House with money left by Thomas Walton a salt merchant of Dunham Woodhouses, for the instruction of 40 boys aged 8–11 years who lived in Altrincham, Dunham, Bowdon and Hale. In 1778 there were 28 boys from Altrincham. Their fathers followed a variety of trades. The curriculum included Latin, writing, accounts and Greek, subjects usually taught in grammar schools. The building proved too small and the school moved to larger premises at Seamon's Moss in 1867. For 180 years the school offered an excellent standard of education until it closed in 1938, Fig. 15.13.

Mr. Oswald Leicester, son of a local influential family opened one of the first church Sunday schools in Cheshire in 1783 (Chapter Nine). Members of the Altrincham Wesleyan denomination started a Sunday school in 1798 in a small room in a house off what is now New Street. A field had to be crossed to get there but it was so popular that it soon offered weekday as well as Sunday teaching. At the foot of the Downs, members of the Congregational Chapel started a Sunday and weekday school in 1839.

In the early nineteenth century two societies were formed in London concerned with providing education for children of poor parents. In 1811 Andrew Bell formed the National Society for Promoting the Education of the Poor in the Principles of the Established Church. The Society aimed *"to discipline the infant poor to good orderly habits, to train them to early piety, to warn against social and moral danger and protect the social order"*. Joseph Lancaster founded another society for the education of the poor, the Royal Lancastrian Society in 1808, and six years later after his departure it was renamed the British and Foreign School Society. In these schools, the children of members of non-conformist denominations were trained to *"accept their station in life and to render them useful and respectable members of society"*. By the end of the 19th century the 7 schools connected with St. George's, St. Margaret's and St. John's (Fig. 11.1) were 'National' schools. Rigby Memorial in Broadheath and the British School on Oxford Road were 'British and Foreign' schools. All that remains of the Oxford Road complex is the Mackennal Institute building, now a dress shop.

Both societies used the Bible as a textbook and were run on the monitorial system. In one room under the scrutiny of one teacher up to a hundred children would be kept in order and taught by child monitors, sometimes as young as six years old. Lessons consisted of reading, writing and arithmetic for all children, girls were also taught needlework. Both societies used punishments and rewards as a course of moral training. Typical misdemeanors in Altrincham were not attending church, swearing, lying, quarrelling, talking in class, 'telling tales', playing truant, being disobedient, eating

Fig. 11.1. **St. John's National School, now a clinic.** *D.G.B.* Church beyond.

Fig. 11.2. **Culcheth Hall School** *D.G.B.*

fruit, throwing litter and coming to school late. Punishments included being washed in public, made to wear a dunces cap, being caned and being expelled. Typical explanations for absences were accounted for by limbs being broken, fever, headache, ague, smallpox, itch (a very common excuse), scurvy and death. Rewards for good work were approbation, prizes and medals.

In 1846 Sir James Kay Shuttleworth, the first secretary of the Privy Council on Education inaugurated the pupil-teacher scheme whereby monitors would be replaced by apprentice-teachers of at least 13 years of age. These children had to pass an annual examination and could compete by examination to be fully trained in a Teacher Training College. In 1862 the staff of St. Margaret's Boys School consisted of a master, a pupil-teacher, a paid monitor and a part-time monitor and in Navigation Road in 1906 there were 4 pupil-teachers.

With the rapid rise in population in Altrincham in the early decades of the nineteenth century many dame schools, boarding schools and colleges were founded. According to Stranger's Guide for 1856 there were 9 schools, 1 college and 23 persons listed as teachers. One teacher, Maria Priestner of Marble Hall, George Street, who ran a school was also a mangler.

By the 1830's public opinion was rebelling against the employment of children and many Acts were passed to control the number of hours children should work. These Acts led to an increasing number of children on the streets creating an urban social problem which it was considered could only be solved by children attending school part time when they were not working. The churches enlarged and built premises to provide the necessary places.

In order to improve standards of education the government introduced an Act offering a system of grants in 1862. For every child under 6 attending regularly the school would be allowed 6s 6d (32½p), and for every child over 6, 4s (20p) per annum. For every child over 6 passing an 'inspection' in the subjects of reading, writing or arithmetic, the school could receive a further 2s 8d (13½p) per subject passed. Because it carried a large portion of the grant, attendance of pupils became very important. The preparation for inspections to obtain grants monopolised the work of both teachers and children; the 'three Rs' had arrived.

Fig. 11.3. Early drawing of Navigation Road Schools.   *Trafford Leisure Services*

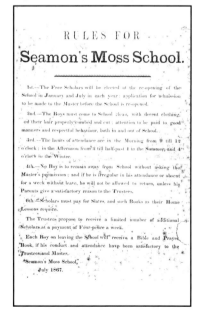

Seamon's Moss School Rules

Fig. 11.4. Altrincham Boys Grammar School   *D.G.B.*

GRANT MADE TO ST. GEORGE'S INFANT SCHOOL, 1865

Average attendance	106	Grant £21 4s 0d	(£21·20)
Passed in arithmetic	22		
Passed in reading	22		
Passed in writing	22	£ 8 16s 0d	(£8·80)
For infants under 6	71	£23 1s 6d	(£23·07)
		Total £53 1s 6d	(£53·07)

There was much truancy and teachers in their spare time visited the homes of the truants. Bad weather and illness accounted for many absences of both staff and pupils, epidemics of whooping cough, measles and smallpox all took their toll. Many children stayed away to help on farms; for example on 26 July 1872 some children were absent in Altrincham gathering strawberries in the fields. Buns were distributed on Friday at noon to those children who had attended school all week.

During the last quarter of the century attendance at school became compulsory up to the age of 10 years in 1880, 11 in 1893 and 12 in 1899. Over the whole country 2,500 School Boards were set up to administer the education of children. Altrincham preferred to appoint a School Attendance Committee in 1891 to ensure attendance and provide free elementary education. A charge however was still made for secondary education.

A school was usually divided into 7 standards from 5 to 11 years. As several classes shared one large room, the problem of noise made learning difficult. Long rigid desks could be uncomfortable, heating was often inadequate. The pupils wrote on slates or drew in sand trays and it was a proud day for the Head of St. Margaret's Boys School in October 1872 when he was able to enter in his Log Book "Dictation is now done entirely upon paper in the Upper Standards, the work is much neater".

Hadfield's Directory for 1886 listed 12 church schools and 8 private schools. The increase in the number of schools provided by all denominations of churches reflected the concern of their members for the young of their parishes. The private schools listed were different from those listed in Stranger's Guide of 1856, which had all proved ephemeral. Culcheth School, on Ashley Road, was founded by Miss Edith Lang and her father in 1891, Fig. 11.2.

By 1898 Altrincham with a population of 12,424 was providing school places for 3,169 children. Attendance was still poor as many children frequently helped in the fields or at home and the average attendance was only 2,232. Children were now required to attend school by law so when a child wanted to leave school to start work he or she had to pass an examination to obtain a 'labour' certificate.

In 1903, Cheshire County Council was made responsible for education and delegated authority locally through the Altrincham, Bowdon, Hale and District Administrative Sub-Committee. Under the chairmanship of Judge Bradbury the Sub-Committee founded a large school complex in 1906 at Navigation Road, Fig. 11.3, for 600 pupils to replace an earlier

Fig. 11.5. **Navigation Road boys with their Union Jacks on Armistice Day, 1918.**   Mrs M. Tyler

Fig. 11.6. **Class of girls and teachers, Navigation Road, 1922.**   Mrs M. Tyler

school founded by the Congregational Church for children of Broadheath.

In the same year schools were founded on Queens Road and Cedar Road near Stamford Park, to replace the schools founded by the non-conformist churches. From 1906 children from the catchment area who were eligible for an advanced type of education called Higher Elementary Education were accommodated in the Cedar Road school until 1910, when a Higher Elementary School (later known as Bradbury) was opened on Queens Road. The County High School for Girls (later Altrincham Girls Grammar School), was opened in 1910 on Cavendish Road with kindergarten, junior and secondary departments. Altrincham County High School for Boys, Marlborough Road, for boys from 8 years old, was founded in 1912 (from 1934 it was known as Altrincham Boys Grammar School, Fig. 11.4).

The non-conformist churches had accepted state education with the benefits of the provision of new schools but the Church of England and the Roman Catholic Church preferred to offer their own religious ideas and lessons. To this end the sisters of the Institute of the Blessed Virgin Mary founded Loreto Convent, Dunham Road in 1909 (Chapter Nine for details).

The state accepted responsibility for wide areas of child welfare. School meals were also supposed to be introduced but one of the first pupils at Navigation Road did not remember anyone staying at school for dinner at this period. Medical examinations were introduced in 1906. St. John's log-book for 15 September

The Hulme Grammar School
MANCHESTER.

Scholarship, Free Place and Entrance Examination,
April 6th and 7th, 1934.

ENGLISH

For boys under ELEVEN years of age.

April 7th, 9-15—10-45.

1. Write about 200 words on one of the following :—

   (a) The happiest day in your life.
   (b) How you spend your spare time.
   (c) Explain the rules of the road to a boy who is using a bicycle for the first time.
   (d) Describe any race you have watched, or in which you have taken part.
   (e) The duties of a Policeman, a Fireman, or a Postman.

2. Write a letter, properly addressed and dated, to a Station Master asking him to reserve seats for you on a train by which you intend to travel. Give all the necessary information.

3. Indicate the subject and predicate parts in the following sentences :—

   (a) Don't be in too much of a hurry.
   (b) I must write my answers carefully.
   (c) How many marks have you received ?
   (d) Untidy corrections involve a loss of marks.
   (e) On this paper several questions have been printed.

4. Write about 5 lines each on 4 of the following, explaining the meaning of the terms ;—

   chemistry, hibernation, temperature, discipline, a three-speed gear, an accumulator, horticulture, biography, biology.

5. Rewrite the following passage in modern English, with correct stops, inverted commas, etc. :—

   Give me the truncheon said Balin to his lady wherewith ye slew your knight anon she gave it him for alway she bare the truncheon with her and therewith Balin smote him through the body and said openly with that truncheon thou hast slain a good knight and now it sticketh in thy body and then Balin called to him his host saying now may ye fetch blood enough to heal your son withal.

D.G.B.

Fig. 11.7. **Part of an entrance examination to a Direct Grant Grammar School, 1934.**

1908 shows Dr. Lawrence had a list of 78 pupils who needed medical treatment. Domestic subjects were introduced to make girls into good wives and mothers and craft lessons given to provide the basis for apprenticeships for boys. National events were celebrated and Fig. 11.5 shows boys from Navigation Road ready to celebrate the end of World War I.

The school leaving age was increased to 14 years in 1918 but the decrease in average family size meant there was no shortage of places. As in other professions women teachers had to retire when they married but after the First World War many spinsters who had lost sweethearts and fiancés trained to become teachers. A teacher of this period is shown with her class in 1922 at Navigation Road school, in Fig. 11.6.

An examination was introduced to find which children would benefit from the teaching at grammar and 'high' schools so that pupils could be offered a grant to support them. The amount of grant varied according to the circumstances of the parents but it was possible for a child to be educated free of charge. This broadened the social base of high schools. In 1924, 16 children from Navigation Road passed an examination to go to Bradbury and 14 were unsuccessful; one girl

passed a County Scholarship examination for the High School for Girls. Fig. 11.7 shows part of a 1934 examination taken successfully by a pupil from Navigation Road to obtain a scholarship to a direct-grant non-County grammar school. Efforts were made to improve facilities in Elementary and Secondary schools with the introduction of art, craft, science and domestic science rooms, *e.g.* as shown in Fig. 11.8, so that learning could take place through activity and experience. Physical exercises were devised to promote better health. Many sports became part of the curriculum. Out of school activities included visits to places of interest such as a telephone exchange, the gas works, even to London.

Forest School, a private school primarily for children in the top half of the ability range was founded in 1924.

With the increasing number of inhabitants due to the post-War I building programme, more schools were needed and in 1932 one was built for juniors in Oldfield Road, and two schools for secondary pupils in Wellington Road in 1938. Just before World War II, ideas for creating a tripartite system of modern, technical and grammar schools for the 11 to 14 year age group were not acted upon in Altrincham.

During World War II Altrincham schools received evacuees and operated a shift system. Pupils attended the school one month in the mornings and the next month in the afternoons. Teachers attended Navigation Road school during holidays to supervise the children of War workers. The canteen there supplied meals for such children from all the schools in Altrincham.

The 1944 Education Act abolished fees in state-run secondary schools and made schooling obligatory to 15 years. Nationwide there was a growing desire for comprehensive education but Altrincham opted to continue to offer 'grammar' or 'secondary' education to pupils over the age of 11 years.

Although secondary education was now free to all, the demand for private education remained and North Cestrian Grammar School was opened in 1951, Fig. 11.9.

During the fifties and sixties the 'bulge', the large increase of numbers of children born after the war, needed school places. With this in mind and because of the high cost of maintaining old buildings the schools connected with St. Margaret's, St. George's and St. John's churches combined in 1968 to found Altrincham C. of E. school in Townfield Road. More places were provided for the Catholic community by the replacement of St. Vincent's School, Fig. 11.10, and the building of Blessed Thomas Holford in 1964. Delahays School was also built in 1964. The use of radio and television made lessons more interesting and the teacher/pupil relationship began to become less formal in many schools. The school leaving age was increased to 16 years in 1972 but many pupils stayed at school to obtain qualifications to take advantage of higher education.

In the 1974 reorganisation of local government education became the responsibility of Trafford Metropolitan Borough. Children with mild learning difficulties are often taught in special classes within their own schools but children with severe learning

Fig. 11.8. **Altrincham Girls County High School** – a cookery class, 1934.

Trafford Leisure Services

Fig. 11.9. **North Cestrian Grammar School, formerly the villa 'Fernlea'**

D.G.B.

Fig. 11.10. **Former St. Vincent's School off Manor Road, due for demolition.**

D.G.B.

Fig. 11.11. **Brentwood School off Deansgate Lane, for disadvantaged children.**

D.G.B.

difficulties have been taught at Brentwood School since its foundation in 1974, Fig. 11.11.

After the bulge had passed a falling population required fewer school places. Bradbury School was demolished in 1985 and the boys and staff were transferred to Delahays School to form Green Lane Secondary School. The boys' school and girls' school on Wellington Road have been merged.

The first government grant for education in 1833 was £20,000 given to the British and National societies for the whole country. In 1986–87 Trafford MBC spent £65,300,000 on education and employed 3,211 people.

An account of education in Altrincham would not be complete without reference to adult education. In 1847 the Altrincham and Bowdon Literary Society was founded and opened a library and newsroom in premises in Victoria Street (Well Street) for use of which a charge of 1d per week was made. The society soon joined the Lancashire and Cheshire Society of Mechanics and Literary Institutes which aimed to provide instruction in those scientific principles which governed the trades of the working man. These premises proved too small for all those wanting to increase their knowledge. A new establishment was built in lower George Street, Fig. 11.12, containing a library, a reading room and three classrooms. In 1877 the Local Board of Health took over the library and enlarged the property 15 years later to include a technical school which flourished until 1923 when it was transferred to the better equipped workshops in Navigation Road School. A new library was built on Stamford New Road in the mid 1970's.

The Bowdon Literary and Scientific Society was formed in 1878. At its 5th session in 1883, 78 members were offered lectures which included:

Oct. 29	Tennyson's Ulysses	Rev. F. Wainwright, M.A.
Nov. 26	Some Experiments in Phosphorescence	S. O'Kell, Esq., F.R.A.S.
Dec. 10	The Moon	R. A. Proctor, Esq., F.R.A.S.

Altrincham was one of only 6 venues in Cheshire where Oxford University offered Extension Courses. W. H. Shaw presented 6 lectures on Florentine History which 580 people attended. Since the beginning of the 20th century, the Workers Educational Association has offered the people of Altrincham courses on a wide variety of subjects from psychology to gardening, often in conjunction with the Extra-Mural Department of Manchester University. Trafford Educational Authority also offers courses in both vocational and non-vocational subjects at the South Trafford College and its annexes. Adult education is still very much part of the Altrincham way of life.

Fig. 11.12. The old Art Gallery, Museum and Library in George Street being demolished in 1975.   *W. Wilson*

Chapter Twelve

ALTRINCHAM AT LEISURE

BASIL MORRISON

For centuries after the granting of a market and fair charter by Edward I in 1290 Altrincham has enjoyed the privilege of a three day fair. Its date was altered in 1319 to the eve, day and morrow of St. James' Day (25 July), the Sanjam Fair. The early fairs were probably for dealing in animals but were also occasions when people met together to enjoy themselves. Eventually they developed into rather boisterous and noisy occasions on the eves of which the town crier would read the proclamation which included the following passage: "... *and that all manner of persons do forbear to carry unlawful weapon or weapons, but that they leave them at their respective lodgings*". There are some who today might say behaviour has not changed much since then! As a result of riotous behaviour Sanjam fair was abolished in 1895.

Perhaps Altrincham was luckier than some other towns of similar size due to the energetic and enthusiastic development of local organisations by ordinary people. Altrincham also has to thank generous-hearted benefactors like Lord Stamford and others who did so much in the latter part of the 19th and early 20th centuries to give the locality its present-day image as a first-class area for leisure pursuits by presenting the town with open spaces in which people could enjoy themselves.

Stretching from Goose Green including Lloyd Street and Stamford Park was the area known as Hale Moss where in former times, near the Pinfold, many forms of amusement were to be found. Cockfighting, hen-racing

and, up to 1753, horse-racing took place. The latter sport also took place at Racefield near St. Margaret's Church. In the last century the area was mainly occupied during the summer by itinerant showmen and actors mingling with the machine-made music of the swingboats, roundabouts, boxing booths and other noisy attractions. Even today, showmen occupy Denmark Street carpark in the spring, carrying on the fair tradition. At one period the fairs took place in Atlantic Street.

The tradition of display was perpetuated by Altrincham Carnival for many years, headed by Ted Fleming and Freddie Fox, who as King and Queen Carnival, helped to raise large sums of money for Altrincham General Hospital. Its popularity then waned, to be resurrected in 1978 by Altrincham Festival Committee organising a procession of colourful floats through the town and a host of interesting events throughout Festival Week to help local charities, Fig. 12.1.

In 1901, to commemorate Queen Victoria's Jubilee, a swimming bath was opened followed in 1909 by a second bath on the site now occupied by Rackham's

Fig. 12.2. Altrincham Sports D.G.B. **Centre**

Fig. 12.1. **Altrincham Festival Parade. Timperley Guides and Brownies Supreme Entry Prize 'Santa's Workshop', 1989**

Altrincham Guardian

Fig. 12.3. **Altrincham Picture Theatre, 1913-66.**   *B.D.M.*

Fig. 12.4. **Altrincham Hippodrome.**   *B.D.M.*

store in Stamford New Road. These two baths were replaced by a new bath in Oakfield Road in 1974. This was extended in 1982 to create the popular Leisure Centre in Oakfield Road providing swimming, badminton and other activities, Fig. 12.2.

At the turn of the century, the cinematograph arrived, a more sophisticated form of entertainment. The first cinema in Altrincham had an interesting history. In 1816 a small Unitarian Chapel was erected close to the corner of Shaw's Road and Central Way with a small burial ground at the front on the corner. The chapel was replaced in 1872 by the fine Unitarian Church on Dunham Road. A shop and house were then erected on the burial ground after reinterment of the remains elsewhere. Later still the house and shop were joined on to the old chapel at the rear, the whole building being used first as a Salvation Army H.Q. until it became Altrincham's first permanent theatre. It was called the Central Theatre from which Central Way derives its name. Following the demise of the theatre it was converted into a cinema and for reasons hardly defying imagination it was affectionately known as "Th' Bug Hut". It was closed down in 1933 as it failed to comply with safety regulations.

In December 1894 a small timber-built theatre was erected called the Princess Theatre which is believed to have stood near Stamford Park. It was managed by the Misses Clegg and Hodgkinson who presented various plays and concerts for some years. According to the Altrincham Guardian of 9 January 1895 it was destroyed by fire. From then on the actors and actresses performed in St. Vincent's School.

In 1913 Altrincham Picture Theatre (979 seats), part of the Moorhouse Circuit, was built on the site of Station House office block. With the coming of the 'talkies', it continued to prosper until it closed in 1966, Fig. 12.3.

Fig. 12.5. **Hale Cinema in Cheshire – black-and-white style, drawn by Basil Morrison.**

Fig. 12.6. **The Regal Cinema.** Stylish 'Egyptian' architecture, where Roberts House now stands. *B.D.M.*

Fig. 12.7. **The Garrick Playhouse and logo.** *B.D.M.*

Fig. 12.8. **The Club Theatre, Oxford Road,** being enlarged in 1983. *B.D.M.*

Just prior to World War I Altrincham Hippodrome (1,000 seats) was erected at the foot of Stamford Street as a live variety theatre and for many years was popular and well attended. It was opened and managed by a Mr. Hargreaves as Altrincham's premier house of entertainment. His son Frank took over the theatre when it was converted to a very comfortable cinema right up to the time it became known as Studio One of the Cannon Circuit, finally closing in 1986, Fig. 12.4. The site is now occupied by a modern office block.

Although the cinema which once stood on the site of the modern block of flats at the corner of Ashley Road and Willowtree Road was known as Hale Cinema, Fig. 12.5, the whole of the seating accommodation was within Altrincham Borough boundary for rating purposes, while the stage and screen were in the rating of Hale Urban District Council! It was a most pleasing building in part black and white Cheshire style suitable to the area. It was opened in January 1923 and demolished in 1979.

Roberts House on Manchester Road, (the present home of the Inland Revenue and Employment Offices) lies on the site of what was reputed to be one of the finest luxury cinemas outside Manchester, Fig. 12.6. The Regal Cinema was opened here on 13 May 1931 by Lord Stamford. It was truly an outstanding cinema which could seat 2,000 patrons. It possessed a beautiful Compton organ, pride of resident organist Norman Cocker and other well-known visiting organists of the time including Joseph Seal, Harry D. Speed and Charles Massey. The theatre was for many years the home of the North Cheshire Amateur Operatic Society for its bi-annual musical presentations. Sadly on the night of 6

January 1956 the whole building was destroyed by fire.

Accompanying the growth of the cinema came the lighting of the dramatic torch in Altrincham with the foundation in November 1913 of the Garrick Society in the cellar provided by Mr. J. W. Byrom beneath his Kingsway drapery store. Some 20 years later fired by encouragement from George Bernard Shaw himself the new Garrick Playhouse on Barrington Road was built and proved to be the first 'little theatre' built for repertory in Great Britain, Fig. 12.7. Designed by T. Harold Hill, built by Charles Pennington of Hale it was opened on 1 October 1932 by Mr. P. M. Oliver the Liberal M.P. for Altrincham. It cost £9,000, seated 500 and had a stage wider at that time than that of the Opera House, Manchester. The Society were proud to proclaim in 1932 *"We have not flung the robe of Thespis about a converted warehouse, nor have we made our temple in some disused ecclesiastical property"*. The Garrick logo, Fig. 12.7, depicting the torch-bearing, kneeling thinker was designed by Miss Ella Slynn, scenic director and teacher in elocution. Today many societies present shows at the Garrick.

There have been many non-professional, private or ecclesiastically-connected dramatic societies in the town,

10 Adelphi Terrace
London, W.C.2
10th July, 1920

If you insist of being an amateur society you must go to the Society of Authors, and pay £5 5 0 for each performance, and be limited to two, or at the outside three performances. I have no power, as a good trade unionist to waive or reduce these terms.

If you would only go into theatrical business seriously you would have to pay no more than 5% on receipts not in excess of £50. It is not essential that your operations should be continuous, or that your profits (if any) should be privately spent instead of being reserved to strengthen the enterprise and finally enable you to have a regular Altrincham Repertory Theatre paying a hiring wage to its artists and employees. But if you are determined to be amateurs you must pay the penalty.

G.B.S.

Fig. 12.9. **Altrincham Football Club Ground, Moss Lane.** Home of 'The Robins'.   *D.G.B.*

Letter by G.B. Shaw to the Garrick.   *Miss M. Ross*

![Dunham Hall and Park]

Fig. 12.10. **Dunham Hall and Park.** *Trafford Leisure Services*

Fig. 12. 11 **Timperley Cricket Club.**   *B.D.M.*

but of those remaining, Altrincham's Club Theatre's meteoric rise in popularity, Fig. 12.8, is worthy of mention. Founded in 1896 when St. Margaret's Church Institute in Market Street was built, it is one of the oldest societies in the county. It was not until 1947 when it was joined by the Club Players from Timperley that the society blossomed under new management since when it has never looked back. The theatre, on Oxford Road, is perhaps not as well-known as it might be. Due to its limitation in size, full houses have been assured for every night of each play, there being no need to advertise and there is a waiting-list for audience membership. In 1962 on the sale of St. Margaret's Institute to Altrincham Council, the Club Theatre bought the Methodist Chapel and adjoining school in Oxford Road and the chapel was subsequently converted into a 129-seat theatre. It was not until 1982 when registration as an Entertainment Club was required under the Greater Manchester Act 1981, that the basic accommodation in the school was completely refurbished. The society's president, Dame Wendy Hiller supports the improvement of cultural amenities of the area, appreciating that, with the professional theatre being beyond the financial reach of many people, the Club Theatre meets an important need. The club's senior vice-president was Mr. Arthur Dakin, an active member since 1918 and the chairman is Mr. David Lane who also had a long association with the theatre.

It has been said that an English town is not a town unless it possesses a football club. In 1903 Altrincham Football Club was founded and was originally known as the Rigby Memorial Sunday School Football Club which was an offshoot from the British Schools in Oxford Road behind which were once Rigby Street and Pownall Street. Some years later it was renamed Broadheath Football Club. Its first ground was at Pollitt's Field until in 1920 the Council offered their present site in Moss Lane, Fig. 12.9, at a rent of £10 per annum. A year later, the club became a limited company and played in the Cheshire League in 1933. Some 28 years later in 1961 Messrs. Noel White and Peter Swales took over the management of the club's affairs. By their energy, and business-like approach, they placed the club firmly on its feet. They borrowed money to build the existing stands and provided many other amenities expected of a club of the standing of the 'Robins'. On the formation of the Northern Premier League Peter Swales became its chairman.

Since well before the turn of the century, many of the breathing spaces laid out as parks and recreation grounds have been given by generous landowners for the benefit of the public (Chapter Seven). Great pleasure has been enjoyed by the public for many years in having access to Dunham Park, Fig. 12.10, with its majestic 250 year old trees, a deer house dated 1740 and an old working saw mill originally a corn mill built in Elizabethan times.

The town prides itself on a fine municipal 18-hole golf course on Stockport Road, Timperley. In the 1890's the land around the present clubhouse was leased to Timperley (private) Golf Club, but in 1934 the whole of Timperley Hall Farm was purchased by Altrincham council. Due to its pleasant aspect and accessibility it is a popular and well-used amenity.

On 7 April 1877, the sporting gentry of the day founded Timperley Cricket Club, Fig. 12.11. whose first ground was in Moss Lane up to 1883 when the present site was acquired at the corner of Stockport Road and Wood Lane. The 21st cricket season saw the erection of the present pavilion, and alterations to part of the old pavilion. The hockey section started in 1886 and is reputed to be one of the oldest in the north-west. A tennis section opened prior to World War I and the club is now a cricket, hockey and tennis club.

The idea of an ice rink for Altrincham, Fig. 12.12, had been for some years in the mind of Mr. Albert Allen, a local business man and builder. In 1948 while taking a petition round Didsbury seeking support for an ice rink to be built there he met Mr. Ken Bailey who was taking part in an ice show. The Didsbury rink was never built due to planning difficulties but Mr. Allen conceived his ultimate dream of an ice rink in Altrincham which opened on 2 December 1960 when 2,000 people came on the first night. It was fitting that the Grand Ice Gala should open with an exhibition from Sjoukie Dijkstra, Champion of Europe and the World who later won a Gold Medal for Holland, her home country. It was equally fitting that the rink's 21st birthday in 1981 should be graced by the reigning British, European and World Ice Dance Champions, Jane Torvill and Christopher Dean, who later became Gold Medallists at the Olympic Games.

The rink serves enthusiasts from as far afield as Stoke, Crewe and North Wales and it has a high reputation promoted by the quality of the teaching staff attracting skaters from all over the world. Some of the most famous skating personalities who were trained here included Sharo Jones and Paul Askham, Karen Barber and Nicky Slater and many other champions. From 1960 the rink was owned and operated by Mr. Allen as chairman with Mr. K. N. G. Bailey as managing director but on 2 February 1987 it was taken over by another local businessman Mr. Derek C. Thompson and it is now known as Altrincham Ice Rink (Trafford) Ltd. with Mr. Bailey as managing consultant. The rink supports Altrincham Ice Speed Skating Club and the Aces Ice Hockey Club.

There are many clubs which cater for activities other than the dramatic arts or sports. Among these are a number of artists' societies, the oldest of which is probably Altrincham Society of Artists founded in November 1937 with Lord Stamford as its first president. Its popularity over the years has rapidly increased and it now possesses over 100 members. There is weekly tuition for members wishing to improve their technique and there are indoor and outdoor exhibitions of work. The society possesses its own studio-clubroom headquarters in Sylvan Grove, Altrincham. There are many other societies—educational, uniformed, social, musical, choral, operatic, history, civic, garden and allotment—too numerous to mention in detail, which provide valuable service to the community.

Fig. 12.12. **Altrincham Ice Rink.**

D.G.B.

Chapter Thirteen

TRANSPORT

THE BRIDGEWATER CANAL

DON BAYLISS

Francis Egerton, 3rd Duke of Bridgewater, devoted his energies to developing his Worsley estates, particularly for coal mining. He, his agent, John Gilbert, and engineer, James Brindley, built one of the most spectacular canal systems of the day. The Act of Parliament which enabled the Duke to start building his contour canal was passed in 1759. The canal was first intended only to carry coals to the developing markets in Manchester by a route through Salford.

During 1759 this first plan was abandoned and a new Act obtained to carry the canal across the Irwell, by a high stone aqueduct at Barton, to Stretford. At Old Trafford, there would be a branch to Manchester. This waterway would tap the growing markets for coal both in Manchester and north Cheshire, across the Mersey. At Altrincham the gentry and businessmen signed petitions supporting the new plan. In the face of this potential competition, the turnpike trusts responded by investing a lot of money in road improvements from Manchester as far as Stretford. The canal reached Stretford in 1761 and the amount of coal which was carried to that place by barge, instead of by road, so alarmed the trusts that the Duke agreed to compensate them annually for the quantities of goods carried by the new canal.

The third Act was passed in 1762 which allowed the canal to progress into Cheshire and so to Runcorn, thus serving north Cheshire and providing a water connection between the river Mersey, above Liverpool, and Manchester. An aqueduct was built to take the canal across the Mersey flats at Stretford in 1763.

The surveying of the land to Altrincham across the bogland of Sale and Timperley Moss and the sandy heath at Broadheath followed. To counter this threat to road traffic and trade, a turnpike trust re-metalled the road from Stretford to Altrincham in 1765, but in this year land for the canal had already been acquired. Much enclosure of these wastes had been undertaken, the ground was firmer and progress speedy. This is an extract from a document of 1765:

"'The measure of land mark'd out for his Grace the Duke of Bridgewater betwixt Riddings Hall and ye Farther side of Broadheath

	£	s	d	
Timperley Moss to				
Hankinson's Inclosure	12	7	6	*(£12·37)*
Hankinson's 1st and 2nd Inclosure	9	7	6	*(£ 9·37)*
Timperley Moss from Hankinson's				
Inclosure to Isaac Royle's				
Inclosure	19	8	1½	*(£19·41)'"*

The canal then passed through other lands owned by Mr. Worthington, Dr. Sedgwick, Jer. Brundrett, John Birch and Elizabeth Broom (4 plots) and through: *"Waste to the Poor House Inclosure, Broadheath . . . and through Charles Greswell's as staked out"*. The surveyors had already been busy.

The canal was opened through Broadheath as far as Lymm in 1765, but the Duke was in serious financial trouble, owing over £60,000 and borrowing large amounts of money from merchants and even small amounts from employees. To raise money, Gilbert was instructed to start a passenger boat service from Worsley to Manchester and Lymm. In 1767 a letter from a writer in Altrincham to a newspaper stated that the Duke had built warehouses for corn and coal wharves "near this place", *i.e.* at Broadheath and that the canal had already bridged the Bollin at Dunham. Coal had dropped in price to one half. The letter went on to state that it was believed the Duke had stayed at Tatton and had been *"towed some miles"* on the canal *"to see the Progress of his Works"*. The whole canal to Runcorn was completed in 1776. By 1781 there were passenger services from Manchester to Runcorn every day. The boats were described as very comfortable and cheap and claimed to offer a cuisine as good as hotels in London! The boats were horse-drawn but also had sails, and travelled at five miles per hour. One service left Castle Quay in Manchester at 8 a.m., reached Altrincham at 10 a.m. and Runcorn at 5 p.m. A boat the other way called at Altrincham at 4 p.m.

The trade on the canal led to the growth of the hamlet of Broadheath. This became the port for Altrincham with a sawmill and foundry, Packet House and Navigation Hotel, a boat house (now a tool hire firm), and a warehouse on the north side of the canal east of Broadheath Bridge, Fig. 13.1. A larger warehouse was built in 1833 (later a flour mill, now Luxiproducts), Fig. 13.2. Broadheath developed a considerable trade in coal, corn, timber, stone and night soil from Manchester for the Altrincham vegetable growing industry. It remained separated from Altrincham by fields. Altrincham became a minor 'canal town' and a few early wealthy canal-commuters and traders using the canal lived there.

The canal was to suffer its first eclipse after the mid-19th century through competition with the railway system. Lord Francis Egerton, Earl of Ellesmere, agreed in 1846 for the new railway to Altrincham (built 1849) to cross the Castlefield canal complex by a massive viaduct in return for 10,000 railway shares and agreement that he would withdraw his passenger boats on the canal. In 1871 the canal was sold for £1,115,000 to the chairmen of the two railway companies operating the Altrincham line who claimed they were acting as

Fig. 13.1. Warehouse, now demolished, east of Broadheath Bridge.

Trafford Leisure Services

Fig. 13.2. The warehouse of 1833, later Hulbert's Flour Mill and now housing a manufacturer of children's items. Note former entrance for barges.

D.G.B.

Fig. 13.3. Former coal staithes at Broadheath, canal to right.

D.G.B.

individuals and not for the benefit of their companies! They formed the Bridgewater Canal Company but, as may be expected investment in the system was negligible and in 1897 the canal was sold to the Manchester Ship Canal Company for £1,710,000.

There was then a growth of trade for 70 years with the rise of the Broadheath machine-tool and other industries, assisted by the presence of the canal and railways for transporting coal and raw materials and some finished goods. After World War II the canal was still carrying half-a-million tons of coal a year, but commercial traffic virtually finished with the demolition of small coal-powered power-stations recently. The coal staithes at Broadheath, Fig. 13.3, have now gone and the coal wharf site has been developed as an office complex. The canal now fulfils a different role, for leisure boating, and fishing. The Broadheath towpath forms part of a walkway round the 'Cheshire Ring' of canals.

COACH TRANSPORT

Altrincham was important as a stage on the mail and passenger coach services to Chester, Warrington and Knutsford. Pigot and Dean's New Directory of Manchester and Salford for 1821-22 mentions that coaches ran frequently from the Waggon and Horses formerly in Old Market Place. The 'Victory' coach stopped on its run from Manchester to Chester every morning at 7 a.m. The return coach in the evening from Chester ran out at 7 p.m. from the Waggon and Horses. Another service is recorded as using a stage at the Navigation Inn at Broadheath (and no doubt calling at Altrincham) and from here the 'Pilot' ran on its way from Manchester to Chester at "half past two o'clock" and returned the next day to Manchester at the same time. At the beginning of the 19th century the Unicorn was a mail stage and mail coaches for Manchester and Knutsford left here at 4.30 p.m.

Kelly's Directory of Cheshire for 1864 states there were horse-drawn omnibus services from Bowdon Station which left for Hale on Monday, Wednesday, Thursday and Friday at 8 a.m. They seem to have made a round trip collecting people to commute to Manchester by train. There was another outward service at 5.20 p.m. which would have taken the same people home from the train.

Fig. 13.4. **Open-top tram No. 345, destination Deansgate, in Stamford New Road.**

MTMS Archives

Fig. 13.5. **Covered-top car No. 643 at Altrincham.**

MTMS Archives

ELECTRIC TRAM OPERATION
RAY DUNNING AND DON BAYLISS

The Manchester Carriage Company in 1897 applied to extend their horse-tram tracks from Stretford to Altrincham and Hale, but this failed. In 1901 there was a proposal for Altrincham and District Tramways company which planned to develop a figure-of-eight electric tram system centred on Moss Lane bridge. This plan was rejected. The outcome of various subsequent parliamentary bills was that Manchester Corporation obtained a long lease on lines to be constructed to Altrincham.

By 17 August 1906 the tramways had reached Park Road, Timperley. The roadway under Timperley and Broadheath railway bridges had to be lowered and Broadheath Bridge widened for the passage of the trams. Lines were then laid down Barrington Road, Sandiway Road, Stamford New Road and Railway Street. On 9 May 1907 seven special cars left Manchester town hall filled with council representatives and other worthies

and a tape was cut as the first tram crossed the Altrincham boundary. At a celebration tea later that day back in Heaton Park a discordant note was struck when Alderman Wainwright, chairman of Manchester Tramways Committee said that he hoped they would eventually be able to convey the people from the crowded district of Hulme *"direct to the gates of that beautiful domain, Dunham Hall"*. Robert Martin, Chairman of Altrincham Tramways Committee reminded the gathering that there would be serious objections by the inhabitants of Bowdon to attempt to popularise Dunham Park. A tram illuminated with 1800 lamps, followed by 5 other cars then left for Altrincham and was cheered into the town.

The service trams reached Altrincham from Exchange on 10 May 1907. The cars ran alternately via Deansgate–Chester Road, and Mosley Street–City Road. Later, a service was also introduced from Piccadilly to Altrincham via All Saints and Stretford Road. The cars ran into Altrincham down Barrington Road, single track with passing loops, and from Altrincham outwards via

Sandiway Road; there were passing loops in Stamford New Road and double track in Railway Street. The minimum fare for adults was 1d ($\frac{1}{2}$p); 5$\frac{1}{2}$d (2p) all the way!

It had been stipulated that 50 horse-power trams should be used on the Altrincham route but those which operated were 40 h.p. and too light for the job. It was a constant struggle for the drivers and it was not unknown for them to fail to stop to pick people up at 'request stops' in order to keep on schedule.

From documents dated Monday 9 October 1911, there were 12 service tramcars on full day service on the Altrincham route consisting of 6 open-top bogie (large) trams, Fig. 13.4, and 6 covered-top open-ended bogie trams. Also there were 6 covered open-ended bogie trams on part-day service.

In October, 1920, car No. 643, Fig. 13.5, was frequently complained about for being noisy. One lady used to dash out of her house, note the tram number and report it. Another lady complained the tram woke her up every morning. An angry councillor said it was an absolute disgrace and eventually Sale and District Council sent a letter of protest but 643 still rumbled on. The destination boards on the side of the trams read: MANCHESTER STRETFORD SALE ALTRINCHAM. When it was decided to paint the boards different colours for different routes, those on the Altrincham route were brown with white lettering.

A 'workman's ticket', which was cheaper than the normal fare could be obtained up to and including 7 a.m.

One of the services offered by the trams was that of Post Trams, carrying mobile post-boxes. The last left Altrincham at 8.26 p.m. arriving in Piccadilly at 9.25 p.m.

The General Manager of the Tramways, Henry Mattinson died late in 1928 and in early 1929 was succeeded by R. Stuart Pilcher. It was not long after this appointment that a tram-scrapping plan came into operation. On 19 January 1931 a regular bus service was worked on the 47, Fig. 13.6, and 48 tram routes, adopting the trams' service numbers. For a time trams operated in the rush hours but eventually the last tram ran on Saturday, 6 June 1931. On the following Tuesday the bus fare was raised by 50% to 6d (2$\frac{1}{2}$p)!

Most of the lines were lifted within a year but those on Sandiway Road were lifted in 1943 to provide steel for the war effort. Other remnants of lines could still be seen on Manchester Road in Broadheath in 1988 when sewerage works were carried out. These lines still remain under the road surface.

BUS SERVICES
MICHAEL DAVIES

Before the First World War there had only been trams or horse-drawn carriages or wagonettes, the former inflexible and unable to serve many localities and the last slow and uncomfortable. One horse-drawn service in the Altrincham area was a double-decked omnibus which ran from the Bleeding Wolf in Hale to Broadheath station via Altrincham station between 1904 and 1907. The first motorbus service, operated from Macclesfield by the British Automobile Traction Company ran to Altrincham in 1913, but this succumbed to war-time conditions before the end of 1914. The subsequent development of bus services began in similar circumstances to that in many other towns after World War I. Men returning to civilian life invested their gratuities and savings in surplus ex-War Department vehicles and provided a much appreciated service to the travelling public.

Following the cessation of hostilities, green 'British' buses, operating from Stockport through the growing

Fig. 13.6. **Fully-enclosed tram, No. 628 on the 47 route.**

MTMS Archives

Fig. 13.7. Part of John Wood's fleet. *A.M.D.*
The 4 large buses to the left are Leyland 32 and 40 seat vehicles; the 3 small vehicles are Oldsmobiles with 14 seats.

areas of Cheadle and Gatley, again appeared on the streets of Altrincham. In 1921, the local furniture remover and charabanc operator, John Wood and Sons Ltd., commenced operations from his Oakfield Road warehouse with a few red and white buses. His open charabancs, each named after a flower, Harebell, Bluebell, White Rose and Camellia were already well-known in the locality. The first regular timetable was issued in August 1921 covering the route to Hale Barns and this was quickly followed by routes to Hoo Green by Bucklow Hill, Arthog Road, Bowdon Vale and Lymm. By 1922, Wood's vehicles were a serious competitor to those of the 'British' company on the Stockport route and his business was further consolidated when he took over a small Timperley operator, the Timperley Motor Company which operated from Lloyd Street to Baguley. Now operating a fleet of over 20 buses he traded from March 1922 as Altrincham and District Motor Bus Services Ltd. (though the buses were labelled Altrincham Motor Bus Services, Fig. 13.7). Wood's vehicles radiated in an arc south of Altrincham from Latchford in the west, to Macclesfield in the east, including Pickmere, Northwich Station, Knutsford, Lower Peover, Mobberley and Alderley

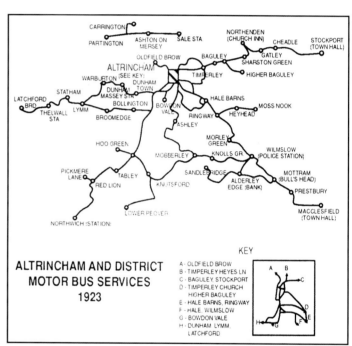

Fig. 13.8. Map of 1925 bus services of John Wood's Company. *A.M.D.*

Fig. 13.9. North Western Tilling Stevens *A.M.D.*
Bus No. 202 of 1926 at the Kingsway Stand.

Fig. 13.10 Altrincham Bus Station on Kingsway, *A.M.D.*
1930-1976. The Billiard hall can be seen on the right. Leyland double decker no. 252 (1949), route 80 to Didsbury and Stockport. Leyland single decker no. 308 (1950), route 99 circular to Delahays Road and Timperley.

Edge, Fig. 13.8. None of Wood's buses ran north of Altrincham apart from an isolated service from Sale Station to Ashton-on-Mersey, Flixton and Partington, as Manchester Corporation Tramways had a monopoly on the Manchester road.

By late 1924 both Crosville Motor Services and the newly formed North Western Road Car Co. (successors to British Automobile Traction from April, 1923), now the principal bus operators in Cheshire were finding the Altrincham and District Motor Services a thorn in their flesh. Wood's next move was an offer to purchase a Northwich operator, the Mid-Cheshire Company, but the two major companies fought him off culminating in a success for North Western, who extended their territory deep into Cheshire from 24 November, 1924. For the next twelve months, Altrincham and District continued to prosper but the days of the medium-sized operator were numbered and the company finally succumbed to North Western's offer of £37,500 for its 26 vehicles and just over 100 route-miles on 1 January 1926.

Petrol-engined vehicles made by the firm of Tilling Stevens were the mainstay of the North Western fleet from the mid-1920's, Fig. 13.9. They were joined around 1931-2 by a large number of Dennis 'Lancets' and these 'cars' (as North Western always referred to their buses) undoubtedly built up the reputation of the company for reliability. An express service to Blackpool was introduced in 1928 and proved very popular with holiday-makers and day-trippers.

Prior to 1926 several locations were used as bus termini. Lloyd Street served Timperley and Baguley (Timperley Motors); Stamford Street, by the Hippodrome served the Stockport direction (British/North Western); Kingsway, by the billard hall—for Altrincham and District's services. Altrincham and District also used a small croft on the opposite side of Kingsway, and it was this area, extended through to Stamford New Road which provided the land for North Western's new bus station opened in 1930, Fig. 13.10. This included a waiting room, enquiry and left-luggage departments, a staff mess-room and administrative accommodation. Altrincham bus station was remodelled during 1962-63. It was closed 13 years later in November 1976 on the creation of the bus-rail interchange, one of several in Greater Manchester County.

During the 1930's, with increasing mobility but only very limited car ownership, North Western improved its services to reach a peak in the summer of 1939 when most local services provided last journeys at 11.30 p.m. from the bus station, and frequencies were such that the public hardly needed to possess a copy of the very comprehensive timetable booklet sold for 2d (1p). Also during this period, the old garage at Oakfield Road proved too small for the increasing size of the fleet, and new premises were built on land at the bottom of Oakfield Street for minor repairs and servicing; major repairs were carried out at the company's H.Q. at Stockport.

During the war years some rural routes including those to Castle Mill, Macclesfield via Dean Row and Bollington, and to Macclesfield via Morley and Wilmslow were suspended and all the express services soon disappeared, including the very popular hourly journeys to Liverpool. After the War, services to London and North Wales returned in time for the 1946 summer season and a Liverpool–Newcastle-upon-Tyne route was reinstated in October 1946. Macclesfield was once more linked to Altrincham by a two-hourly service commencing in June 1947, but Castle Mill no longer attracted the huge pre-war crowd to its bathing pools though it retained, for a few years, a twice-weekly service to and from Altrincham on market days via Hale and Ashley.

Travel by bus over Britain as a whole reached its zenith in the period 1949–51 from which time commenced the long downward spiral with fares steadily climbing to compensate for lost passengers. A typical example was Altrincham bus station to Bowdon Vale ($1\frac{1}{2}$ miles). The fare fell from 3d (1p) in the 1920's to $1\frac{1}{2}$d ($\frac{1}{2}$p) from 1933 to 1950, since when it has steadily risen to its 1990 figure of 50p, an 80-fold increase!

The most important other regular bus operator was Manchester Corporation Tramways Department. On his appointment in 1929, the new manager, Mr. R. Stuart Pilcher advocated replacing the tramways with buses in view of the ageing condition of the tramway stock and the impending electrification of the railway. An express bus service was introduced on 16 May 1929 from The Downs tram terminus to Manchester, Rochdale and Littleborough. In March, 1930 the Corporation modified its express service to operate a purely local limited stop service from Altrincham to Manchester, while still maintaining a minimum fare to protect the trams. However, the restriction was lifted in 1931 when the tramway service was reduced and buses on the 47 and 48 routes took over the majority of the journeys to Manchester. Double-decked buses were introduced in November 1930 and from January 1931 trams ran at the morning and evening peak hours only, Fig. 13.11. They were finally withdrawn on 6 June. (The Manchester bus services 263 and 264 still run from Lloyd Street and the old Downs terminus.)

In 1929 Sykes of Sale had commenced a service from Manchester to Hale Barns via Sale and Altrincham. This became a joint operation with Manchester Corporation but Sykes's part, including two buses, was eventually purchased by them on 14 May 1933. Through journeys from Manchester to Hale Barns continued until the end of 1939, when wartime conditions brought about their suspension. Two other pre-war operators remain to be mentioned. Norman Juckes operated popular Sunday afternoon 'Cheshire Tours' in open charabancs, fare 3s 0d (15p), and trips to Blackpool at weekends, fare 5s 0d (25p) day return; 7s 6d ($37\frac{1}{2}$p) period return). On the occasion of Altrincham Show he ran a shuttle service from the Downs to the showground at the Devisdale, fare 6d ($2\frac{1}{2}$p), for a journey of half a mile, this fare producing a very good return for Juckes and

Fig. 13.11. **Manchester Corporation Downs Terminus shortly before trams were withdrawn, March 1931.** Note two 'low-bridge' type buses. Tram car No. 711 to football match.

A.M.D.

not a few grumbles from those making the trip! Juckes's wife ran a china shop on the Downs and this doubled as a booking office for the bus operation. The second operator was Jackson's Tours which operated from premises between Moss Lane and Mayor's Road and was the only small coach operator offering a service in the immediate post- World War II period. From two elderly vehicles of c.1932 vintage his fleet rapidly expanded with the post-war travel boom to be eventually part of the Shearings empire. No further major changes took place in the public transport scene until the early 1970's, with Manchester Corporation operating a frequent service to Manchester. North Western provided all local services into the rural areas until March 1972, when the company ceased to exist after a very successful 49 years' service.

The depots in the area were transferred to 'SELNEC' the South East Lancashire and North East Cheshire Transport Authority. The long-familiar red and cream livery quickly gave way to SELNEC'S orange and white, and these colours were used by the newly created Greater Manchester Passenger Transport Authority on that body's assuming control of SELNEC following local government re-organisation in 1974.

Sunday 26 October 1986 brought about Government de-regulation and led to the biggest changes since the Road Traffic Act of 1930. The first effect of the new Act was the appearance of a fleet of mini-buses, known initially as 'Altrincham Hoppers' but soon to change to 'Little Gem', operated by GM Buses Ltd., successors to GMT. A rival concern Bee-Line started in January 1987 and this concern fought a fierce battle with GMB for traffic on several routes, mainly in the Timperley and Wythenshawe districts. A system of tendering for the more lightly-trafficked routes was introduced, a subsidy being paid to the successful tenderer by the GM Passenger Transport Executive or Cheshire County Council as appropriate. This has resulted in a great number of operators' vehicles coming to the interchange from places as far away as Burnley, Middleton, Chester and Birkenhead, but perhaps the most remarkable is the re-appearance after an absence of over 16 years of

vehicles of the North Western Road Car Company Ltd., reformed in 1986 from part of Ribble, (a National Bus Company subsidiary); and in 1988 their buses started regular operations from the interchange to Manchester and Trafford Park. Their depot is in Broadheath but the former red livery has given way to heavy blue and red. The bus scene in Altrincham continues to be one of endless variety and the introduction of the Light Rapid Transit or Metro-Link in 1992 will bring even more changes.

RAILWAYS
ANDREW MACFARLANE

Nineteen years after the opening of the historic Liverpool & Manchester Railway, the Manchester South Junction and Altrincham Railway (MSJ&A) arrived in Altrincham. Its main purpose was to provide a link from London Road station (now Piccadilly) to the Liverpool & Manchester Railway at Ordsall Lane, Salford. The branch line to Altrincham, then a small market town of about 4,000 people, was almost an afterthought. Before the line opened, the original promoting companies, the Manchester & Birmingham Railway and the Sheffield, Ashton-under-Lyne & Manchester Railway, became part of the London & North Western (LNWR) and the Manchester, Sheffield & Lincolnshire Railway (MSLR) respectively. Lord Francis Egerton guided the Bill authorising construction through Parliament on 29 January 1845, provided land for the line alongside the Bridgewater Canal and agreed to withdraw the competing passenger-carrying flyboats which plied the canal. The Bill received Royal Assent on 21 July 1845, and a contract to build was awarded to John Brogden of Sale in October. The original intention was that Deansgate Row, Navigation Lane and the Stockport turnpike would all bridge the line. To save money, level crossings were installed and present-day motorists have this decision to thank for the delays they suffer!

The first train ran on the Altrincham branch, Fig. 13.12, at noon on Whit Monday, 28 May 1849.

Railway officials, local dignitaries, friends and relatives were drawn in two first-class carriages hauled by an engine borrowed from the LNWR. One coach carried the Stretford Temperance Band wearing blue uniforms. At Sale the train was greeted with canon salutes and cheers from the workmen lining the route. The train made a stop at Timperley (Brooklands Station did not open until 1859) and after arriving at Altrincham, the band led the procession to the Unicorn where the party ate and drank. After a drive out to Rostherne everyone returned to the Unicorn for more eating, drinking and speech-making. The train returned to Oxford Road at around 10 p.m.

The first public train left Altrincham at 8 a.m. on Friday, 20 July 1849, hauled by an engine of the type shown in Fig 13.13. A young lad called Isaac Warburton ran from his home in Langham Road, Bowdon, to Altrincham Station where he was able to buy the first ticket. The first Altrincham station was just south of the Stockport Road level-crossing. An extension to the Bowdon terminus at Lloyd Street was opened in September 1849. A turntable was installed here in September 1858. The cost of building the whole line had been £575,000. The line had an immediate effect on the area; land and property values rose, and new villas and terraces were built on The Downs.

The second line to penetrate the Altrincham area was the Warrington & Stockport Railway. The section from Timperley Junction to Warrington opened on 1 May 1854. Next to be opened was the Cheshire Midland Railway from Altrincham to Knutsford on 12 May 1862, to Northwich from 1 January 1863 and extended by other companies to Chester (Northgate) by 1874. Next on the scene was the line from Deansgate Junction to Stockport (Tiviot Dale) by the Stockport, Timperley & Altrincham Junction Railway opened on 1 December 1865. An Act of 1863 led to the formation of the Cheshire Lines Committee (CLC) to manage the companies owning the line from Godley Junction (on the Manchester–Sheffield route) to Deansgate Junction and the Altrincham to Chester line. The CLC was jointly owned by the Midland Railway, the Great Northern Railway and the MSLR. The Warrington and Stockport

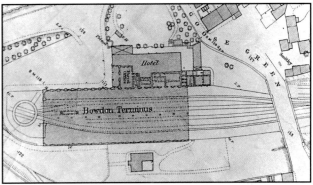

Bowdon Terminus Map.   *Ordnance Survey – D.G.B.*

Fig. 13.12. **Railways in the area.** Dates show   *D. Walton* when sections of the line were built.

Fig. 13.13. **"Venus".** Engine, brightly polished, with top hatted driver   *A.M.* exposed to the elements in 1849.

Railway became part of the LNWR from July 1864 and the link from Skelton Junction to Broadheath Junction opened on 1 February 1866. A curve between Timperley Station and Skelton North Junction opened on 1 December 1879. The final main section of the local network was the CLC main line from Skelton Junction through West Timperley, Partington, Glazebrook and Warrington (Central) to Garston on the outskirts of Liverpool, which opened on 1 March 1873.

In 1880 the two "Altrincham" and "Bowdon" stations were closed and replaced with a new 4-platform station between the two called "Altrincham and Bowdon" which opened on 3 April 1881. The old Altrincham station was demolished and Bowdon Station converted into carriage sheds.

The late 1870's saw the introduction of an Altrincham to Stockport (Tiviot Dale) service which operated until April 1931. Latterly this service was operated by a Sentinel-Cammell steam railcar, Fig. 13.14, which was nicknamed the "Baguley Bus". A daily service from Oxford Road to London Euston via Altrincham began in the 1880's and survived until 1933.

The Royal Jubilee Exhibition of 1887 was held on the site of the 1857 Art Treasures Exhibition at Old Trafford and was opened by the Prince and Princess of Wales (later King Edward VII and Queen Alexandra). The following day they visited Altrincham and joined the royal train at Altrincham and Bowdon station for the 10 minute journey to the temporary Exhibition station.

By 1899 the line was carrying over 5 million passengers a year plus an immense number of season ticket holders (commuters) in its 81 daily trains and was making a profit of £75,000 a year. In May 1907 £668 was spent installing gas lighting on the Altrincham line and in September 1916 the MSJ&A company spent £10 on 'accommodation' for the female carriage cleaners at Altrincham who had replaced the men fighting in World War I.

1923 saw the 'Grouping' of most of the railway companies into the 'Big Four' and from 1 January the Altrincham line's two joint owners, the LNWR and the

Fig. 13.14. **CLC Sentinel steam railcar, No. 600 at Cheadle CLC Station in July, 1938, on the Altrincham line.** *A.M.*
The coach had a steam engine at the far end on this photograph.

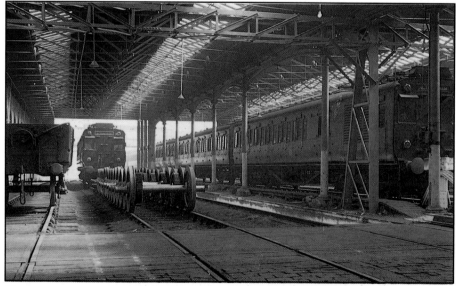

Fig. 13.15. **Interior of carriage sheds, formerly Bowdon Station, now a car park.** *A.M.*

Fig. 13.16. **EX–LMS Class 8F, 2-8-0.** No. 48717 passing Altrincham with the 12.40pm Tunstead to Lostock ICI hopper train (limestone) on 16 July, 1963.

A.M.

Great Central Railway (which the MSLR had become from 1897) became part of the London Midland & Scottish Railway (LMSR) and the London & North Eastern Railway (LNER) respectively. So the MSJ&A continued an independent existence administered by the two companies. The same applied to the CLC which also became jointly owned by the LMSR and LNER.

In 1928 the LMSR/LNER Joint Committee recommended that the Altrincham line be electrified to provide a cheaper, cleaner and more frequent service. 1500v d.c. overhead transmission was chosen. The first electric train ran over the whole line on 14 April 1931, driven by George Graver of Hale, a driver for 29 years. The first day of public operation was Monday 11 May. Bowdon carriage sheds were converted into a depot for the new trains, Fig. 13.15, and most of the old steam-hauled carriages were sold to the CLC. Within a few weeks the old engine shed at Altrincham (its site was under the flyover) was demolished. The journey to London Road was cut eventually to 22 minutes despite stops at three new stations, Navigation Road, Dane Road and Warwick Road. A suggestion for a station between Timperley and Brooklands has not yet been acted upon! A peak of 8 million passengers a year was reached in the years before World War II.

The 1930's saw the introduction of the ICI hopper (steam-hauled) trains from Tunstead Quarry in the Peak District to the Northwich area carrying limestone, Fig. 13.16. Currently 3 trains of up to 22 wagons each carrying $43\frac{1}{2}$ tons are operated per day in each direction, pulled by heavy diesel locomotives.

1 January 1948 saw the nationalisation of the railways and the MSJ&A and the CLC both became part of the London Midland Region of British Railways.

The Lymm line was heavily used on Saturdays in the summer during the late 1950's and early 1960's for passenger trains carrying holidaymakers from Yorkshire to the North Wales coast resorts. Some of these trains called at Broadheath Station to pick up or set down in the days before mass car ownership. However, the writing was on the wall for the Lymm line, passenger services being withdrawn on 8 September 1962, and Broadheath and stations to the west closed from Monday 10 September. The track on the curve from Timperley

Fig. 13.17. **An a.c. electric train, 1989.** D.G.B.

Junction to Broadheath Junction was lifted. The line from Skelton Junction to Warrington remained in use for freight for two more decades and during the 70's was heavily used by coal trains. Complete closure of the Skelton Junction to Warrington line took place with effect from 8 July 1985. The course of the line west of Sinderland Crossing is currently proposed for re-use as part of an ambitious Trans-Pennine cycleway linking York and Liverpool which would also use the towpath of the Bridgewater Canal through Timperley and Broadheath.

The next passenger service to fall under the 'axe' was that from Stockport to Warrington Central via Skelton Junction, withdrawn from 30 November 1964 and stations including West Timperley were closed. Again the line remained in use for freight until the closure of the steel works at Irlam in the early 1970's. Part of the line, from Skelton to Partington, remains in use as a single track to serve the Shell plant at Carrington, and trainloads of liquid propylene are received from South Wales. The section from Skelton Junction to Northenden Junction and beyond also remains in use and since May 1989 has been used by the Chester to Manchester service which has been diverted via Stockport to Manchester Piccadilly. A new station may soon be opened in the Timperley / Baguley area.

The early- and mid-1960's saw the disappearance of goods facilities from stations including the complex of sidings at Broadheath, the marshalling yard at Skelton

Fig. 13.18 **Motor and motorcycle manufacturer's works at the turn of the century, by West Timperley Railway Bridge.**

J. Edwards

Junction and the goods yard at Altrincham. The street tramway for carrying coal and coke from Altrincham goods yard to the gasworks in Moss Lane which opened in the 1890's closed in 1957 when gas production ceased on the site.

By the late 1960's the original electrical equipment on the Altrincham line was nearing the end of its life, and work began on re-electrifying the line on the standard system of 25,000v a.c. Coloured light signals replaced the old semaphore 'arm' type along the line and in February 1971 the control area of the Manchester London Road signal box was extended to Deansgate Junction. Re-electrification cost £1,000,000 partly paid for by the sale of the old overhead copper wires. The last of the old d.c. trains, ran on 30 April 1971, and the first of the new a.c. trains, of the type in Fig. 13.17 ran on 3 May 1971. Fortunately three of the old carriages were saved from the cutter's torch and now reside on the Midland Railway Trust's line at Butterley, near Ripley in Derbyshire. Two of the coaches are owned by the Altrincham Electric Railway Preservation Society.

1976 saw the creation of a bus-rail interchange by the transfer of Altrincham bus station to the railway station forecourt, which involved the controversial demolition of the forecourt canopy. Altrincham level-crossing became pedestrian-only. Work has recently started on conversion of the Altrincham line into part of the first line of the Greater Manchester Light Rapid Transit system. This will use the existing line from Altrincham station to Cornbrook Junction, where the LRT will dive under the Liverpool line and follow the former alignment into Manchester Central, now G-Mex, where there will be a new station. From here the LRT will take to the streets. The voltage chosen for the new system is 750v d.c. and the existing overhead supports will be retained. Opening is planned for early 1992 and the new service should usher in a new era of convenience, speed and frequency in the same way as the opening of the old line in 1849 and electrification in 1931. The alternative meaning of MSJ&AR should still ring true: 'Many Short Journeys and Absolute Reliability!'

MOTOR VEHICLE MANUFACTURE

Altrincham firms made two of the three makes of motorcycle produced in the Manchester area, the Eagle and the Ruby (the other was the D.O.T. of Cornbrook); the Eagle company also made cars.

THE EAGLE COMPANY

Ralph Jackson started making bicycles in West Timperley in 1885 and in 1896 he branched out into motorcycle and car manufacture and founded the Eagle Engineering and Motor Co. He obtained patents for a silent chain-drive and an epicyclic gearbox. One car was a 3-wheeler which cost £100 and was powered by a 4½ h.p. De Dion single cylinder engine and a 2-speed chain drive. Percy Edwards joined the firm in 1910. A new workshop was built, a single-storey hangar-type building with large windows down the side, a pit in the middle, a showroom and open forecourt, and large rear sliding doors where parts could be delivered. Cars and motorcycles were produced, Fig. 13.18, but World War I put an end to the manufacturing business. Little alteration to the building has been made by the successor company, Jackson and Edwards Ltd., except a new frontage and showroom. The firm has been recently operated by Mr. John Edwards, son of one of the original partners.

THE ROYAL RUBY COMPANY

This firm started in Cannel (Canal) Street Ancoats prior to World War I. One of the orders during the war was for motorcycles for the Imperial Russian Army. The machines they made were of high quality and heavy construction with chain drive and JAP engines. After the war, they had works in Bolton and Altrincham, but the firm closed in the 1930's. The Altrincham works were on Moss Lane, and were later used by Banner Shirts and Elitex Fabrics.

Chapter Fourteen

HOUSING DEVELOPMENT FROM 1801

GILLIAN FITZPATRICK

By 1801 the pattern of society and housing in the centre of Altrincham had already been established. The upper and middle classes lived in good quality housing around Old Market Place and in Market Street and Church Street. Lower Town housed poorer families in small properties in George Street, the bottom of The Downs and Goose Green where there were numerous small squares and alleyways. There were 340 houses with a

population of 1,692 and until that time very little development had taken place away from the central area. The pattern had been largely set by physical factors, the better drained land round the market place being higher and more sought after. This pattern was to continue for the next hundred years.

During the early years of the 19th century a few larger villa-type houses were built in both a northerly direction around Sandiway and in a southerly direction along The Downs and Norman's Place. However, the gradual expansion of genteel Higher Town was more than matched by the proliferation of small cottages for the poorer classes especially in two areas, Pinfold Brow (now Lloyd Street) and Chapel Street.

By 1831 the population had almost doubled to 2,708 and concern was already being expressed by this date at the bad quality of some of this cottage housing (this 'concern' was to be continued for the next 120 years until the houses were demolished). There were no regulations on non-Stamford Estate land as to how or where houses should be built, and much development consisted of small 3- and 4-room cottages with little light, little space and totally inadequate drainage facilities. Typhus occurred in many years and in November 1831 there was an outbreak of cholera in the area; while its true causes were not fully recognised it was realised that it had started in the poorer areas. It was fear of it spreading to the higher classes which later prompted the setting up of a Local Board of Health on the recommendation of the Central Board in London. The Local Board, however, found themselves powerless to rectify all that was needed and as a result of a request made to the Privy Council in London, legal powers were granted under the Cholera Prevention Act of 1832.

A preliminary survey was made of the town in 1849 by Isaac Turton, Overseer of the Poor. His alarming statistics prompted the request for a Government Inspector to make a full Inquiry under the powers of the Public Health Act of 1848.

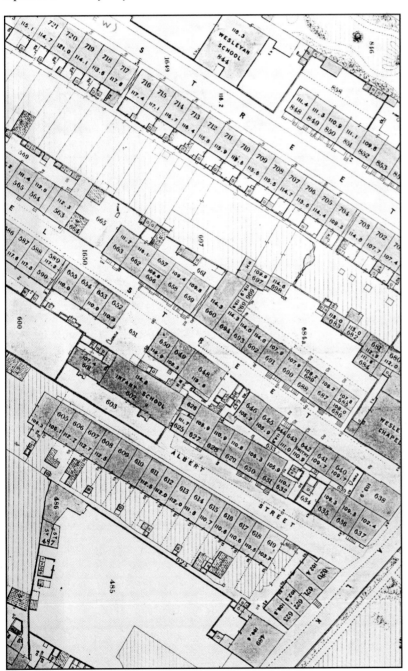

Fig. 14.1. **Chapel Street area, Altrincham Local Board of Health detail plans, 1852.**

Trafford Leisure Services

Fig. 14.2. **Hope Square.** *Trafford Leisure Services*

Isaac Turton's survey showed that there were 781 inhabited houses, 165 of these having been built since 1841 with a further 37 in the course of being built, housing an estimated population of 4,872 in 1849. This figure was probably too high as the 1851 census showed a population of 4,488. The greatest concern was shown regarding 26 recognised common lodging houses which provided from 4 to 10 beds (in mostly 2-bedroomed property), with an average of 3 people to a bed making a population of 546 lodgers per night, including many vagrants. There were also 10 courts and alleys containing 67 houses, mostly lodging houses, with a resident population of about 368 people. Turton went on to cite the worst examples as being in New Street, which was not paved, sewered nor drained, yet consisted of 104 houses; Chapel Street with many cellar dwellings only partly drained; and Newtown, which had no drains or roads, with 25 houses, a smithy, a joiner's and a wheelwright's.

Sir Robert Rawlinson, the Government Inspector made a full report in 1851 which makes grim reading.

His report more than substantiated the preliminary survey of 1849, and the plans which accompany the report show very clearly the types of houses being described, Fig. 14.1. One of the areas picked out for its appalling sanitary arrangements was Hope Square off New Street with its open middens almost entirely enclosed by terraced housing and Fig. 14.2 gives some idea of what this area was like in the 1850's. The most immediate result of the report was that the Local Board of Health was given full powers to remedy these problems and the Board first turned its attention to providing good drainage, from a plan prepared by Rawlinson.

As referred to above, the convenience of the railway was now attracting many wealthy people to the town in the middle years of the century. Many of them were merchants in Manchester who could now take advantage of the healthier climate of the higher parts of the Altrincham area, particularly Bowdon. The prevailing winds meant that Altrincham was never as subject to the smoke-laden fogs which affected

Fig. 14.3. **Lyme Grove.** *Trafford Leisure Services*

Fig. 14.4. **Barrington Road.**   *Trafford Leisure Services*

Manchester and the northern towns. The main areas of Altrincham to be developed were the small patch of land to the west of the town *e.g.* Townfield Gardens, and The Mount; the southern end of The Downs area; Lyme Grove; around St. Margaret's Church in St. Margaret's Road, Bentinck Road and Groby Road. As can be seen in Fig. 14.3, Lyme Grove has retained much of its mid-19th century charm and is illustrative of the substantial type of housing built in these areas.

Dunham Park made an effective barrier to any further expansion to the west side of the town, whilst the northern end around Broadheath was already establishing itself as an industrial area and the eastern parts were considered unattractive for better housing. For these reasons the bulk of this type of housing became limited to the southern areas, soon reaching Bowdon and Hale with little possibility of further spread south since it was halted by the ill-drained land of the Bollin valley.

The first byelaws with respect to 'New Streets and Buildings' made in 1878 perhaps say as much about the type of houses that had been built as about any that were about to be, *e.g.* all new buildings had to be built of stone, brick or other incombustible material, every habitable room had to have at least one openable window amounting to 1/10 of the floor space and every new house had to have efficient water supply and drainage with any privies to be at least 6 feet away from the building. For the first time all new building plans had to be submitted to the Guardians of the Altrincham Union acting as the Rural Sanitary Authority.

It is by no means certain that all new houses did comply with these rudimentary conditions and as they did not apply to existing buildings the problems of

areas like Newtown and Chapel Street persisted. However, the 1880's and 1890's saw a massive house-building programme of fairly substantial, well-built terraced housing, mainly for rent to the lower middle and working classes. This development covered much of the eastern part of the town including areas of what had been formerly Hale Moss, in particular the Stamford Park area and roads running off Hale Road. Development also occurred in the northern part of the town in Broadheath in the Navigation Road area and more centrally round Barrington Road. This type of housing is a familiar sight in many parts of Altrincham and Fig. 14.4 shows a house built at this period.

There was another type of house provision at this time. Although it does not aspire to the fame of Port Sunlight and other similar ventures it was designed on the same principles by a benevolent employer who recognised that a well-housed workforce was likely to be more productive. Perhaps more cynically, the point has been made that a workforce on site is less likely to be late! Linotype and Machinery Ltd. moved to Altrincham in 1896 and the works opened in the following year employing on average a workforce between 1,200 and 1,300 men.

The 40 acres of land on which the estate was built had belonged to the Earl of Stamford, and part was owned by A.C. Sparkes (Chapter Nineteen). The estate of over 170 buildings was planned very much as a model village, retaining many of the original trees and providing integral areas for playing fields, recreational areas and allotments. Fig. 14.5 shows an original plan of the estate. The architects of the cottages were Stott and Sons of Manchester who designed the dwellings as pairs, some with shared central gables and steeply pitched roofs. The overall effect, seen in Fig. 14.6, was

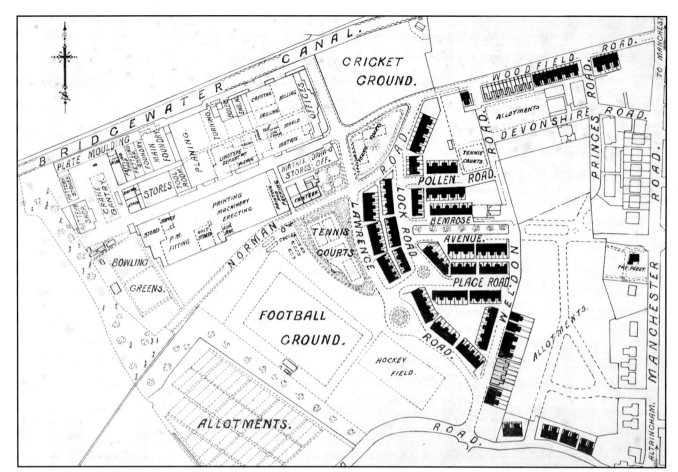

Trafford Leisure Services

Trafford Leisure Services

D.G.B.

Fig. 14.5. (Top) **Plan of Linotype estate, 1897.**

Fig. 14.6. (Middle left) **Linotype estate house – design for front elevation.**

Fig. 14.6. (Middle right) **Linotype estate houses.** Note alterations in windows and doors compared with the original design.

Fig. 14.7. (Left) **The Crescent, Oldfield Brow.**

Trafford Leisure Services

pleasant to look at and must have been very different from that which many employees must previously have experienced. The larger cottages contained bathrooms though it was not until 1964 that they were put in some of the smaller ones, the architects being Cocker, Clews and Cocker of Altrincham. A further 49 houses were built on the estate in the 1920's.

By the turn of the century the population had increased to 16,831 and although there had been a lot of development, private building was declining and more houses were still required. Under the Housing of the Working Classes Act of 1890, Altrincham Urban District Council built its first council estate of 85 dwellings made up of 28 flats and 57 non-parlour type houses. These were built in 1905 close to the centre of the town in the Urban Road area. The Council proudly, if rather unimaginatively, named the roads of the estate Urban Road, Urban Drive and Urban Avenue. At the end of World War II a further 19 dwellings in the form of 'pre-fabs' were added to the site with a life expectancy of 10 years. They are still there. Expansion had been planned in the Gladstone Road area but only a few houses were built before 1914. Most of this area was developed in the 1920's, World War I having put a stop to most building.

The biggest post-war development of housing was at Oldfield Brow. Towards the end of World War I Sir John Leigh had proposed to buy the Oldfield Hall estate from the Stamford estate and present it to the Council as a park. The Council itself had already been considering purchasing it and using the land for housing but were fortunately deterred by the cost and had not reached any decision. At the same time the Countess of Stamford had written to the Council saying it had been the late Earl's wish to donate land for a park on the coming of age of the 10th Earl. However, considering all the circumstances she decided to let Sir John Leigh present the park and at the same time she would offer land equal in value to be used for housing the working classes. In January 1920 a report was submitted outlining the Council's scheme and eventually a site bounded by Seamon's Road and Oldfield Road was agreed upon. The plan accepted was that of the council Surveyor, Harry Brown and included open spaces, allotments, playgrounds, public hall (never built) and green and 476 dwellings of which 50 were to be flats and the remainder a mixture of parlour and non-parlour type houses. 407 houses were built between 1921 and 1931, Fig. 14.7, and after 1945 a further 73 flats were built on the site.

The second major housing development of the 1920's and 1930's was that of the Sinderland estate on the north side of the canal in Broadheath. This estate comprised 322 new houses, mostly of the smaller non-parlour type. Many families were rehoused to this estate from slum clearance schemes in the centre of the town especially from the Chapel Street and Police Street areas. This was the last large-scale housing development in Altrincham itself for 30 years, land having become scarce and most subsequent development both private and municipal was concentrated in Timperley.

However, the area which had first been mentioned in the 1830's as a problem was still to be dealt with. World War II had halted any progress with slum clearance which had been initiated by the Housing Act of 1936. Immediately before the War the Council had acquired the land around New Street and Chapel Street and had demolished about 60 houses, rehousing their tenants. In 1954 a thorough survey of the area bounded by Regent Road, Lloyd's Square, Chapel Street and New Street was made by the Medical Officer of Health, Donald Longbottom. He recommended that demolition was the only course of action-under Compulsory Order if necessary. Not only were many individual houses deemed unfit for human habitation but the whole area was considered to be of such bad arrangement as to be *"injurious to the health of the inhabitants of the area"*. In all the scheme affected 102 families comprising about 380 people. Fig. 14.8 shows a typical example of the type of building described in the report.

Although most of the tenants were rehoused elsewhere, particularly on the Broomwood estate in Timperley, a few residents, mainly older people were rehoused in flats and maisonettes built at the rear of the site. The 1960's saw a similar scheme carried out in the Newtown area. The land was acquired for slum clearance under Compulsory Purchase Order, and the older houses were replaced by flats and maisonettes. Provision of the Pownall Day Centre was included in the original plans. The whole complex was designed by Bradley, Cuthbert and Towell and the main contractors were Harry Daniels and Son (Building Contractors) Ltd. The whole plan which was built in two phases consisted of 96 units of accommodation and was opened about 1969. Fig. 14.9 shows part of this complex shortly after it was built.

At the other end of the scale the 1960's had also seen a trend for demolishing larger old houses and replacing them with higher density units giving a much greater return to the developer. Concern was being

Fig. 14.8. **New Street.**   *Trafford Leisure Services*

Fig. 14.9. New Street flats.

Trafford Leisure Services

***Fig. 14.10* William Walk.** *Trafford Leisure Services*

expressed that these developments, *e.g.* modern flats on The Downs, did not fit in with the mellow Victorian and Edwardian character of brick houses. This concern led to the creation of conservation areas which included The Downs and Goose Green in 1973. Goose Green had been curiously cut off from other residential areas in the 19th century. The railway had isolated it from its neighbour Pinfold Brow and the making of Stamford New Road in 1880 had isolated it from the George Street area. In the 1850's it had been certainly as densely populated as Chapel Street, the 1851 census showing a population of over 100 in what were then tiny cottages. Its social characteristics are described in Chapter Eight. Perhaps because of its small size it was recognised that these early -19th or even late-18th century buildings could be conserved structurally even if not kept to their original use as domestic dwellings. Goose Green is now largely commercial.

The Greater Manchester Council Structure Plan, approved by the Secretary of State in 1981, required Trafford to release enough land between 1978 and mid-1986 for 5,800 dwellings. As far as Altrincham was concerned this resulted in the Broadheath/Sinderland Local Plan which allowed for 1,045 houses, later increased to 1,130 houses, to be built in that area, and included the improvement of some older property.

Development has already started in that area with the White Moss estate. The 1980's also saw a refurbishment of property rather than wholesale demolition and rebuilding, especially on the eastern side in the Stamford Park and Borough Road areas. Here landscaping and large scale repairs have brought improvement to these properties.

Individual units have been built *e.g.* on Oakfield Road and in the old Newtown area which have been kept far more in keeping with the general character of the area. Fig. 14.10 shows an example of this. Plans are now in the pipeline for the development of the eastern part of the town. These plans will undoubtedly affect housing especially in the Manor Road area, predominantly an area of Victorian and Edwardian property. It is hoped that Altrincham's housing of the future will complement the variety of generally pleasant housing which remains in the town from the last 200 years.

Chapter Fifteen

BUILDINGS

ROWLAND FLEMING

Altrincham today is predominantly a town of Victorian domestic architecture. It has not the graceful cohesion of styles of a Cotswold village or Lakeland town, nor the beauty of their natural stone, but like them it reflects the building materials available locally or economically from other areas to meet the needs of its 19th century growth. Large sandstone quarries near Runcorn provided stone for the characteristic towns of south Cheshire and Altrincham has a few red sandstone buildings, such as the former bank, now the County Galleries in Railway Street, and the former Byrom's department store in Kingsway, now a men's clothes shop. It is likely that the sandstone boundary walls of the larger Victorian houses of Bowdon came from a small local quarry in Timperley. It was behind the yard of C. Marston on Stockport Road in the village centre and closed in 1910, leaving a memory in the names of the Quarry Bank Hotel and Stonemasons Arms. Clay was available, however, and many small brickworks flourished near the town. As transport improved more bricks came by canal from Staffordshire and Welsh

slate by rail, soon to be ousted by even cheaper machine-made clay roofing tiles from Stafford. When the council built Altrincham's first large housing estate in the 1920's the first houses had slate roofs but the second phase had clay tiles.

Altrincham has some handsome Georgian town houses and florid Edwardian villas as well as the bulk of Victorian properties which swept away the old plastered and thatched houses huddled round Old Market Place. Upper Altrincham has preserved the character of the original town centre of Higher Town and here there are several buildings of note. Originally the central point of the market place had been the buttermarket and courthouse, adjacent to the market cross. A town hall, Fig. 15.1, was built by Lord Stamford in 1849 adjacent to the Unicorn public house to replace the courthouse demolished at that time. At first-floor level in the town hall wing an oriel window lit the council chamber. The bell-tower above was copied from the one on the former buttermarket of 1684 and contained the bell from there (cast at Little Budworth) presented by Lord Delamer, now in the possession of the Court Leet. There was a large arched doorway on to the road used as the entrance for carriages. After Altrincham became a U.D.C. in 1895 the administrative centre shifted in 1900 to a new town hall in Market Street, (Fig. 7.2, Chapter Seven), robustly designed in the Jacobean style by Manchester architect C. H. Hindle and later sympathetically extended by F. H. Brazier, a local architect. The continuing presence of public buildings and other buildings of quality here has kept this part of Altrincham the centre for administration and professional services.

(Top left)
Fig. 15.1. **The town hall of 1849 is on the right.** *D.G.B.*

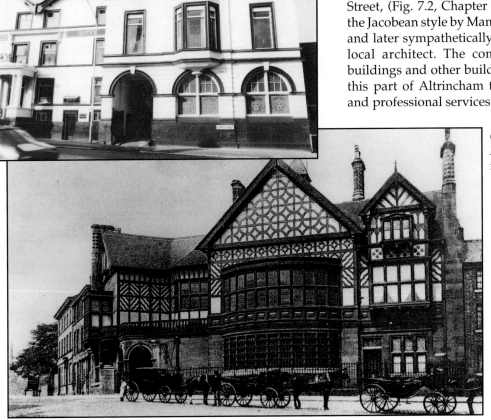

Fig. 15.2. Lloyds Bank.   *D.G.B.*

During alterations in 1988 to shops on the eastern side of the Old Market Place that had formerly been houses and cottages, some 16th century internal wattle and daub walls were found (Chapter Sixteen). On the west side is Lloyds Bank, Fig. 15.2. Though a striking building in red sandstone and traditional Cheshire black and white it dates only from 1887. It was formerly Brooks Bank, built by George Truefitt for Sir William Cunliffe Brooks. The mullioned windows of stained glass are 35 feet high. On the south side of Old Market Place is a graceful group of late-19th century brick-built shops and offices with stone plinth, decorative stone bands and timber-framing, a counterfoil to the bank and also built for Cunliffe Brooks. A number of shops and offices of the 1870's lie on Kingsway, built of red sandstone with an arcaded ground floor and much decoration, Fig. 15.3. On the corner with Post Office Street are Morrison's former auction galleries, Fig. 15.4, built in the 1890's for Cunliffe Brooks in header bond brick with some stone dressings. The upper timber framing is very decorative.

Along Market Street the early-19th century merchants' houses exude an air of former prosperity. People of the highest social class once lived here, Fig. 15.4 (distance). The houses, now all offices and shops are pale red brick with slate roofs, 3-storeyed, some with stone bases, prominent eaves, cornice and parapet, panelled doors, fanlights and columns. Some originally had large gardens and fields behind. The 2-storey attractive former Stamford Estates office was built around 1780 as a gentleman's house, (Fig. 5.6, Chapter Five). Later it was used as a solicitor's office until Lord Stamford made it the office from which his extensive estate was administered. Now owned by the National Trust, it is similar in construction and detail to the Georgian houses on the Downs. It is built in Flemish bond brick, *i.e.* with each course comprising alternate header and stretcher with thin mortar joints. The door is flanked by fluted columns and there is a fanlight over. Inside there is a large foyer from which an elegant semi-elliptical staircase leads upstairs. From one of the upstairs rooms there is access to a barrel-vaulted store-

Fig. 15.3. Shops and offices at the top of Kingsway in an arcaded style. *D.G.B.*

Doorway Stamford *D.G.B.*
Estates Office.

Fig. 15.4. Morrison's former auction galleries on Market Street. Nicholls, *D.G.B.*
Lindsell and Harris's in middle distance on Market Street.

Terra cotta moulding *D.G.B.*
– William Cunliffe Brooks,
Lloyds Bank.

Balshaw's Yard   *C.J. Hill*

Fig. 15.5. Market House, and glass covered area.   *D.G.B.*

Fig. 15.6. **Station Buildings, now Stamford House,**   *D.G.B.*
built by J.H. Broun.

Fig. 15.7. **Stylish houses on The Downs.**   *D.G.B.*

room in which the Worthingtons, the Earls' stewards, kept the papers of the Stamford Estates. There was formerly a carriage entry at the rear into Market Street.

The Market House of 1879, Fig. 15.5, is constructed in yellow Flemish bond brickwork and has a striking clock tower, classical detailed cornice and pilasters with fluted bases. It has weathered well. A glass roof was added in 1930 to cover adjoining land and to extend the market.

One of the first multi-storey office blocks in the provinces was Station Buildings, now Stamford House, Fig. 15.6. It was the conception of a local businessman, J. H. Broun and opened in 1905. Mr. Broun and his architect, John McNamara, were enthusiasts for classical detail and the building is a mixture of styles with bold projecting cornices, curved pediments and Ionic pilasters, all surmounted by a slated mansard roof. The offices were heated by coal and the roof is pierced by chimneys on all sides. Prior to Station Buildings, Mr. Broun had built the main Post Office on Stamford New Road in 1899 and the adjoining Mossburn Buildings, all equally florid with terra-cotta mouldings and signed on the façade with his initials 'JHB'. Most of the decorative elements were factory-made terra-cotta blocks. These were probably supplied by Shaw's Glazed Brick Co. of Darwen, Lancashire, who produced this type of block until about 1980. A drawing would be prepared from the architect's sketch plan and each individual block would be numbered from the drawing. The numbered blocks were then delivered to the site

ready for fixing. The firm was able to supply copies of the blocks many years later if required. Mr. Broun also built the terrace of three-storey houses on Willowtree Road, characterised by his choice of materials which would weather well. But he may have driven hard bargains with his builders. Watson's, the firm that built Stamford House and operated from a yard in Ashfield Road went into liquidation shortly afterwards. Mr. Broun's most distinguished construction, however, was his own home. Unusual for the time, it was a fine bungalow on a superb site in Ashley Heath overlooking the Bollin. Sadly it was demolished in the 1960's, but at the time it gave Mr. Broun his local nickname of "Bungalow Broun".

In the residential areas south and west of the busy central area, it is pleasing that some of the Georgian and early Victorian houses have been well preserved on The Downs, Fig. 15.7, and elsewhere. They are constructed from handmade bricks laid in Flemish bond. The cambered window arches are formed by purpose-made 'gauged' bricks. This distinctive pattern of solid brickwork continued until the end of the 19th century and the advent of cavity walls. The windows are comprised of small Georgian panes with delicate glazing bars. Door surrounds with pilasters and fanlights over panelled doors are characteristic of the period. In Norman's Place, near the General Hospital, are several handsome houses. Richmond House was built in 1820. The house next door, The Elms, was built in the

Fig. 15.8. **Spring Bank House.**   *D.G.B.*

Fig. 15.9. **Architects' offices, Messrs. Hartington, Fleming and Worsley, Ashley Road.**

Fig. 15.10. **Oldfield Hall**   *Trafford Leisure Services*

Fig. 15.11. **Linotype building and clock tower, Norman Road.**   *E.R.F.*

Fig. 15.12. **Budenberg**   *E.R.F.*
Gauge Company

mid-18th century, originally as two houses and one of the first homes in Altrincham to have electric lighting.

The area was more open than today and when interviewed late in life, a local builder, John Berry, born in Bowdon in 1842, recalled that in his youth the owner of Spring Bank, Ashley Road, used to shoot in a wood where Byrom Street now runs. Spring Bank House, Fig. 15.8., was demolished in 1991. Ashley Road later formed a natural boundary between the crowded terraces of workers' houses to the east and the larger houses of Bowdon.

Typical of the latter are the 1860's houses on the east side of Ashley Road, between Peter Street and Hale Road junction, Fig. 15.9. They have 3 storeys with cellars and attics. Ground floor entertaining rooms are lofty with deep moulded skirting and decorative plasterwork to ceilings and moulded panelled doors. The staircase's rich carving stops below the small, plain attic rooms lit by skylights where servants lived.

No 'stately home' remains within Altrincham since Oldfield Hall, Fig. 15.10, was demolished in 1916. It was built in 1616 in sandstone and stood in 14 acres of what is now John Leigh Park, Oldfield Road. Nearby is the giant Linotype works in Woodfield Road which once made most of the world's printing machinery. This is distinguished by an impressive clock tower, Fig. 15.11. So, too was the British headquarters of the German precision gauge makers, Schaffer and Budenberg. Its clock tower, Fig. 15.12, incorporates a full length column of mercury, over 32 feet long, used to calibrate their gauges. The building dates from 1913–14, and was constructed to the designs of Alfred Steinthall of King Street, Manchester. Gerrard's of Swinton were the builders. The buildings were built to a high standard reflecting the quality of the materials and of the builders. The main façade to Woodfield Road is of Accrington Brick with terra-cotta dressings and unusual cast iron panels spanning the brick piers at first floor level. Due to the choice of materials the buildings have weathered well, the only disfigurement being the camouflage paint on the factory chimney which was intended to conceal it from German aircraft in World War II.

The tower of St. Mary's Church, Bowdon dominates the skyline of the southern approaches to Altrincham, and there has been a Christian church there since Anglo-Saxon times. Altrincham's parish church, St. George's was built as a chapel-of-ease to St. Mary's in 1799. With the Victorian growth of Altrincham came a surge of church building. St. George's was enlarged twice although the results do not show themselves to their best from the principal view on Church Street.

In contrast, St. Margaret's on high ground near the Dunham Road boundary with Dunham Massey, is striking. Built in 1855, its ashlar and rusticated stonework, slated roof and Perpendicular proportions are harmonious. Originally the tower was surmounted by a steeple with delicate flying buttresses and pinnacles. The interior is very imposing with hammer-beam oak roof members carved with angels. The architect was William Hayley, of Manchester, and it cost £20,000.

Ten years later, St. John's was built on the corner of Ashley Road for £7,000 in natural stone with a distinctive spire and a roof of mixed Welsh and Lakeland slate. The Methodists built a most imposing church in Enville Road, Bowdon. The foundation stone for St. Vincent's Roman Catholic Church was laid at the corner of Groby Road in 1904. Traditional in form, but striking in appearance, it is built of Ruabon brick with red terra-cotta dressing. The Unitarian Chapel is a modest but pleasing building. External walls are distinguished by their header bond providing a foil for the stone tracery of the windows. The slated roof is timbered over the nave.

Whereas Victorian Altrincham could spend £20,000 on a church some £600 bought its hospital on Lloyd Street for patients with contagious diseases, products of the poor drainage and sanitary conditions of the time. In 1869 the foundation stone was laid for a new hospital at the corner of Regent Road. This was completed the following year and is the basis of the present Altrincham General Hospital.

In 1855, on Stamford Street, Springfield House, a "Collegiate Institution and Boarding Establishment for Young Ladies" provided an appropriate form of education conducted by Mrs. and Miss Oliver. The building was on 3 floors, the main entrance being at first-floor level, approached by an imposing staircase at either side with wrought iron balustrades. The classical proportions and pedimented façade must have been in sharp contrast to the small thatched cottages within the area at that time. The building was subsequently used for commercial purposes, but was demolished comparatively recently in 1978. One hundred years before the foundation of Springfield, Mr. Thomas Walton of Dunham Woodhouses left a sum of £1000 in his will (and subsequently further funds) to his executors, who founded a school in 1759 at Oldfield House for a sum of £2,000. After 100 years Oldfield House closed and Seamon's Moss School for 40 boys was built on the present site on sloping ground fronting Oldfield Road, in a wooded setting and surrounded by a high sandstone wall. It closed in the mid-thirties and has since been used for community purposes but sadly it has not been well maintained, Fig. 15.13.

Despite its ancient past, Altrincham is architecturally, predominantly Victorian and modern.

Fig. 15.13. **Seamon's Moss School.** The inscription over the door reads "This School was founded by Thomas Walton, Gent. AD1759. This building was erected AD1867".

D.G.B.

Arcading – Kingsway   *D.G.B.*

Chapter Sixteen

A BURGAGE IN THE MARKET PLACE

JOYCE LITTLER

The large black deed box containing deeds about 6 Old Market Place had lain for many years in Lloyd's Bank vault, disturbed only occasionally by solicitors requiring one of the many documents it held, but otherwise forgotten and unexamined in detail. The property had a site, size and rectangular shape of part of a mediaeval burgage (a term used in the deeds), hence the title above, Fig. 16.1. Since 1892 it has been occupied by a business known as Whitwham's, Fig. 16.2.

The earliest and principal document in the box was dated 1729. This was a marriage settlement, Fig. 16.3, signed and sealed by the bride, Elizabeth Astley and her father Edward (a yeoman of Altrincham), the groom, Thomas Ashley, and his father John (a woollen draper/clothier of Altrincham). The last mentioned was living at what is now 6 Old Market Place. Edward Astley gave the groom, Thomas Ashley, £200 for his daughter's dowry. These people were obviously well-to-do, Edward's £200 would today be valued between £10–12,000. John Ashley, a wealthy clothier, gave his son Thomas half his house and half his estate with the other half in trust for twenty-one years. John Ashley and his wife (also named Elizabeth) retained all the rents and profits from the estate and security of tenure of the house for their lifetime, together with a dowry of £10 per annum for John's wife Elizabeth after John's death, and for the widows of all heirs to the estate in perpetuity. All the conditions of inheritance were made legally binding in the deeds and were observed for the next 88 years. The house consists of two gabled parts, one behind the other, Fig. 16.4. Later information suggests that John already lived in the front part of No.6 (under the front gable), and Thomas in the rear part.

Although the documents are dated 1729, they also refer back to two previous generations, to John's father, James, and grandfather, also John; then to the well-known Civil War general, Sir William Brereton, from

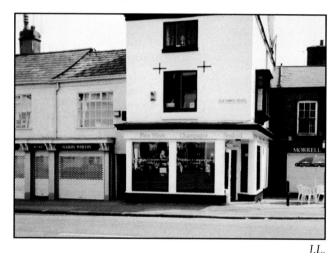

J.L.

Ordnance Survey

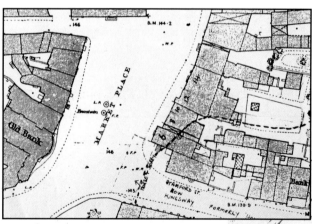

Fig. 16.1. (Above) **Map of Old Market Place, 1876, showing the long narrow shape of the burgages.**

The thick dotted line estimates the original shop edge of Hollow Bank. A suggested position of the 'Horse and Jockey' is marked at the top of Kingsway.

Fig. 16.2. (Top right) **No. 6 Old Market Place. Whitwham's Fine Wine, Champagne and Seafood Bar.**

Fig. 16.3. (Right) **The Marriage Settlement between Thomas Ashley and his father John, and Elizabeth Astley and her father Edward in 1729.**

true performance of the covenant herein contained on the part and behalfe of
and hereby to be observed and kept he the said John Ashley
Ashley doth hereby bind himselfe his heirs Executors and Administrators
unto the said Edward Astley in the penal summe of five hundred pounds of
of Great Britain to be paid to the said Edward Astley his Executors Administrators
for the true performance of the covenant and payment herein contained on the
behalfe of the said Edward Astley his Executors and Administrators or any of them to be
observed paid performed and kept, he the said Edward Astley doth hereby bind himselfe his heirs
Executors and Administrators unto the said Thomas Ashley in the penal sum of five hundred
pounds of lawfull mony to be paid to the said Thomas Ashley his Executors Administrators
or Assigns In Witness whereof the parties aforesaid to these presents their hands and seals
interchangeably have set the day and year first above written

Sealed and delivered by the parties John Ashley
Thomas Ashley Edward Astley and
Elizabeth Astley in presence of

Geo Taylor

John Ashley

Thos Ashley

Elizabeth Astley

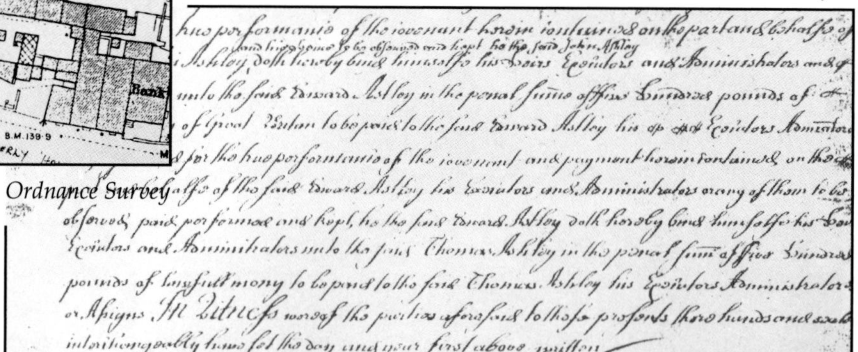

J.L.

J.L.

Fig. 16.4. The rear of No.6 and gables from the north side.

The bricked-up doorway may have been used by the clothier to haul in woollen goods to the store room behind it.
The narrow extension is 19th or 20th century.

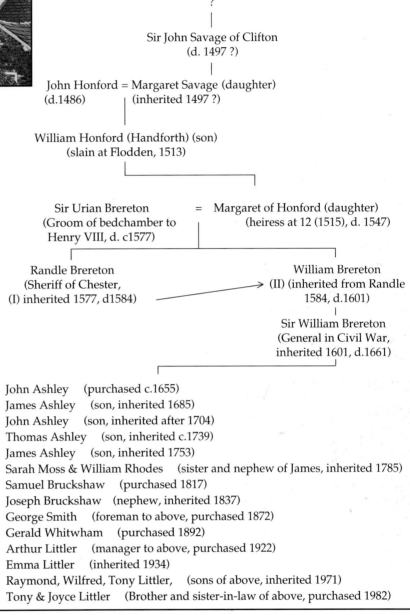

TABLE 1   OWNERS OF No. 6 OLD MARKET PLACE

?
|
Sir John Savage of Clifton
(d. 1497 ?)
|
John Honford = Margaret Savage (daughter)
(d.1486)   (inherited 1497 ?)
|
William Honford (Handforth) (son)
(slain at Flodden, 1513)

Sir Urian Brereton   =   Margaret of Honford (daughter)
(Groom of bedchamber to   (heiress at 12 (1515), d. 1547)
Henry VIII, d. c1577)

Randle Brereton   William Brereton
(Sheriff of Chester,   ⟶   (II) (inherited from Randle
(I) inherited 1577, d1584)   1584, d.1601)
|
Sir William Brereton
(General in Civil War,
inherited 1601, d.1661)

John Ashley   (purchased c.1655)
James Ashley   (son, inherited 1685)
John Ashley   (son, inherited after 1704)
Thomas Ashley   (son, inherited c.1739)
James Ashley   (son, inherited 1753)
Sarah Moss & William Rhodes   (sister and nephew of James, inherited 1785)
Samuel Bruckshaw   (purchased 1817)
Joseph Bruckshaw   (nephew, inherited 1837)
George Smith   (foreman to above, purchased 1872)
Gerald Whitwham   (purchased 1892)
Arthur Littler   (manager to above, purchased 1922)
Emma Littler   (inherited 1934)
Raymond, Wilfred, Tony Littler,   (sons of above, inherited 1971)
Tony & Joyce Littler   (Brother and sister-in-law of above, purchased 1982)

whom the grandfather of John (1729) had purchased the property, Table 1. Sir William died in 1661 having inherited his father's estate in 1601, thus there was a time scale for the date of purchase. Because he was a large landowner and the house (No.6) and cottages adjoining were all that Sir William and the previous inheritors owned in Altrincham, it has been possible through Inquisitions Post Mortem (documents recording death, heir, and extent of Crown lands held) to trace the ownership back to 1509.

The Mayoral Lists of Altrincham (see Table 2 and Appendix 2) name a John Ashley as Mayor in 1656 and 1677; his son James Ashley, Mayor in 1685 (the year his father or elder brother died); and a John Ashley, Mayor

in 1718. This represents three generations of Ashleys, all of whom were connected with No.6. The mayor had to be a burgage-holder of Altrincham, giving extra significance to the reference in the deeds of No.6 as "a burgage".

Thomas, the bridegroom in 1729, was, and remained, a woollen draper/clothier like his father and possibly followed in the footsteps of his grandfather James and great-grandfather John Ashley. The clothier was the financier and organiser of the local woollen industry, purchasing fleeces and paying the local cottagers to complete each stage of the manufacture. In 1753 Thomas Ashley died aged 45 years and Elizabeth Ashley, his wife, died 10 years later aged 55 years.

Weaver   *J.L.*

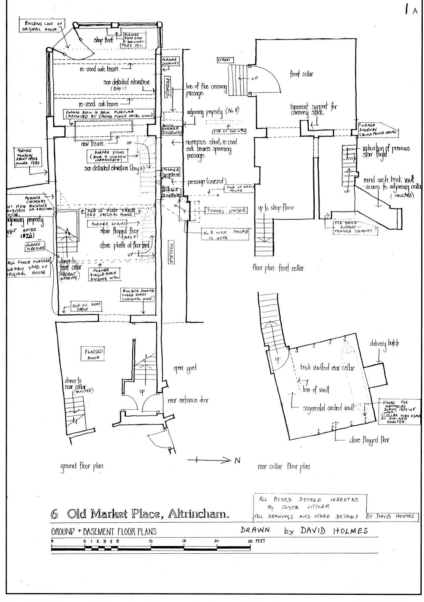

6 Old Market Place, Altrincham.

GROUND + BASEMENT FLOOR PLANS   DRAWN by DAVID HOLMES

Fig. 16.5. Ground floor and basement plans of No. 6.   *David Holmes*
All boxed details and dotted outlines refer to evidence found of former structures.

Their grave is in Bowdon churchyard. Also at Bowdon are the Astley graves of Elizabeth's (Ashley, née Astley) brothers, (named as trustees in the marriage settlement), and her father Edward who died in 1740, in his 99th year. Thomas's son James inherited No.6 and the rest of the estate. A document of 1766 describes him as ". . . Grocer formerly of Altrincham but now of Mile End London".

In 1795 Aiken had written that there had been formerly a thriving worsted industry in Altrincham, until Irish worsteds began to be imported. The local worsted trade suffered and became centralised in east Lancashire and west Yorkshire, so the Ashleys were wise to change their type of business. Grocers were becoming very wealthy because of the many exotic imports coming into the country following the opening up of the colonies and a business in London was particularly rewarding. From various addresses of people in James Ashley's will, he seems to have been in business in the Eastcheap area and had become a very wealthy man. To him is attributed many improvements and extensions to No.6 (and what were by then known as the neighbouring cottages, Nos.8–14), because in 1772 he raised a mortgage of £1,200 (worth about £60–70,000 today) and repaid it all with interest in two years (together with a posthumous debt of his father's of £50!). In 1772 No.6 had a tenant, Michael Goulden, a grocer, but the business may well still have belonged to James Ashley. Judging by the changes made in the building, together with the rear vaulted cellar, the rectangular front cellar linked by vaulted tunnel to another vaulted cellar under No.8, a prosperous business needing an unusually large amount of storage space is indicated.

James Ashley died in 1785 without children or brothers so the property and lands were inherited (according to the precepts laid down in the deed of 1729) by his sister, Elizabeth Moss and his nephew, William Rhodes (a bankrupt). The Ashleys also appear in the rentals of the manor of Dunham at this period paying their 3s 0d (15p) chief rent each for their "own lands in Altrincham". By the time of the Land Tax return of 1815, the tenant is given as Samuel Bruckshaw, also a grocer. In 1817 Elizabeth Moss and William Rhodes (now a discharged bankrupt) sold No.6 to Samuel Bruckshaw, and presumably the business too as he continued as a grocer, baker and corn merchant. In his will twenty years later he is described as a chapman, a travelling salesman. Samuel became Mayor in 1820, and an old printer's block of the building shows an architectural style which suggests that it is of that date.

No building is shown attached on the south side (as is the case today) but there is evidence that formerly the 'Horse and Jockey' stood next to No.6 across what is now Kingsway and that it stood well forward into the Market Place by the whole of its depth, adjoining the south wall of No.6 where this extended forward. About 1823 the old inn was demolished when Hollow Bank was filled (described below) to make Stamford Street (now Kingsway).

Just after Queen Victoria came to the throne in 1837, Samuel died leaving the property, land and business to his nephew Joseph Bruckshaw who was said in the will to have been trained by Samuel to take it over and who had lived at No.6 for many years. The censuses of 1841, 51, 61 and 71 give a few interesting facts about him. He was 37 when he took over, a bachelor who remained so all his life. Like so many family businesses, he employed his own extended family, his first cousins and later his second cousins. One cousin, Elizabeth Brundrett, became his housekeeper, remaining in that capacity until he died. George Smith of Dunham also worked for him all those years, as assistant and finally as foreman; he too remained a bachelor.

In 1841 Joseph Bruckshaw, nephew of Samuel, became Mayor. He continued the grocery, corn and porter business until he was 72. In 1872 he sold the property and business to his 48 year old foreman George Smith, and died the following year. Joseph is buried with Samuel and his wife in St. George's church yard. George Smith then raised a mortgage of £1,000 with Eliza Brundrett and gave her security of tenure at No.6 for the remaining years of her long life.

By 1878 George Smith had let the grocers shop to Worthington and Hulme who continued as grocers. In 1888 Robert Worthington of Partington, in partnership with James Hulme of Dunham Massey, employed assistants, Gerald Whitwham and Luke Winstanley of Agden. The latter had by 1890 taken over the business in partnership with Gerald Whitwham. According to his directions the properties were sold off when George Smith died in 1892 and Gerald Whitwham took the opportunity to purchase No.6 and the business. He became well-known in the now greatly expanded town, as a meticulous man with an eye for quality and a wide range of good wines. He became a local councillor and continued the traditions of No.6 by becoming Mayor in 1911.

In 1915 Arthur Littler and his young wife Emma, came to Altrincham from Chester to take up the position of manager of Whitwham's. By 1916 he had a lease and by 1922 he had purchased the property and business.

In 1934 Arthur Littler died aged only 44 years. Emma inherited the firm and property and ran it through the 1939–45 war with her youngest son Tony until his call-up in 1944. Returning from the services after the war, her three sons, Raymond, Wilfred and Tony, gradually took over the day-to-day work, eventually expanding into catering and wholesale wines.

When Emma died in 1971 the three brothers inherited all the property and land and the business. Eventually each took over a separate part of the firm, Raymond the catering, Wilfred the grocery and Tony the wines. In 1973 Raymond Littler became the last Mayor of Altrincham, concluding the line of mayors associated with No.6. In 1982 Raymond and Wilfred retired and the shop part was closed, ceasing to be a grocers, for the first time in 230 years. No.6 was bought by Tony and Joyce Littler.

For five or six years it became the packing department for the greatly developed wine section of the firm which had now expanded to such an extent that it had become a firm of wine shippers and brokers.

THE BUILDING

In July 1987, it was decided that the shop at No.6 should be opened again. Simultaneously, Barry Whitby, the furrier next door at No.8, decided to expand into his property at No.10 but everything came to a sudden halt when plaster removed from the inner wall, opposite the shopwindow of No.10, revealed an ancient 8 foot section of wall, timber-framed, with wattle and daub panels and an old door exactly fitting a doorway which was only 4ft 8ins (142cm) high; at the bottom of it was a cat flap! At Nos. 8 and 10 the recently extended shop now shows the timbers and on one wall part of the wattle panel has been left exposed under glass.

Alterations were begun at No.6 but came to a halt when a large bulge was found behind the Victorian shelving when it was removed in the shop. The architect and consultant engineers were called and after some time decided that though the bulge was serious, the old place could be saved.

The ground floor plan of No.6, Fig. 16.5, shows a building with narrow frontage onto the Market Place. The area of No.6's plot was documented as 10 square perches of statute ($5\frac{1}{2}$ yards) perch measure, which bears an uncanny resemblance to the 2 perches X 5 perches of the size of a burgage mentioned in the Charter of AD1290. It might be thought that No.6 was a whole mediaeval burgage plot but this is misleading because we have to reckon not by modern statute measurement but by the ancient Cheshire large measure, in which a perch was not $5\frac{1}{2}$ but 8 yards. This made a plot 2 perches wide to be 16 yards or 48 feet (not 11 yards of statute measure). Four properties Nos.8, 10, 12 and 14 occupy 2 burgage ends as follows:

Nos.   8, 10   2 x 24ft = 48ft i.e. 16 yards
       12, 14   2 x 24ft = 48ft i.e. 16 yards

No.6 is also half a burgage, the rest ran alongside and is represented by the shops on Kingsway, e.g. (Morrell's, Fig. 16.2).

∴ No.6's 24ft frontage plus Morrell's shop 24ft width gives one whole burgage width of 48ft.

All these properties originally had burgage lands behind extending 120ft (5 Cheshire perches). The process of dividing burgages along their length and also transversely was taking place at least as early as the beginning of the 16th century and led to the area becoming very built-up.

In 1760 James Ashley made extensions to the properties and removed the timber-framing, replacing the timbers with brick.

The construction of a timber-framed house is

Fig. 16.6. **The re-used piece of timber in Bay 1,**   *J.L.*
inserted to absorb movement. The 'VII' is a carpenter's mark indicating that it would fit into a socket with that number.

Fig. 16.7. **The numbered, re-used wall timber of**   *J.L.*
Fig. 16.6. It fitted exactly into a socket numbered 'VII' in the removed, recessed beam. Another timber fitted socket 'XIII'

divided into a series of bays. At No.6 there are three bays, Fig. 16.5; Bay 1 is on the North wall from the front window to the pillar supporting the central chimney; Bay 2 on the North wall, runs from the same pillar as Bay 1, back to the dotted lines marking the end of the front gable; Bay 3 is the North wall of the rear house under the rear gable. Brickwork in Bay 1 was unbelievably haphazard, of all shapes, sizes and ages, mortared with an astonishing casualness of bonding. Pieces of timber had been incorporated and these had prevented cracks from running upwards. One of the timbers bore a carpenter's mark "VII", Fig. 16.6, which fitted perfectly into a re-used oak beam removed from the ceiling above it. The socket into which it fitted also had a scratched mark "VII" beside it, (Fig. 16.7). Another piece was also found which fitted number "XIII" socket.

The removal of the bulge in Bay 1 revealed a doorway and old lintel near the end of the brickwork by the front window. Mysteriously, there had been no doorway in the inner wall which was entirely composed of old bricks and mortar, yet on the other side of the wall this doorway was clear to see and was entirely filled with 19th century bricks. The conclusion was that it had been refilled at some time from outside and that it had been a doorway before the 1760 de-timbering, possibly even from before the building of the rear gable, Fig. 16.8.

The plaster-work in Bays 2 and 3 clearly showed the string marks (string—a sloping joist supporting the steps in wooden stairs) of two flights of stairs rising towards each other, one in the rear house and one in the front.

On the south wall opposite Bay 3 were smoke marks along much of its length, well outside the removed chimney-breast and covering the broken ends of the single brick wall. Samuel Bruckshaw was described as a "baker" and his ovens may have been there. In the south-east corner of the front gable was a sharply defined smoke mark which appeared to have been channelled to the corner under a hood or other such means, possibly a large open corner fireplace. No chimney now remains there, and there seems little likelihood that it was smoke from the bakery, but from another chimney which was probably removed when the rear gable was added.

A large back-to-back chimney was built under the front gable, perhaps at the same time. It went through the building at every level and a support for this was built in the cellar. Although in 1669 Sir Peter Leycester commented on the lack of chimneys in Altrincham and the preponderance of cottages where fires burned in the centre of the floor and smoke escaped through a hole in the roof, it is probable that No.6 would have had chimneys for most of its life.

At some time, probably in the Victorian period, the back-to-back chimney was removed at ground level, the remaining stack on the floors above being supported with a large oak beam. This was insufficient for the weight above it and has been the main cause of structural problems, which have been exacerbated by the traffic which has thundered by in more recent years. Recently two extra girders were put in to flank the beam on large new brick pillars to take the strain.

The flooring of the rear gable was of very old flags, no doubt there for centuries but now encased in concrete. Mr. John Archer the architectural historian commented on the excellent construction and condition of the rear vaulted cellar and the vaulted passage from the front cellar, which leads to another vaulted cellar in similarly good condition under No.8. (There is another vaulted cellar under No.14 and a square cellar under No.12.) It was the three cellars which led to him pointing out the wealth of the owner, Fig. 16.9.

It was found that whereas all other walls rested on large stones or the ground, the rear wall of the rear gable went down at least 8ft below ground and probably more. Further investigation indicated that the house, even as a single gable, had overhung Hollow Bank, possibly being a 2–2½ storey house at the front and a

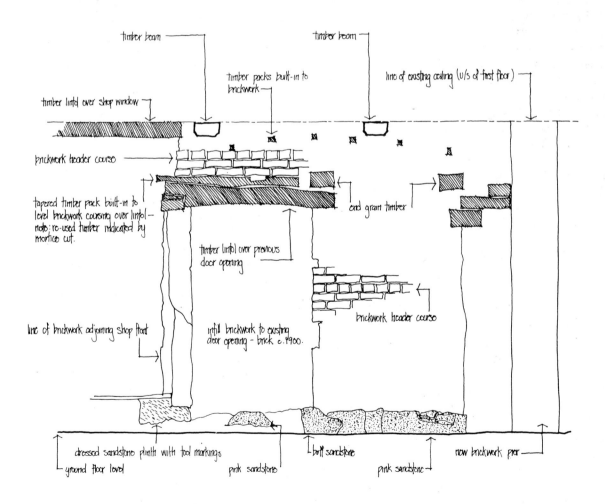

Fig. 16.8 **Architect's drawing of Bay 1.**   *David Holmes*
After the bulging wall was removed the old doorway on the left was revealed.

3-3½ storey house at the back. No cellar was built under the rear gable which probably gave more stability. At some stage the whole of the long yard behind was infilled to a considerable depth (recent architectural investigation had already shown this fact).

The work of restoration continued, and some amounts of daub were found between the bricks and about half a cupful was saved for investigation.

No.8 was extended over the passage, all the supports for it being of the old timbering.

A printer's block showing No.6 was inherited with the building when it was acquired by Arthur Littler in 1916. It was always thought to be a flight of someone's fancy, but in recent months it has been found to be accurate and detailed, many of the doubted structural features having been verified during the repairs and

Fig. 16.9. **The rear vaulted cellar.**   *J.L.*
What were thought to be 'ham hooks' were found to have been put in by Emma Littler during the 1939-45 war when the cellar was used as an air raid shelter. Hammocks were slung across the cellar between the hooks.

Fig. 16.10. **Printer's block on an old bill head of about 1945.**   *J.L.*
The shop doorway is in the centre and no building is attached.

John Archer and an archaeologist were quite definite that this was from the wattle and daub panelling which had been part of the house walls when they were timbered. It confirmed John Archer's original dating of 15th or 16th century at the latest, and that although modified the house had never been pulled down and has probably always been at least 2 storeys high. The panels and timbering were probably removed about 1760 and the timbers put to use elsewhere in the house. The thatching was removed also and the roof raised, old timbers were re-used here too, and these remain. The building had been extended forward 2 feet and

investigations to the building, Fig. 16.10. The old place has now been repaired and strengthened and remains in many ways, an eighteenth century adaptation of a mediaeval building occupying half a burgage. Eventually, refurbishing completed, the shop was re-opened in 1988 as "Whitwham's Fine Wine, Champagne and Seafood Bar". Most customers are surprised when they visit it to enjoy their modern tastes, to realise the antiquity of the place and the complexity of the lives of its owners and tenants over the last few hundred years revealed by "the old black box".

Chapter Seventeen

PAST PERSONALITIES OF ALTRINCHAM

BASIL MORRISON

Among the notable benefactors who have left their stamp on Altrincham, the principals were undoubtedly the Earls of Stamford and Warrington, in particular, **Roger Grey**, the tenth and final Earl, Fig. 17.1. He was born at Whitehall Court, London on 27 October 1896, educated at Eton and New College, Oxford and died unmarried on 18 August 1976 at the age of 79. The Earl's predecessors had done much to enrich Dunham Massey and Altrincham and a great many of the roads in the Altrincham area are named after, and in the memory of, the Stamford family and their forebears. By the nature of the bequest under his Will of his estate to the National Trust, Roger Grey bequeathed a gift of quite outstanding value for posterity.

Roger Grey became Altrincham's Charter Mayor when the town became a Municipal Borough in 1937 and was only the second member of the Grey family to hold this office. Without the Earl's aesthetic influence and the continuation of the stringent building regulations handed down by the Stamfords, much of the residential part of the town might be far less attractive today. A rather lonely man, but possessed of great kindness, an intense civic pride and an unmatched knowledge of Cheshire, he always lived up to his father's favourite saying—"to love and labour is the sum of living".

In 1849 **George Faulkner Armitage**, Fig. 17.2, was born at Townfield House, Church Street. He qualified as an architect and designer of furniture, commencing in business at his residence, Stamford House, Church Street, Fig. 17.3, at a site now occupied by the Cresta Court Hotel and Welman House. His house was originally the Stamford Arms and Bowling Green Hotel. To extend his social and other activities, Mr. Armitage purchased Sandiway House, an adjacent residence together with 1½ acres of land in 1901. He maintained a

Trafford Leisure Services

Fig. 17.1. **The Charter Mayor. The Right Honourable Roger Grey, Earl of Stamford, D.L., J.P.**

Trafford Leisure Services

Fig. 17.2. **George Faulkner Armitage**

Fig. 17.3. **Stamford House, Church Street.** *B.D.M.*

staff of 6 comprising 3 gardeners, a coachman, a laundrymaid and a housemaid, Miss Hazelhurst. She worked for the family from 1924–1937. The last years of her life were spent at Bickham House, Bowdon to which she left a bequest of £500 in her Will.

Prayers each morning were 'de rigeur'. They were held behind locked doors and woe betide anyone who was late. The moral rectitude of the day was exemplified by the quaint incident which took place following Mr. Armitage's death. In his Will, he left £75 each to Miss Hazelhurst and to the remainder of the staff with the exception of one man who despite being a very good employee for many years had had to get married, which had apparently upset Mr. Armitage, a strict and religious disciplinarian. Miss Hazelhurst out of her own bequest purchased a suit of clothes for the man.

Mr. Armitage designed and furnished many large country houses and London clubs. The dome to the Manchester Jubilee Exhibition in 1887 and the exquisite carvings to the choir stalls in Chester Cathedral were his work. His designs for the Council Chamber for the British Commission at the Paris Exhibition in 1900 won him a Gold Medal. In the 1920's his business was taken over and became Armitage and Wolfe—later Wolfe and Alexander and currently Shaw and Alexander in Manchester. The beauty of Armitage's work can be seen in the memorial cross in the Rest Garden opposite St. Margaret's Church, the erection of which he superintended without fee or reward having already subscribed handsomely towards the cost.

Prevented by ill-health from taking on active service during World War I, George Armitage was the only person to have been Mayor of Altrincham for 6 consecutive years, from 1913–19. In 1931 he was appointed Chairman of the Magistrates for the Altrincham Petty Sessional Division. Due to heavy traffic passing his front door he took unkindly to the motorcar and preferred his oldfashioned single horse brougham in which he took his daily drives. He was the last of Altrincham's gentry to possess this mode of transport and died in 1937.

At the turn of the century, when Cotton was King, one of the best known of the many 'merchant princes' in Manchester was **Mr. Samuel Lamb**, who lived at 'Denzell' on Dunham Road, a mixture of Victorian, Gothic, Flemish and Renaissance styles, Fig. 17.4, surrounded by its magnificent 10-acre garden. He was a wealthy shipper in Manchester and purchased the property about 1905. Samuel Lamb and his family became well-known in the district for their great philanthropy and support for Congregationalism and Liberalism, and by throwing open the beautiful gardens at Denzell to the public at weekends. His daughter, Miss Sybil Lamb, a Culcheth Hall School old girl, carried on her father's good works. After his death in December 1936 she and her brother, Mr. C. J. Lamb gave Denzell and its grounds to Bowdon Urban District Council in memory of their parents. Another of the family's gifts was a large bracket clock in the council chamber in Altrincham Town Hall.

Many businesses established in early times are still flourishing today. **Isaac and George Worthington** established a partnership of attorneys-at-law in 1785 in premises now occupied by the National Trust Offices. No. 7 Market Street, dating perhaps from the mid-18th century, had by 1795 become the residence of one of the partners who merely had to cross the road to get to his office. The firm moved to No.5 Market Street which had been the property of the Nicholls family.

Devereux Jones Nicholls appears in the partnership with Hugo and Robert Worthington in 1814. His son William Devereux Nicholls purchased No.5 Market Street from Lord Stamford on 31 August 1854 and in 1856 and 1857 held the position of Mayor of Altrincham. He was the senior partner in Nicholls Worthington who conducted most of the town's legal business and were also the first legal advisers to the Local Board of Health in 1851. He was responsible for the formation of the Mayor's Land Charity, a body of trustees to ensure that the profits from land endowed to the mayoralty by the Earl of Warrington should not be solely at the mayor's disposal. The trustees allocated income for the good of the community after making a small allowance for the personal use of the mayor.

Fig. 17.4. **A view of Denzell from the South**

B.D.M.   **F.R.B. Lindsell**

In 1871 **Joseph Harris** was taken into the partnership. His family name in the firm is continued today through his great grandsons, Mr. J. L. (Ian) Harris and Mr. G. Oliver Harris as Nicholls, Lindsell and Harris. Joseph held the Clerkship to the Justices for the Petty Sessional Divisions for more than 30 years and was succeeded by his son Harry Leonard Harris and in 1930 by his grandson Joseph Graham Harris who retired in 1963.

Frederick Raymond Barber Lindsell entered the legal partnership in 1883. He identified himself vigorously in the political life of the area as a staunch Conservative becoming the agent to Mr. Coningsby Disraeli at the General Election in 1895. He was instrumental in providing swimming baths in Stamford New Road and served on the Court Leet becoming mayor in 1896. He was also chairman of the management committee of Altrincham Provident Dispensary and Hospital, one of the present wards being named after him. He died in 1917 aged 66. The bi-centenary of the firm was held at their offices on 8 March in 1985.

Having had a close connection with the business life of Altrincham for nearly 70 years and involved in local affairs, it is not surprising that the name of **Eustace George Parker** is respected today, Fig. 17.5. Born in 1848 at Aston Manor and educated at King Edward Grammar School he eventually joined his father and applied himself to the manufacture of quality watches. In 1863, he and his brother took over the jewellery business of William Boddington in Church Street. Ten years later, in 1873 Mr. Parker acquired a business in Knutsford which had been established in 1760. After 5 years the Parkers moved into George Street and then purchased Tower Works at the corner of Stamford New Road and Grafton Street where the present business is carried on by Mr. Eustace Parker's grandson Mr. Brian Parker and his son John.

There were few better horologists, valuers and jewellers than Eustace Parker. The present mayoral chain of Altrincham was his personal handiwork, which he bore round his own shoulders with distinction in 1889–1890. He did much as an Overseer of the Poor and was a strong supporter of Altrincham Agricultural Society Show becoming chairman of the committee. It was the largest one-day show in the country; it closed in 1966.

Mr. Parker was an important freemason, served on the board of Altrincham General Hospital and was a life member of the Conservative Club. He was associated with St. Margaret's Church, St. John's Church, Hale Barns Mission Church and Ringway Parish Church. He was the founder and first captain of Ringway Golf Club. Eustace Parker died in 1932 at the age of 84.

Peter Morrison, a farmer, came from Scotland in the 1840's to live at Grange Farm, Bowdon described on an old map as being on Morrison's Lane. His son David, Fig. 17.6, born in 1850 after being in one or two businesses became apprenticed to Mr. H. G. Syers an estate agent on Kingsway. Three years later in 1875 he commenced business on his own as an accountant and estate agent on The Downs, moving later to George

B.D.M.

Fig. 17.5. **Eustace George Parker J.P., and the medal of Altrincham Agricultural Show he supported.**

Fig. 17.6. **David Morrison** *B.D.M.*

Trafford Leisure Services
Fig. 17.7. **Sir William Henry Veno.**

B.D.M.
Fig. 17.8. **Miss Mary Howes Smith.**

Street and opening a sale room as an auctioneer at Station Buildings, Moss Lane in 1905. He moved to larger premises at No.2 Old Market Place and in 1920 to the old Post Office premises at the corner of Post Office Street (Fig. 15.4). His son, David Stanley Morrison who died in 1974 was followed by his grandsons Philip and Basil and their sons and the business continued to grow embracing offices in Lancashire and Cheshire. In 1895 David Morrison was Mayor, chairman of several local committees, chairman of the Auctioneers and Estate Agents Institute in Manchester and a prominent freemason. His son Stanley was Mayor in 1926–27 and chairman of the Auctioneers Institute in 1934–35. His grandson, Basil, was chairman in 1960–61. David married in 1877 and died in 1929, the second of 6 generations of Morrisons.

William Henry Veno, Fig. 17.7, was born in Scotland in 1866, and started in business at only 15 years of age. He left home at 17 to become a sailor returning to resume business 3 years later. At about 25 he again visited the United States where he was a manufacturer of proprietary articles. While there he was engaged by the Republicans to stump the southern and western states for the election of President McKinley. After the successful election he returned to Manchester spending over £300,000 in placing on the market Veno's Lightning Cough Cure. In the 1920's Lady Veno helped her husband by standing on a box in Altrincham Market whistling loudly the tunes of the day to attract customers.

Following his knighthood in 1918 for public and philanthropic services Sir William sold his business for £600,000 and then immersed himself in serving the public. Sir William lived latterly at Woodlands, Dunham Park and was a Freeman and Liveryman of London. He died in 1933 at the age of 66 at Woodlands in tragic circumstances, his body being found in the grounds beside which lay his shot gun.

John Henry Grafton's name is perpetuated in Grafton Street and the Graftons office block and shopping mall. He lived for many years at Overdale, Bradgate Road and was a supporter of St. Margaret's Church. In 1896 he acquired the old Wesleyan Chapel in

Regent Road as a Mission Church to be attached to St. Margaret's. After considerable alterations it was reopened as All Saints Church. Following his death, and the removal of St. Margaret's Church spire in 1927 it was decided to extend the west end of the nave. It appears his widow verbally agreed to bear part of the cost but she died leaving no record of her intentions in her Will and the work was left incomplete.

Mary Howes Smith was headmistress of the County High School for Girls from 1913, Fig. 17.8. She possessed an outstanding educational background obtaining a history degree at Newnham College, Cambridge. After several years teaching in London, she came to Altrincham. To some this remarkable woman may have seemed autocratic with her pince-nez, long links of beads and flowing gown. Her love for her school and the people of the district endeared her to everyone she met. During her period in London she was appointed by King George V to teach English and History to his daughter, Princess Mary who later became the Princess Royal. While in Altrincham she continued travelling to London to continue this work.

Another famous woman was **Alison Uttley**, born Alice Jane Taylor in 1884 at Hilltop Farm at Cromford, Derbyshire. She went to Cambridge, and then taught English and Physics at a school in Fulham from 1908, describing the house in which she lived in 'Traveller in Time'. In 1911 she married James Uttley, a civil engineer and came to live at No.10 Higher Downs. After his death in 1930 she found it necessary to support her son and herself by writing over 50 books, mainly for children including 30 'Grey Rabbit' titles. She received an honorary degree of Doctor of Letters from Manchester University. She moved to Beaconsfield in 1936 where she lived for 40 years until her death in 1976 at the age of 91. On her gravestone in Penn churchyard are the words "Alison Uttley, a spinner of tales".

Juliana Horatia Ewing the authoress, 1841–1885, lived at 14 Higher Downs, then Downs Villa, only for 12 months from 1877–1878 but her contribution to the lives of children are worthy of mention. She was the second child in the large family of Rev. Alfred Gatty, vicar of Ecclesfield near Sheffield and her mother,

Margaret was a well-known writer of stories for children. Margaret's father was Lord Nelson's chaplain and friend and this resulted in the Gatty children being named Horatio or Horatia according to their sex. Juliana's stories were drawn from life and always had a moral background. The title of one, "The Brownies" suggested the name for Sir Robert Baden–Powell's junior Girl Guide movement. Her style appealed to Tennyson, Kipling and even Queen Victoria. She came to Altrincham to join her husband Major Ewing who was posted to Manchester in the Pay Corps. When he was posted to Malta she was not able to join him and died of cancer at the early age of 44 and is buried at Trull near Taunton.

Many people remember the **Noble** brothers, furnishers, in George Street (adjoining the present Leeds Building Society) who once filled their shop window with hand-painted £1 notes for a sales promotion, to the consternation of the police. **Godfrey William Bonson**, born on 9 June 1858, was trained at Gillows in London and later at Kendal Milnes in Manchester. He built the Midland Bank block, in which his furniture shop was one unit, at the corner of Stamford New Road and Moss Lane. He was Mayor in 1909 and died in 1932.

Dr. Adolf Brodsky, the Russian-born violinist was born in 1851 at Taganrog and at 9 entered the Vienna Conservatoire. He joined the Leipzig Conservatoire, 17 years later as senior professor of the violin. In the following year he was privileged to give the first performance of Tchaikowsky's violin concerto which had been pronounced as too difficult by one of his contemporaries. In 1895 he returned from America as leader of the New York Symphony Orchestra to be offered the prestigious position as leader of the Halle and senior violin professor at the Royal Manchester College of Music which had started with Sir Charles Halle as Principal. Sadly it was Brodsky's task to conduct Mozart's Requiem at Sir Charles's funeral the same year. He succeeded Sir Charles in the Halle and also became Principal of the College. He lived for twenty-five years at 3 Laurel Mount, Bowdon, on the wall of which is a 'Blue Plaque' to this effect. One of his students, Archie Camden said as an epitaph: "His was the true spirit of music. It was noble without the trappings of nobility; compassionate without the slur of sentimentality; stylish without extravagant showmanship".

There were 11 members of the **O'Brien** family, mother, father, 8 sons and a daughter. The father, Henry Francis O'Brien, born in 1868 founded the firm of that name, manufacturers and refiners of lubricating oils in Broadheath in 1890. The family originally lived at Hawthorn Bank, Grosvenor Road where a photograph was taken in the garden in 1914 of what they called the 'V-group' showing all the family, Fig. 17.9. In 1929 they moved to Leys Road,

Timperley and 23 years later in 1937, on the occasion of Mrs. O'Brien's birthday decided to repeat the photograph. They were very musical, playing many instruments including the 'musical saw'! They were a generous family and gave their service to many charitable efforts.

Helen Allingham (neé Paterson) 1848 - 1926 became a water colour painter of national renown whose delightful rural scenes are found on many greetings cards. Her family lived for a short time at No. 16 High Street (now Market Street) where a 'Blue Plaque' in her memory can be found on the wall of what is now an office of Bellway Homes. She also lived on St. John's Road before moving to Birmingham and London. She became the first full woman member of the Royal Watercolour Society.

Ronald Gow was a pupil and later a teacher at Altrincham Boys Grammar School. Locally known for his literary and cinematographic activities including the early use of film for reconstructing scenes from prehistory, he later became nationally known as a dramatist. He married Wendy Hiller and one of his best known plays was an adaptation of Walter Greenwood's "Love on the Dole" for the stage. For many years he lived at No. 63. Stamford New Road, now Barclays Bank, and his fame will be honoured by a 'Blue Plaque' on the wall of the bank.

There were many other notable local people. George Massey introduced gas into Altrincham in 1844 and is mentioned in Chapter Ten. In Chapter Nineteen details can be found of industrialists such as George Richards and others who made Broadheath's name world famous.

Fig. 17.9. The O'Brien family – the 'V' photographs. *B.D.M.*

Chapter Eighteen

PAST FAMILIES

JANET HARDMAN

The study of past Altrincham families through Wills, parish registers, census enumerators' returns and other sources shows that the population character and structure was of a complex nature not revealed by the overall figures printed every 10 years in the censuses. The population was composed partly of families who remained here for generations but others who came into the place subsequently left it. Several people came to Altrincham concerned with the trade brought by the Bridgewater Canal after it reached the town in 1765. One of these was James Gratrix who came from Didsbury and had a saw mill near the canal wharves (the mill was not knocked down until the 1960's). Gratrix was made Mayor of Altrincham in 1794. One of the houses associated with the canal, opposite Navigation Road, has just been demolished for office development, Fig. 18.1. The interesting history of its occupants can be traced to the present. Christopher Mort was the first wharfinger to be appointed at Broadheath. He had worked for the Duke of Bridgewater for 50 years by the time he died in 1806. Born at Astley, near Leigh, he came with his wife Mary and three daughters who had been baptised at Peel near Worsley. A son, Thomas was baptised at Bowdon in 1771. At that time there was also a John Mort in the town, perhaps related, a weaver turned draper who had a business in Church Street together with his son also called John. The latter married Mary Brundrett in 1799. Another John Mort became a prominent figure in local affairs and was Mayor in 1858–59.

Two later wharfingers were William Collier and then Thomas Leigh from Worsley. By 1906 there was Edward Green and subsequently Peter Higson whose name appears on the tender of Fig. 18.2. In the 1920's came James Lincoln Baxendale, now called manager, with his wife Allie. He is pictured in Fig. 18.3 on one of

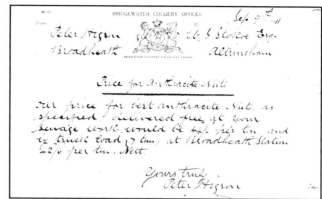

Fig. 18.2. **Tender for coal, 1911.** *J.H.*

Fig. 18.3. **Mr Baxendale and horse behind Bridgewater House.** *J.H.*

Fig. 18.4. **Garden of Bridgewater House.** *J.H.*

the horses, Bluebell, at the back of the house ready for the 1928 Altrincham carnival. The house then had a beautiful garden and his children Allie and Bill are pictured with the gardener, Mr. Gallagher in Fig. 18.4. They left and went to live in Timperley when Mr. Baxendale decided to start his own coal business, which became well-known locally. He became Mayor in 1959-60. Bill was killed in World War II but Allie (now

Fig. 18.1. **Bridgewater House, 1989 before demolition.** *J.H.*

Hamilton) still lives in Timperley and although only three years old when they left Broadheath still remembers the house with affection. Her most vivid recollection is of watching the organ grinder and his monkey from her bedroom window as he played outside the Packet House Inn opposite. A sister Pat (now Williams) was born later and also still lives in Timperley.

Many of the merchants and tradesmen arriving in the late 18th century lived in Church Street. John Holden, a woolstapler who had been born in Saddleworth, built two houses on land opposite to the Bowling Green Inn, called Stoney Acre which he had bought from William Parkinson. Holden also owned land in Ashton-under-Lyne. He only had one daughter and when he died in 1799 everything he possessed was sold. Bequests were made to a number of people including a niece Hannah who was married to John Derbyshire. He was the son of a maltster, also called John Derbyshire who had been Mayor of Altrincham in 1775 and had premises and a dwelling near the site of the Railway Inn on Stamford Street.

At this time of population increase through in-migration and natural causes, non-conformity grew rapidly and there had been a Wesleyan chapel from 1788. A demand arose for an Anglican church in the town as distinct from St. Mary's in Bowdon and this resulted in the building of a new chapel-of-ease, St. George's. The first baptism here was of George, son of James and Rebecca Walthew on 15 December 1799. James was the Overseer of the Poor and one of a family of plumbers and glaziers. He had been Mayor in 1792.

In the early nineteenth century Altrincham was noted for its worsted and some cotton industries. After 1800 there were two or three textile factories in the town (Chapter Five) but many people would have worked in their cottages with the whole family often involved. To make a living, this occupation would often have to be combined with working a small plot of land or keeping a few pigs or cows. Richard Knight was such a weaver who was also a part-time farmer. He supplied the workhouse with milk. By 1851 there were only 18 weavers mainly in silk and cotton. Four of these had been born elsewhere, three were brothers, John, James and Charles Dean and there was another John Dean, probably a cousin. The brothers James and Thomas Harrop were two other weavers.

The Warmishams were another family in the wool and worsted trades. Robert Warmisham of Baguley married Ellen Shelmerdine at Northenden in 1741 and they moved to Altrincham about 10 years later and had at least nine children. Four of these were Robert, John, Isaac and Elisha. The first of these, Robert, became a worsted manufacturer. His son, John, was a saddler on Church Street and had retired by 1861. The second son, John, was a weaver who died in 1778 when only 28 years of age leaving a widow, Sarah, and son John, who himself died only 22 years later leaving his widow and three children paupers. Sarah remarried in 1781 this time to Joseph Gleave, a shoemaker. The third son of

Robert Warmisham, Isaac, became a woolcomber and died in 1793 when 50 years old, leaving a widow Ellen with three children. He did not leave a Will but Letters of Administration were granted to Thomas Ashley, a woolcomber and chief creditor. Isaac had two sons, Isaac and Thomas. The first son, Isaac, married to Mary, appears in the paupers accounts from 1819–21 as receiving about £6 a year. There must have been sickness in the family as there was also a bill for £3 8s (£3·40) for a Dr. Broadbent (more than half the poor relief received for one year) and another of 10s (50p) for coffins for his children (though there was only one named in the burial register, Ruth, aged 21 months). The second son, Thomas, was a weaver in New Street in 1851 and he had a son of the same name who also carried on the same trade. The fourth son of Robert Warmisham, Elisha, was another woolcomber and he died in 1796 aged 50 years. His widow, Maria, was left with three children aged 4, 6 and 10 and all were listed as paupers in 1800–1801. Maria died in 1805. By 1861 the name Warmisham still survived with three bricksetters, one porter and one blacksmith. At the turn of the century Joseph Warmisham a bricksetter (and perhaps a descendant) lived on Navigation Road. He was also a fireman, part-time in those days. In 1906 the pay for this job was 3s (15p) for the first hour and 1s 6d (7½p) for each subsequent hour. Perhaps he was connected with the Warmishams who put in tenders (shown in Fig. 18.5) for roofing and tiling to the Council at this time.

One of the old trades connected with textiles was that of bobbin turning. Several people of this trade are known before 1800 and the trade is mentioned in directories after 1800 but there were few left by 1851. Two of these were William and James Johnson both living in Chapel Street. They were descended from one of several families of this name all in the same trade in the late 18th century. Another bobbin turner in 1851 was John Hamilton who lived in Police Street.

Basket-making was the occupation of three generations of Amerys. George who married in 1766 had at least 10 children who did not all survive to

Fig. 18.5. **Letterhead of the Warmishams**

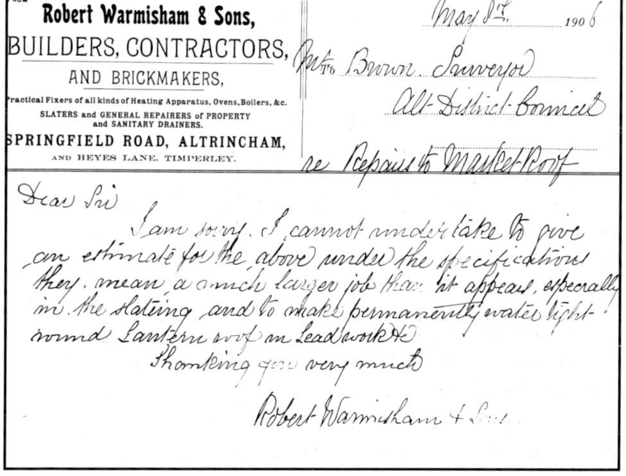

MEMORANDUM.

FROM Robert Warmisham & Sons,
BUILDERS, CONTRACTORS,
AND BRICKMAKERS,
Practical Fixers of all kinds of Heating Apparatus, Ovens, Boilers, &c.
SLATERS and GENERAL REPAIRERS OF PROPERTY
and SANITARY DRAINERS.
SPRINGFIELD ROAD, ALTRINCHAM,
AND HEYES LANE, TIMPERLEY.

J.H.

adulthood. His son George was still working in 1851 and lived on Peel Causeway. His grandson William who lived in Victoria Street in 1861 combined basket-making with letter-carrying.

In 1851 nearly 45% of the people living in Altrincham had been born outside the parish of Bowdon and had come from all parts of the British Isles, and other countries as well. Many of the working class incomers crowded into the George Street/New Street area. Most marked were the number of servants (384) and labourers (402) listed in the total population of 4,488. Isaac Turton was one of the newcomers. Born in Halewood near Liverpool, he became the constable of Lymm, married a local girl and then moved to Altrincham in the early 1830's to become assistant Overseer of the Poor (Chapter Fourteen gives details of his very important report of 1849 on the poor state of health of many people in the town and its insanitary conditions). One of his sons worked as an estate agent. Another, George, by the end of the century was Assistant Overseer to the Council and responsible for the collection of rates.

Although many new families had come to live in Altrincham since the late 18th century, at the same time some were moving away. The industrial revolution changed the whole work pattern and several occupations were particularly affected. Some families moved out from Altrincham to better themselves in the large cotton mills in Manchester. Hulme was a popular place to settle, still semi-rural and some gardeners moved and carried on that activity there. Others changed their occupations to warehousemen, porters and later some worked on the railways.

James Layland was a weaver who came to Altrincham from Manchester about 1764. His son, John, also a weaver, married Mary Priestner in 1789 and though some of their descendants were to be found in Altrincham throughout the 19th century, some went back to Manchester. William Layland, a son of John and Mary, was living in one of the cottages in Lower George Street in 1839 and was also working a piece of land near to what is now Greenwood's shoe repair

shop. William had two sons, James, a wood sawyer who lived in Navigation Road in 1851 and John, a shoemaker, who lived in Chapel Street and eventually became a Chelsea Pensioner. James had two sons, Charles was a joiner and Ralph an upholsterer.

Some families were prominent but then faded out, such as the Slaters, a family of bakers. Many of their children were baptised at Hale Presbyterian chapel but few survived their childhood. The oldest known, John, died in 1783, then James, in 1801. James had a son, also James, and a brother, Thomas, both of whom died in 1811. Thomas who was buried with his father does not appear to have had any children and left his property (near Lloyd Street) to his nephew Daniel who by then had moved to Manchester. The rest of the estate was left to his nephew James and niece Ellen who had married another baker John Pickstone. By 1851 the name Slater cannot be found in the town.

Some idea of the variety of people and trades can be obtained by looking at the records for one street, for example Stamford Street. In a tithe schedule of 1839, 8 of the houses were listed as owned by John Barratt, a grocer and maltster on Market Place who also owned a number of other properties and land in the town. The only named occupier of the houses was William Whitehead. In 1851 the publican of the Malt Shovels, Fig. 18.6, was named as George Birch from Withington. The rest of the cottages along from here were inhabited by two sisters, Alice and Mary Smith, dressmakers; Isaac Hamilton, bricksetter; John Bradbury, brickmaker; Joseph Whittle, groom; Thomas Bates, railway worker; and George Smith a land surveyor. The fronts of these cottages lay on the south side of the street next to the block in which is Walton's model shop, across Station House carpark exit. Just behind these buildings was Police Street, where Station House now stands. Behind the Malt Shovels the end plots had a house, yard, workshops and two fields which had been owned by John Mitchell a thread manufacturer (who had married an Ellen Cooke in 1784 and had been the Mayor in 1811 and again in 1815). After he died his sons, James, John and Henry Mitchell continued as tenants, lived next

Fig. 18.6. **Malt Shovels and shops today.**   *J.H.*

Fig. 18.7. **Abraham Gibbons c.1880** *J.H.*

door to each other and also continued the business of thread manufacturers. By 1852 the properties belonged to Samuel Barratt (who in 1864 was recorded as living at High Bank). More property owned by John Mitchell in Victoria Street (occupied by John Holt and Joseph Smith) was then sold to an Isaac Gaskaith. Perhaps business had not been good as the estate was valued at under £600. The three Mitchell brothers nevertheless continued in manufacturing until at least 1860.

The Gibbons were originally a family of farmers. Abraham Gibbons, usually known as 'Ibby' is pictured in Fig. 18.7 about 1880 in Market Place doing his milk round. He had descended from a farming family in High Legh and there had been a large number of Gibbons in Bowdon parish for many years, farmers or gardeners. Born in 1827 he started his working life as a shoemaker but later had a shop on Chapel Lane (Regent Road) selling milk and provisions. His brothers Isaac and Jacob were grooms and sister Elizabeth a dressmaker. His father William, a gardener and weaver was born in Dunham near the Rope and Anchor and probably moved to Altrincham after his marriage to Ann Langford in 1812. One of Abraham's sons, Richard

Freeman Gibbons was a clerk in a shipping office in Manchester and after his marriage to Alice Hulme lived in lower George Street in cottage No.10 which stood opposite the old library. In 1906 the rent for this was 3s 6d (17½p) a week. At No.4 Isaac Dean was paying 5s (25p), Joseph Whyatt at No.6, 6s 9d (34p), Ann Riley at No.8, 3s 3d (16p), Mr. A. Chapman at No.12, 4s 0d (20p), Mrs. Speke at No.14, 5s (25p), and Mrs. Loftus at No.16, 4s 9d (24p). One of Richard Gibbons' sons, Leslie Harold was a plumber and lived on Mayor's Road. His wife Annie now aged 84 is still living there. Another son, also called Richard Freeman Gibbons, worked at Waterhouse's Cornmill in Brewery Street and his son Alan Gibbons owns the shop called Weetman's near Hale Station.

The name Brundrett was one of the most common and can be found as far back as 1641. Many members of this family were farmers and market gardeners. A Jeremiah Brundrett appears in the list of Stamford estate tenants in 1701 mentioned in Chapter Four. Aaron Brundrett, born in 1737, the son of Jonathan and Ellen married Martha Barlow in 1761 and was a woollen weaver but later became a chapman (a dealer in small goods) and probably had a shop in the Market Place area. He was also the Postmaster (probably the first) and the Mayor in 1790. He and his wife had seven children but only two survived them. By the time his father died the son and heir, Jonathan, was living in London and does not appear to have returned. His sister, Mary was still at home with her mother and they inherited the house, means of support and the use of Aaron's pew, No.81 in St. George's Chapel. There must have been burial clubs at the time of Aaron's death because the Amicable Society, mentioned in his Will, was to pay out immediately for mourning. He also left £10 to his niece Hannah Drinkwater. His estate was valued at under £3,500, a substantial sum and he was listed as being one of those eligible for jury service, *i.e.* a burgess holding land in the town.

A few other family names to be found frequently 200 years ago which have survived to the present day are: Ashley (Chapter Sixteen), Barlow, Garner, Holt, Pickstone, Royle, Warburton and Worthington. The study of families as can be seen above helps to bring the history of the town to life particularly as it deals with named people from all walks of life.

THE INDUSTRIAL DEVELOPMENT OF BROADHEATH

DR. CURTIS SPARKES

Broadheath, during its industrial history, was to become one of the most remarkable areas in the world. Developed on a 'greenfield' site, situated on a former heath, Figs. 19.1 and 19.2, its manufactured goods achieved worldwide recognition. The engineering items produced included, among many others, a range of famous printing machines and pressure gauges, which were exported to almost every country in the world, but its greatest achievement was to attain international fame for machine-tools.

In the middle of the 19th Century there were no indications of the pending industrial expansion which was to take place as there were only a few warehouses, a saw mill, coal wharves and a foundry, later known as the Borax Works, which employed a few moulders.

What developed was a massive complex of firms, in which there were to be five which became internationally famous. These were Richards, Linotype, Churchills, Budenbergs and Kearns, each of which had a different history. These will be recorded in some detail, together with a brief mention of some of the smaller, but also important firms.

THE ROLE OF LORD STAMFORD

One of the most interesting factors in the case of Altrincham and its surrounding areas was the control on the use of the land exercised by the late Lord Stamford. His family had devised special types of

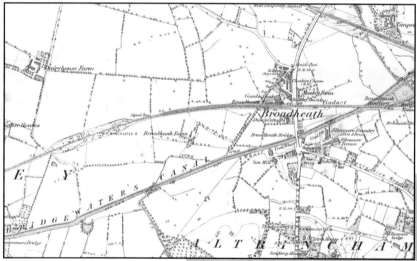

Fig. 19.1. **Map of Broadheath in the 1880's, before becoming industrialised.**
Duke's Cottages were formerly the workhouse.
Ordnance Survey

Fig. 19.2. **View over Broadheath from St. Margaret's Church.**   C.A.S.
Linotype chimney is in the centre of the picture

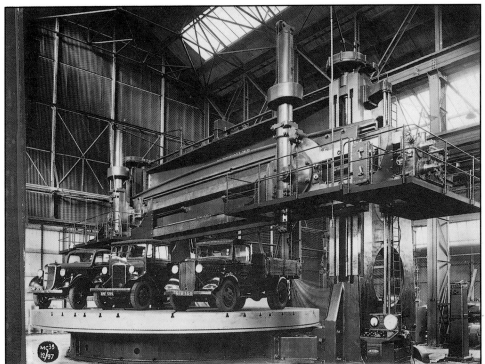

Fig. 19.3. **George Richards Co. Ltd. produced this boring and turning mill in 1946.** The lorries are to show the size of the mill.

C.A.S.

covenants which had been carefully prepared to ensure that the final decision on the use of any land and the nature of the buildings to be erected rested completely with the Stamfords. In fact, Lord Stamford could override any plans agreed by the local Council and certainly exercised this authority when he thought it was necessary to protect his rights.

At the outset industrial development was not held by the Altrincham and Bowdon residents in high regard, but Lord Stamford saw this in a more realistic way. He recognised the implications of this momentous event and decided that any industrial development of industry in Broadheath should be limited to the north side of the canal and railway. The canal, railway and roads, combined with low interest rates, offered ideal conditions for acceptance by industry and created a great attraction for development. For a full list of firms, see Appendix 3.

THE FIRST FACTORY – GEORGE RICHARDS

In 1884 an American engineer, George Richards, opened the first factory in Broadheath. He started his original works in Manchester which he named Atlantic Works, symbolising his separation from America where he was born. When he moved to Broadheath he gave his new business the same name, also the street in which it was located. Fig. 19.3. shows a typical machine tool produced by this firm.

TILGHMANS

In 1873, the Tilghmans, two American brothers, founded a small factory in London. Seven years later they moved

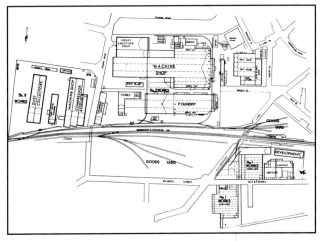

Fig. 19.4. **Site plan of Tilghmans** *C.A.S.*

to Sheffield to continue their shot blast equipment manufacture, especially for use in the local file industry. The Tilghmans had discovered in their house in the United States, that their windows became opaque due to the action of sand blowing against them. From this simple observation grew their sand blast business. Sand was later replaced by cast-iron shot when it was discovered that sand led to the operators developing lung problems.

A most interesting letter sent to the Tilghmans in the States in 1895, from one of their representatives who knew the Richards company in Broadheath, suggested that the latter firm was in financial trouble, also that it was not being well managed. Furthermore that the plant and equipment was in poor condition and most of it was outdated. In the light of this letter Tilghmans then made an offer to George Richards of £25,000 for the company. This deal was finally concluded but the money never reached George Richards himself,

Fig. 19.5. Thornton & *C.A.S.* Pickard manufacturing Co. Ltd.

Fig. 19.6. **The Broadheath Blockade. Mr. A.C. Sparkes and Farm Hands, 1905.** *C.A.S.*

who apparently suddenly left this country for Belgium and never returned. In these circumstances, in order to protect their financial interest in Richards company, Tilghmans appointed their American friend Matheson as Managing Director in 1896. At the same time they moved their factory in Sheffield to Broadheath and combined it with that of George Richards. To accommodate the two companies they built a second factory in Broadheath, Fig. 19.4. This move proved beneficial to Tilghmans who quickly achieved worldwide recognition for their products.

EARLY SMALLER FIRMS

Messrs. Luke & Spencer, makers of grinding machines and grinding wheels, opened their works in Atlantic Street, in 1884, quickly followed by Thornton & Pickard known internationally for photographic apparatus, Fig.19.5. Thornton, the firm's founder, invented the technicolour process.

Factories needed power and this was quickly recognised by the Altrincham Electric Supply Ltd., when they built their power generating station on the canal bank, to supply not only the growing industrial demand, but also the town, an early benefit to the residents of Altrincham.

Industrial development continued when Radium (Broadheath) Ltd. started a business producing a process for suede and leather dyes, also the manufacture of all kinds of leather dressings and finishes for the shoe trade. They were followed by the opening of Charles Madan & Co., makers of steam injectors, when they moved from Manchester and built a new works on the canal side of Atlantic Street. These injectors were soon being supplied to most engineering firms making steam equipment, but most important they were fitted to the Royal Naval vessels in service during the First World War.

These companies were joined by the Leather Company (Altrincham) Ltd., who manufactured hydraulic leather packings. They had started in Stretford in 1888 and were the largest manufacturers of this type of packing. Their Grafton Street works in Altrincham also employed 35 people.

The J. W. Record Company was established in 1911 by John Westmorland Record to produce high quality measuring instruments. They carried out large contracts in both World Wars and at one time were employing over 600 people. Their famous graphic recorders achieved a very high reputation by being some of the most sensitive in the world.

By the end of the 19th and beginning of the 20th century, the industry of Broadheath was growing at an extremely fast rate. Some of the larger firms are now described below.

LINOTYPE AND MACHINERY COMPANY

The event which was to have a major impact on Broadheath was the arrival of the Linotype and Machinery Company in 1896, Fig. 15.11. This company expressed a wish to acquire about 40 acres of land. Of this, 30 acres were purchased from Mr. A. C. Sparkes, the grandfather of the writer. The sale of this land, which lay on the south side of the canal, was in direct conflict with the ideas of Lord Stamford who wished to restrict all industrial development to the north side of the canal. The Linotype and Machinery Company overcame this objection by proposing to use only 4 acres of the land for their buildings. The remaining 36 acres would be developed into a unique housing estate for the factory employees, while retaining a rural air in line with the advanced designs of the day of garden suburbs. Thus, one of the country's first carefully planned housing estates (described in Chapter Fourteen) was built with tree-lined avenues between the rows of houses. Tenants' houses of different designs reflected the position of the employees within the factory. Furthermore each road was named after a Director of the company, *i.e.* Lock, Lawrence, etc. From an industrial point of view this was a new approach to factory planning in the region and was a very practical example of the way a forward looking company could design a manufacturing complex which would fit into a rural area.

The Linotype Company were faced, however, with two unexpected problems. First, their idea was to bring coal from Manchester to their own power station which would be built alongside the canal. In view of the size of the boilers required, it was necessary to erect a very large and tall chimney, still a dominant landmark. Not only did this bring strong protest from the local people, but the project almost had to be abandoned because of the difficulty of making a satisfactory foundation. The second problem, was their idea that having bought the land they had a complete right to its use. This view was not shared by the previous owner, Mr. A. C. Sparkes, who was now developing property in Broadheath and needed the right of access to move building materials through the Linotype grounds. The company objected to this and this led to my grandfather creating the famous Broadheath Blockade intended to impede the company's access to their plant, Fig. 19.6.

Part of the Linotype's business success was in making type for most of the world's printing presses. A line of letters was made from a bowl of molten metal. This was then fixed to large cylinders which rotated to print the letters on the paper from a supply of ink. The whole process required a large number of complicated and accurately made pieces of machinery. It needed a high degree of engineering skill to design and build these machines. However, the desire for more news to be produced even faster, contributed to the decline of this Broadheath firm.

When the era of electronics, satellites, television, computers and word processors came along, it was a totally new field in contrast to heavy engineering skills which had been used by the Linotype company. While these new devices were gaining momentum, Linotype was cushioned from the final impact by the resistance of the printers whose union operated virtually a closed shop and refused to accept the new techniques and with a continuing need to supply spare parts for their existing machines which were now distributed all over the world. It is also a criticism of the education authorities and universities in particular that they found little of interest in research problems, or offered any suitable training programme for the new print industry that was emerging. The molten metal and original complicated mechanically operated printing machines were replaced by the micro-chip and the need was for a much smaller manufacturing plant and buildings. Hundreds of staff were finally laid-off and today a more hi-tech company trading as L&M Ltd. is engaged in the manufacture of a modern type of printing equipment.

BUDENBERG GAUGE COMPANY

Following the building of the Linotype factory and their unique housing estate on the south side of the canal, there were no further developments until the arrival of the Budenberg Gauge Company in 1912. This famous pressure gauge firm was founded in Germany in 1852, then came to Manchester, and finally to a new factory in Woodfield Road as Schaffer & Budenbergs. The design of their buildings illustrate that it was possible for industry to design not only a first class office block, but one which was very aesthetically pleasing. With considerable justification there have been requests over many years for a Conservation Order to be granted for the preservation of this extremely pleasant building, Fig. 15.12.

This company achieved worldwide recognition, not only for the excellent pressure gauges they produced, Fig. 19.7, but for their excellent company relationships.

Fig. 19.7. **Example of early (left) and later (right) Budenberg pressure gauges.** *Budenberg*

The firm proved for many years to be one of the most successful family owned businesses in this country. In keeping with the current modern business practices re-organisation is now taking place in this remarkable company.

CHURCHILL MACHINE TOOL COMPANY

Charles Churchill was born on 8 July 1837 in Hampden, Connecticut, U.S.A. He came to this country at the age of 25 to install machinery made by his father. Shortly after his arrival he commenced importing tools and machinery and founded the Charles Churchill Company in 1865 in Manchester.

In 1901 he acquired a small factory in Griffin Court, Salford, and in 1904 moved to larger works in Pendleton, which he rented at an annual rent of £90. The need arose for more accurate machinery, not only for established industries, but also for the promising prospect of the infant motor car trade. Mr. Churchill then founded a new company on 1 January 1906 to carry on the business of machine tools alongside his original Charles Churchill Company. By 1906 it had produced over 200 machine tools of various types at the Pendleton works including precision grinding machines. The demand for these machines continued

Fig. 19.8. **Churchill Machine Tool Company Works, 1950.** *C.A.S.*

to increase and in April 1918 it was decided to purchase a plot of land in Broadheath from Lord Stamford. On this 11 acre site the firm commenced building a factory early in 1919, which they completed during the same year. This was to be called the Churchill Machine Tool Company, Fig. 19.8.

As their range of high quality and modern grinding machines expanded, so did their name become well-known throughout the industrial world. The company was honoured for their war effort by a visit from the late King George VI and the present Queen Mother, the then Queen Elizabeth, in July 1946. So successful did the company become, that at one stage they were employing over 1,500 people. However, in 1961 the company was incorporated with the Birmingham Small Arms Company (BSA) which also had a large manufacturing unit, together with an excellent sales organisation. In 1967 the BSA Company, including Churchills, was taken over by Alfred Herberts to help to fill their order books following a rapid diminishing of orders for their own machines. In spite of considerable pressure from the local unions and a visit of a delegation from Altrincham Town Hall to discuss the subject with the then Chancellor of the Exchequer, the Rt. Hon. Anthony Barber, efforts to keep Churchills in Altrincham were without success. The works finally closed in 1976 and although a small number of employees went to Coventry, the Churchill Machine Tool Company ceased to exist in 1987.

H. W. KEARNS & CO. LTD.

H. W. Kearns company opened their factory in Atlantic Street in 1907 and were to become one of the world's leading machine-tool makers. The writer was with the company for 50 years, finally retiring as Managing Director. The founder was born in London in 1846, obtained a Degree in Chemistry at London University and then became involved in the manufacture of baby food in London and later in the dyeing industry. H. W. Kearns eventually had four sons and one daughter. The eldest son, Joseph, and his second son, Lionel (later to be Sir Lionel), went to Cambridge to study engineering. Old H. W. Kearns' interest in dyeing and his association with a company in Rawtenstall, induced the family to

move to that area and in view of his sons' interest in engineering he bought £30,000 of shares in the machine-tool company of William Muirs in Manchester. He soon held an important position on the Board and later became its Chairman.

Muirs' factory was situated in one of the poorer parts of Salford, a location which H. W. Kearns thought would never attract the best kind of labour, or provide the ideal conditions for making accurate machinery. In the light of a disastrous experience trying to make baby food in similar circumstances in London's dockland and this being reported in the press, he proposed to Muirs' Board that they should move the factory to the suburbs. He was out-voted on this and immediately withdrew the £30,000, which he then invested to build a new works of his own.

Kearns was friendly with Matheson, who was now the Managing Director of George Richards and Tilghmans. Within one year of buying the land from Lord Stamford he had built an excellent factory in Atlantic Street for the production of machine-tools. He also brought with him from Muirs 28 men, including an old draughtsman named Simons, who said he had been taught to draw in a sand tray in a small school in Salford and that Mr. Muir had sent him to a specialist to have the bumps of his cranium felt to see if he would make a suitable apprentice!

Meanwhile, a few years earlier Richards had signed an agreement to build a remarkable forerunner of the modern machining centre which had been designed by Frank Pearn, a Manchester manufacturer in 1895. Kearns became aware that Richards were becoming disenchanted with this agreement and so they approached Pearn and made a new agreement with him to produce his machine. However Kearns terminated this contract within 12 months and decided to concentrate on a new type of universal horizontal boring, milling and drilling machine which they were developing. Meanwhile, Richards continued to develop a wide variety of other types of machine-tools, including the horizontal boring machine. However, the relationship between the two firms became very bitter when Kearns in 1920 accused Richards of infringing their patent. This resulted in a case being taken to the Law Courts in London. Eventually the expenses involved reached a level where both companies suddenly realised that if they were to continue there was a very serious threat that either one or both would face bankruptcy. At the last moment they made an out-of-court settlement. The agreement incorporated an instruction that no member of either company would be allowed to visit the other's factory, though this had no effect on the friendly relationship between their employees.

Unfortunately Richards became the first victims of unforeseen events which overtook the whole of the machine-tool industry of this country. During the nationalisation of the coal and steel industry, the Staveley Coal & Iron Company were taken over and received substantial compensation for their assets. This left that company with money, but no business portfolio. To develop one they selected companies from the

Munitions work. *C.A.S.*

machine-tool industry and within a few years had taken over 30 of the country's most important machine-tool firms for their Group, Richards being one of the first. Richards soon lost control of their factory to London and with the Staveley Design Centre being in Bedford, this led to a reduction in the rate of design and development of Richards machines.

By late 1950's, following a disastrous effort to re-design their range of horizontal boring machines, there was a decline in their customers' confidence and in the firm's future. By early in 1960 the Staveley Directors decided that Richards needed a stronger management team and proposed moving the plant and personnel to a new site.

At this point in time it is necessary to outline the events at Kearns. H. W. Kearns under the Chairmanship of Sir Lionel Kearns had continued to build an international reputation for its range of horizontal boring machines. By the late 1930's they were building between 200 and 300 machines a year with a staff of 500. In the 1950's they constructed the world's first punched card numerically controlled NC horizontal boring machine. In fact, this was 20 years before the Japanese entered this field which they now dominate. The prototype machine, with tape control required 2 to 3 miles of tape to complete its operation; a late model is shown in Fig. 19.9. By the 1950's Kearns was approaching the end of a strong family control, which it had enjoyed under Sir Lionel Kearns. However, to the outside world Kearns was a very successful and well managed company in contrast to the situation then prevailing at George Richards.

Sir Lionel's death in 1960 was followed by a change in the policy as to whether the company should become involved with another machine-tool company or arrange for a takeover. This change in the outlook of the Kearns family had not been lost on the Staveley Board. Richards losing money, Kearns profitable, the two companies being only a few hundred yards apart in Broadheath, both making horizontal boring machines—this was to Staveley's management almost too good an opportunity to miss. Their intention was to buy-out Kearns and close Richards, but to Staveley's astonishment the Kearns Board rejected this offer and decided to sell to

Fig. 19.9. **One of the last Kearns Richards boring** *C.A.S.* **machines.** (The car is to show the size of the machine).

Tube Investments. The public announcement of this agreement was to be made within a few days, when, to the complete surprise of the city and the remaining members of the Kearns Board, the family decided to accept the offer from Staveley. Within a few months the Kearns Directors were replaced and a massive redundancy policy implemented. Technically the two companies' designs were totally different and in spite of all efforts to persuade the customer that all was well, orders continued to fall. In fact, the customers were as puzzled over the unexpected events as were both companies' employees.

This change of ownership took place in 1965 and within five years the two firms were facing total closure. For a brief period of time the joint companies were taken over by a management buy-out but unfortunately this did not succeed and the remnants of the firms were acquired by FMT, a group of companies with headquarters in Brighton and Newcastle-upon-Tyne.

TODAY

Of the five companies described in detail, only Budenberg remained a family firm until recently, but has now been taken over. Churchills have ceased to operate, while the Linotype & Machinery Company are working at a very much reduced level, but still supplying items of modern printing equipment. Kearns Richards, as mentioned above are now part of the FMT Group, which has closed all the production facilities in Broadheath. Retail warehousing, offices and some industrial units have now been built on the sites once occupied by some of the world's most famous machine-tool and engineering companies. At its peak Broadheath employed over 10,000 highly skilled engineers, perhaps more in fact than at present employed in Trafford Park today. The remarkable complex at Broadheath deserves its rightful place in the industrial history not only of Altrincham but of Britain.

Chapter Twenty

ALTRINCHAM IN WORLD WAR II

Reminiscences by TONY LITTLER

The declaration of War on Sunday, 3 September 1939, though a great tragedy, came as no surprise following the political situation which had developed during the previous 12 months. Buildings were surrounded by sandbags; trenches dug in parks; air-raid shelters prepared and distributed to those who needed them; gas masks, identity cards and ration books issued, Figs. 20.1 and 20.2. In the last few days of peace the reservists of the armed forces had been recalled for duty and hundreds of thousands of children were evacuated from the cities.

Young men and women not old enough for military service, those in reserved occupations, the elderly and, the unfit, felt it their patriotic duty to join one of the many voluntary organisations which had been formed or re-invigorated. Some of those in Altrincham were as follows.

The Auxiliary Fire Service (A.F.S.), later called the National Fire Service, had their headquarters at the Unitarian School in Sylvan Grove. The Local Defence Volunteers (L.D.V.), later called the Home Guard, and since the T.V. programme of that name, now called 'Dad's Army', had their H.Q. in the Y.M.C.A. in Oxford Road, which stood where the service road, Rigby Street, now lies between the last shop and the row of houses on the left going from the town towards Hale Road. The Red Cross had their H.Q. in Heald Road, Bowdon. The Women's Voluntary Service (W.V.S.) had their H.Q. over Hawker's, the men's outfitters, at the corner of Cross Street and Stamford New Road, now McDonald's. Altrincham Land Club was formed by men and women who gave their time at weekends to help local farmers. They were organised by Mr. and Mrs. Ross. Mr. Ross worked at Lloyd's Bank, outside which the members assembled at 8 a.m. on Sunday, dressed in an astonishing variety of 'farming' clothes and head-gear, with the inevitable 'wellies' (rubber boots) on their feet, astride their faithful and often antique bicycles (new ones were unobtainable). Altrincham Pig Club was popular because when one's pig was slaughtered one could keep half in addition to the meat ration. The Ministry took the other half. The pigs were mainly fed from swill collected from family and friends, who in their turn then received an odd slice of bacon to supplement their rations, and many a bucket of evil smelling liquid was located outside people's back doors. Not everyone had space to keep a pig so they were kept in the grounds of Sandiway House on Church Street, near the George and Dragon.

The junior organisations were mainly pre-armed service cadets. The Army Cadets were at Hale Drill Hall, its site now occupied by the Ashley Hotel in Hale village. The Sea Cadet Corps attached to the Royal

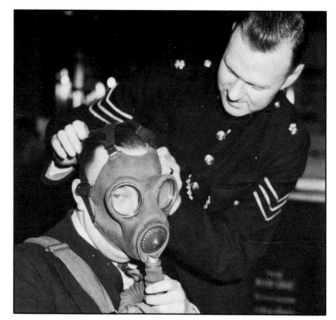

Fig. 20.1. **Gas mask for those on duty.** *Trafford Leisure Services*

Fig. 20.2 **Ration book** *J.A.L.* **Shrapnel** *Dr D.M. Brooke*

ARP (Air Raid Precautions) Van. *Trafford Leisure Services*

Navy met where they meet today at T. S. Talisman by Broadheath Bridge. One of the founding members was Ted Sloan, the licensee of the old Stamford Hotel in Railway Street, demolished when the Graftons was built. He was a strong supporter of the Sea Cadets. The Air Defence Cadet Corps became the Air Training Corps (A.T.C.) with its H.Q. at Altrincham Grammar School. The girls' section was the Women's Junior Air Corps, whose H.Q. was at Navigation Road School.

Bombing was a serious problem for the civilian population. Air raid shelters were of several different types, large public ones, in underground vaults; low, single storey, windowless buildings above ground capped with a slab of concrete 9"-12" thick, and with an entrance at both ends, (there was one in Lloyd Street); home-made timber, or corrugated iron Anderson shelters which could be sunk in the garden; Morrison shelters, which were heavy steel tables in the home under which one could crawl; or cellars adapted for the purpose. In Chapter Sixteen reference is made to a vaulted cellar which was used under Whitwham's shop in Old Market Place. This was on the advice of the authorities who gave assurances of its safety. It was made habitable and newly-whitewashed; stone flags were carpeted; it was furnished with a cupboard for tinned food; emergency lighting and heating were installed. There was an assortment of seating which left little room for beds so four large hooks were put into each of the opposing walls, (shown in Fig. 16.9, Chapter Sixteen) and at night hammocks were slung between. If the sirens wailed a warning during the day, serving staff, customers and office girls (with their ledgers to carry on working!) were all ushered down into the cellar until the 'All Clear' siren sounded and everything returned to normal . . . until the next warning.

One of the worst raids was that of the Manchester Blitz. The following account describes the role of the Altrincham Auxiliary Fire Service (A.F.S.). The first night of the Blitz, 22 December 1940, started on a Sunday evening. In the event of a raid on Manchester the plan was that fire brigades from concentric districts round Manchester moved towards the city, each circle moving nearer to the centre to take the place left by the previous circle of brigades. This meant that the outer circle in which Altrincham lay drew from an ever-widening area as the fires increased in size and number. This happened on the night of the Blitz; the Altrincham brigade moved towards Manchester and visiting brigades moved here. The incoming engines were identified as they came down the Dunham road and some crews were sent to Sylvan Grove to be fed, and others routed to Sale.

A motley collection of crews assembled that night, especially when those from Wales arrived with magnificent solid-tyred engines. The firemen wore enormous brass helmets, sitting back-to-back on some engines, a practice discarded some years before when local brigades acquired newly-designed engines. They had never heard bombs or anti-aircraft gunfire and were very startled at first. As the Sylvan Grove base ran out of food, so Whitwham's grocery shop was opened up. The shelves and counters were stripped bare as though a swarm of locusts had been there, (it was all replaced of course) but it proved its worth that night by being just round the corner from Sylvan Grove.

The second night of the Blitz (when many land-mines were dropped on the greater Manchester area), was even worse than the first. These were large mines dropped by parachute which exploded above ground creating widespread damage and causing many deaths. Some places where bombs fell at various dates were:

1. The corner of Moss Lane and Oakfield Road opposite Royle's car body shop, Fig. 20.3.
2. Near Skelton junction.
3. In Bath Street.
4. In Charter Road.
5. In South Downs Road.
6. In New Bridge Hollow (the bridge over the Bollin before Lymm Corner).
7. On O'Brien's oil works in Brunswick Road.
8. On the railway embankment nearby.
9. In Dunham Park (a very large number of incendiaries).
10. In Wright Street and Huxley Street behind the Cheshire Cheese Hotel at the junction of Sinderland Road and Manchester Road, a land-mine which killed several people and devastated the area, Fig. 20.4.

Fig. 20.3. **Bomb damaged corner** *Trafford Leisure Services* **of Moss Lane and Oakfield Road.** 'S' on lamp post points towards shelter. Note stripes on lamp post to make it clearer in the blackout.

Fig. 20.4. **Land-mine damage in** *Trafford Leisure Services* **Broadheath**

11. On the house next to the 'Swan with Two Nicks' at Bollington. Rumour had it that it was the pub itself – what a disaster!

The most awesome and potentially most dangerous bomb was the one on O'Brien's oil works which fell into one of the storage tanks at about 9 p.m. one night and set it alight. All night long the firemen played their hoses on the surrounding tanks to keep them cool and prevent them exploding. Others tried various means of dowsing the flames in the burning tank, such as by using foam, but without success. The strong wind blew away the foam as they tried to direct it into the hole and the flames continued to leap through the hole like an enormous bunsen burner. The foam which was on a limited allocation to all brigades had soon been used without effect, and to obtain more required a Home Office permit as vast amounts were being used in the cities. The fire continued all that night and during next day; the cooling hoses also had to continue with no solution to dowsing the fire yet found. Eventually more foam arrived.

In the end O'Briens themselves solved the problem. Metal tubes with hooked-over ends were made in a Broadheath works; these were hooked over the top of the burning tank with the foam hoses attached to the other end. They worked! In about half an hour the blanket of foam had put out the blaze—and not a moment too soon, for dusk had come and soon the bombers returned searching for the fire to finish the job they had started the previous night. Thankfully they left without dropping any more bombs on O'Briens.

Bombs were not the only things which rained down. One night it sounded as though an express train was heading for Dunham Road. The noise had come from an anti-aircraft shell with trajectory problems. The shell came in an arc over Altrincham landing on the railway station, breaking all the glass and severing one of the stanchions which held up the footbridge over the lines. Anti-aircraft fire meant a great deal of shrapnel fell into the streets, peppered buildings, vehicles and people, a dangerous hazard known in many cities to have caused deaths and severe injuries.

Blast from the explosions always seemed to have unpredictable effects, some being quite long distances away. This was most noticeable in the case of the land-mine which fell in Huxley Street and Wright Street in Broadheath, no doubt intended for the industrial area. The whole area was very severely damaged as can be seen in Fig. 20.5, and a number of people killed. The blast sucked out windows over a wide area round Broadheath including West Timperley, Manchester Road, Church Street, Kingsway, George Street and Regent Road in Altrincham. Buildings on both sides of Whitwham's had their windows blown out but Whitwham's, though taller and standing further forward into Old Market Place, had not one window damaged.

Another target seemed to be the railway line. That may have been because of a particular train which came through regularly at night with very heavily laden open wagons, shaking the station and town as it rumbled by, struggling·up the steepening gradient towards Hale. The boiler fire was being well-stoked but despite covers over the top of the cab they were insufficient to hide the fire from the air and everybody was very relieved each time it went safely through the town. We were told it was the 'Brunner Mond' (the old name for I.C.I.) train which carried limestone from Derbyshire to Northwich from which sodium carbonate is extracted to make glass, needed in vast quantities after raids shattered windows. It was only later it was learned the train was carrying armaments at night.

The blackout was a very serious matter, every tiny chink of light having to be covered. In the darkness even a glowing cigarette could be seen for miles and many is the time that one would hear the cry from a patrolling Air Raid Warden *"Put that b . . . . . light out!"* Wardens and others were constantly patrolling, checking that there were no chinks of light and taking action if found. Enemy agents were around and light was an easy way to guide in the bombers. Vehicle headlights were so well shaded that it was not easy to see where one was going and even pedestrians had to carry shaded torches.

The attempts to keep information secret were made by posters saying 'Walls have Ears', 'Careless Talk costs Lives', etc.; by radio reports of raids (if reported at all) having no place-names merely indicated as being in the N.W. or S.E., etc.; by removing all signposts to baffle any invading armies (this didn't help the resident armies either, both uniformed and civilian . . .). Early one Sunday morning shortly after Dunkirk the sound of tramping feet woke the residents of Altrincham. There were soldiers as far as one could see in all directions. Later it was learned that on arrival in Manchester they had been told to march to Hale. Unfortunately they should have been sent to Hayle in Cornwall. The ladies of Hale sent out an appeal for food and equipment with a splendid response.

Everyone was affected by rationing of basic foods although the amounts varied from time to time depending upon availability and the current success or failure of the U-boat blockade on the convoys of supply ships. All rationed goods from grocers were allocated by weight, for example 1 oz. of tea, 2 oz. of butter, 4 ozs. of margarine or cooking fat, 2–3 ozs. of bacon, 8 ozs. of sugar, all per person per week. Many canned goods were rationed on a points system, each can having a specific number of points which were cut out of the ration book when the goods were purchased. All the coupons cut out were then counted in their categories and sent to the Food Office. Clothing, hats and shoes also had a points system. At certain times bread and potatoes were rationed too, but on the whole vegetables were in sufficient supply not to need rationing. Meat was rationed by monetary value of approximately 1 shilling (5p) per person per week, so that the quantity one could buy would be more for a cheap cut then for an expensive cut. Offal remained unrationed but scarce and was allocated by the butcher. Long queues formed when it was available, mostly for 'regular' customers only. Imported fruit became very scarce but the poor greengrocers did their best to allocate it fairly. Some people obtained goods and petrol over their rationed quantities on the 'black market'.

There were national and local morale-raising 'weeks': 'Wings for Victory Week', when all were encouraged to give money for more Spitfire fighter planes; 'Navy Week' to give money for an aircraft carrier; 'Dig For Victory Week' to encourage the digging up of even more lawns and flower beds to grow vegetables. One such week was said to be due to Mrs. Churchill having learned that soap was scarce in Russia; so 'Soap For Russia Week' was launched. As soap was in fairly good supply a box was provided in each grocer's shop into which the customers could put soap for the Russians.

Great courage was often shown. It was especially seen in that particular type of English lady who never panics and is always in charge of every situation, like one in the Altrincham area who during a raid was upstairs in bed. She awoke to hear urgent knocking on the door so went to the top of the stairs as her manservant answered it. *"Who is it Charles?"* she called. *"It's the firemen milady, they say the roof is on fire and they want to come inside with their hoses to put it out"* he said. She was unperturbed and after a few moments reflection she called loudly *"Very well, but tell them to WIPE THEIR FEET FIRST!!"* Another similar lady in Regent Road also told of a fire asked, *"Do they have to bring the engine?"* When assured they did, replied *"Well tell them not to ring their bell—after all it is Sunday!"*

Some buildings were commandeered for war-time use. Large houses on both sides of Regent Road were used to accommodate American Officers, 50–100 of whom lined up for roll call each morning down the middle of the road. The Americans also had the 'Doughnut Dugout' near the corner of Cross Street and Stamford New Road, near the present Gas Showrooms. Chewing gum and nylon stockings which they always seemed to have were a great attraction to the local girls—but it did not make the Yanks popular with the local boys.

The British regular army had a detachment at Stamford House in Church Street, now the site of the Cresta Court Hotel but previously the house of George Faulkner Armitage, the architect. By coincidence the C.O. was a Colonel Armitage, thought to be a nephew.

'Bowdon Croft' on Green Walk, Bowdon, was used as a hospital. Shaftesbury Avenue, Timperley, newly completed, was closed along its whole length becoming an R.A.F. Maintenance Unit. Lorries were parked diagonally along each side of the road—all very convenient for the 'Hare and Hounds'. Similarly the Observer Corps in Dunham were convenient for 'The Vine', and the Home Guard at Ashley for 'The Greyhound'. No.2 Maintenance Unit at Sinderland Camp was, as it had been in the 1914–18 war, one of the largest ammunition dumps in the country.

In Dunham Park was a German prisoner-of-war camp guarded by the Polish army. By the main entrance gate almost opposite Denzell the prisoners had built a superb model said to be of Hitler's Eagle's Nest at Berchtesgarten. It is a pity that it was not preserved as no trace is now there. Nearby was a training place for

Fig. 20.5 V.E. Day Celebration, Oldfield Brow. *Trafford Leisure Services*

Special Operations Executive personnel. Ringway airport, opened just before the war, was a hive of activity with many different aircraft from various Allied air forces constantly landing and taking off, and SOE trainees practised parachute jumping from here. Paratroops trained in Tatton Park where gliders were hidden among the trees.

Altrincham and surrounding areas were designated 'safe' for young evacuees and people with spare bedrooms had to take them. Although some returned home after a short time many stayed for most of the war, well integrated into their foster homes. One was adopted by the family.

Firms in Broadheath worked tirelessly producing equipment for the war effort but many smaller companies were also involved. Royle's car body shop in Oakfield Road near Moss Lane, repaired aircraft and it was a very usual sight to see the odd Oxford or Anson and later a Mosquito, stuck in the middle of Oakfield Road whilst they manoeuvred it in or out of the building. Arden and Bull's garage at 18 Old Market Place (now the Job Centre), employed numerous girls filling practice shells. Byrom's, the large drapers on Kingsway who occupied all the large building which used to be called Byroms Building, perfected a new type of blackout which won them contracts for war factories.

With all the foregoing voluntary and industrial activity, all the effort given by Altrincham servicemen (of whom I was one) and service women, the Merchant Navy and Auxiliary Forces, the town was fully committed to supporting the war effort. Altrincham throughout showed its community spirit, Fig. 20.5.

It is perhaps appropriate to mention feats of bravery in other conflicts. The story of World War 1 remains to be told in detail, but two events stand out. First the loss of 50 men out of 161 who enrolled from only 66 houses in Chapel Street, and, second, the awarding of the V.C. to Captain E.K. Bradbury of the Royal Horse Artillery, killed in France. After World War II, Private W. Speakman of the Royal Highlanders was awarded Altrincham's second V.C., in the Korean War in November 1951, for leading, while severely wounded, a group of men on repeated grenade charges from a heavily shelled position. Altrincham has much to be proud of in War.

Chapter Twenty-One

ALTRINCHAM TODAY

NIGEL STOCKS

This brief survey looks at Altrincham in its three economic roles as a place of work, a place to shop and a place to live. Many may think that represents a drab way to describe a lively town, more familiar to them for its social life, its entertainment, its Victorian architecture and its traffic. However it is the economy of a town that supports its other activities and indicates the directions in which they may change; and, not least, it is the readiest source of relevant statistics. Even then, current comparative figures are hard to find, and in economic terms it is often not sensible to distinguish Altrincham from its close companions, Hale and Bowdon.

ALTRINCHAM AS A PLACE TO WORK

In 1981, 23,000 people were employed in Altrincham, Hale and Bowdon. This was approximately one quarter of the total number employed in Trafford as a whole. Jobs in manufacturing industry provided a quarter of all employment. Office jobs made up more than 20%. Shop jobs provided more than 10%. Since then, in line with national trends, the proportion of jobs in manufacturing industry will have declined, and the proportion in offices risen. Actual numbers in various types of jobs in 1981 are shown in Tables 1and 2. Since then, in line with national trends, the proportion of male jobs will have fallen.

The majority of these jobs are concentrated in just two areas - Altrincham town centre, and Broadheath.

TABLE 1   EMPLOYMENT IN ALTRINCHAM, HALE, AND BOWDON IN 1981 BY TYPE OF JOB

	Males	Females	Total
Industry	4,360	1,290	5,650
Warehousing & Distribution	640	260	900
Shops	890	2,050	2,940
Offices	2,690	2,290	4,980
Construction	940	140	1,080
Miscellaneous	3,210	4,310	7,520
Total	12,730	10,340	23,070

Broadheath is the second most important industrial area in Trafford after Trafford Park. Four fifths of all jobs in industry and warehousing and distribution in Altrincham, Hale and Bowdon are to be found in the area, Fig. 21.1. Altrincham town centre is the main focus for shop and office jobs. It is not however a significant focus for industry.

Fig. 21.1. **Atlantic Street** – retail warehouses have brought more activity to Broadheath   *D.G.B.*

Trafford Leisure Services

Fig. 21.2. **Oakfield Road industrial and service premises**

TABLE 2   EMPLOYMENT IN ALTRINCHAM TOWN CENTRE AND BROADHEATH IN 1981 BY TYPE OF JOB

	Town Centre			Broadheath		Altrincham
	Male	Female	Total	Male	Female	Total
Industry	3,710	940	4,650	110	110	220
Warehousing & Distribution	530	210	740	-	-	-
Shops	30	20	50	580	1,560	2,140
Offices	190	160	350	1,260	1,170	2,430
Construction	500	60	560	140	20	160
Miscellaneous	400	220	620	1,110	1,170	2,280
Total	5,360	1,610	6,970	3,200	4,030	7,230

The majority of the industrial, and a significant proportion of the miscellaneous service activities operating from the town centre are located in the Oakfield Road - Manor Road-Moss Lane area, Fig. 21.2, to the east of the railway line and the main shopping area. With the notable exception of the NW Gas head office and the bus depot, Fig. 21.3, the majority of these firms are small businesses employing relatively few people.

As a service centre, Altrincham contains the majority (68%) of the 538,000 square feet of lettable floorspace available in office blocks in Altrincham, Hale and Bowdon. It is nonetheless the smallest of the three main office centres within Trafford, after Trafford Bar and Sale town centre. The broad distribution of office floorspace in the Borough as at 1987 is shown in Table 3.

TABLE 3 DISTRIBUTION OF LETTABLE OFFICE FLOORSPACE IN TRAFFORD

	Total Supply (sq. ft., nearest 1,000)	Share of Supply
Trafford Bar	1,229,000	51%
Remainder of Stretford and Urmston	98,000	4%
Sale Town Centre	400,000	17%
Remainder of Sale	167,000	7%
Altrincham Town Centre	368,000	15%
Remainder of Altrincham-Hale-Bowdon	170,000	7%

The majority (78%) of the available floorspace in the town is concentrated in ten self-contained blocks in a relatively small area at the northern end of the main shopping area, Fig. 21.4. The amount of lettable floorspace in the town has more than doubled since 1971 from 163,000 square feet to 368,000 square feet. Much of this growth, amounting to 154,000 square feet of floorspace, has been concentrated into the period since 1978. Before then, Sale and particularly Trafford

Fig. 21.3. **Shearings Bus Station, Moss Lane.** *D.G.B.*
The servicing end

Fig. 21.4. **Attractive new office block on** *D.G.B.*
Stockport Road

Bar were more popular locations for office development.

Outside the town centre, in the rest of Altrincham, Hale and Bowdon there have been only two small additions to the stock of floorspace since 1974, amounting to less than 10,000 square feet in total, Fig. 21.5. As an office centre Altrincham is in direct competition with a number of other commercial centres in the south Manchester area, including Sale, Stockport, Cheadle, Wythenshawe and Wilmslow. These centres are located fairly close to one another and offer similar attractions to commercial companies. They function essentially as a single market providing accommodation suitable for small and medium sized companies expanding within or intending to move into the Manchester area. The comparative size of these competing centres as at 1987 is set out in Table 4.

TABLE 4 SIZE OF ALTRINCHAM AND ITS COMPETING OFFICE CENTRES

(square feet)	Lettable Floorspace
Altrincham Town Centre	368,000
Sale Town Centre	400,000
Trafford Bar	1,229,000
Wythenshawe	120,000
Manchester International Office Centre	126,000
Stockport Town Centre	1,066,000
Cheadle Town Centre	51,000
Cheadle Hulme Town Centre	72,500
Wilmslow Town Centre	377,000
Knutsford	177,000

A comparative survey in 1987 showed that rents for newly built floorspace in Altrincham, at around £7.50 per square foot, were comparable with those achieved for similar quality floorspace in Manchester City centre and in centres like Sale and Cheadle. Rents were well above those obtainable in Stockport (up to £5 per square foot) and other parts of south Manchester, but a little behind those for Wilmslow (£8 per square foot at least).

The rate of letting, trends in rents, and the volume of planning applications show that office development interest in and immediately around Altrincham Town Centre continues undiminished. Office development is notoriously a boom and bust activity. At some stage, a period of market saturation will occur and persist perhaps for some years, though it is not yet in sight.

ALTRINCHAM AS A PLACE TO SHOP

Altrincham is by far the largest and most important centre in Trafford, Fig. 21.6. It has over the last fifteen years grown to become one of the largest and highest quality shopping centres in the whole of the Greater Manchester and north east Cheshire area. It is one of three centres, along with Stockport and Bolton,

Fig. 21.5. **Small offices, Hale Road.**
D.G.B.

Fig. 21.6. **Lower George Street**   D.G.B.

recognised in the Greater Manchester Structure Plan as of sub-regional status. Though still the smallest of the three, Altrincham has established itself in particular as a fashion and comparison goods centre. A major redevelopment, of the northern end of the main shopping area, the 'Petros' scheme, completed in the mid 1970's, Fig. 21.7, encouraged major national multiples to establish themselves in the town, attracted by the quality of the centre and their belief in its future growth.

The town now serves a dual shopping function, providing for the day to day food and household needs of people living nearby, and for the occasional major household durable and comparison goods requirements of people living in a wide prosperous catchment area of suburbs, small country towns and Cheshire countryside.

The town centre contains a total of approximately 705,000 gross square feet of retail floorspace, of which 529,000 *gross* square feet, or 75% of the total, is occupied by durable and comparison goods outlets. Table 5 compares the size of Altrincham, in terms of *net* sales space, with its main competitors.

TABLE 5   SIZE OF SHOPPING CENTRES – ALTRINCHAM AND MAIN COMPETING CENTRES

(net square feet of sales space)

	Convenience Stores	Durable Comparison Stores	Total
Altrincham	107,000	317,700	424,700
Other Sub-Regional Centres			
Stockport	98,000	639,100	737,100
Warrington	N/A	N/A	850,000
District Centres			
Sale	107,200	158,500	265,700
Wythenshawe	115,800	98,400	214,200
Wilmslow	89,400	210,000	299,400
Knutsford	30,600	67,800	98,400

Fig. 21.7. **The Petros area.**

There are currently some 440 separate trading outlets (excluding the market) operating within the town centre. Major multiple retailers represented include Marks and Spencer, C & A, W H Smith, Woolworths, Mothercare and Boots. There is also a Rackhams (House of Fraser) department store and two main supermarkets, Sainsbury and Safeway. Altrincham is perhaps most notable for the number of local independent shops it has retained or attracted during its period of growth, and for its very popular 3 day market.

Since 1971 retail floorspace in Altrincham town centre has grown by 40%. The Petros redevelopment scheme at the northern end of the town contributed a substantial proportion of this growth. Sainsburys in Lloyd Street, opened in autumn 1985, provided most of the remainder. A study carried out for the Borough Council by Bernard Thorpe and Partners estimated Altrincham's 1984 turnover at £93 million, divided approximately equally between convenience goods and comparison goods. There is substantial potential for comparison goods businesses to increase their turnover levels in line with future increases in spending. Bernard Thorpe and Partners estimate that Altrincham could experience an increase of over £19 million between 1984 and 1996.

A comparative survey in 1987 showed that rents for prime shops in Altrincham at around £70 per square foot are higher than in most competing centres, reflecting the strong retailer demand for property in the centre. Only Manchester City centre and Stockport achieved higher rental levels of around £75 per square foot for prime property. Warrington achieved rental levels of around £45 per square foot. Vacancy levels in the town have been modest in recent years, with rates as low as 6%. Shops occupy 60% of the available units in the town (of which 85% are occupied by comparison goods retailers). Service outlets occupy almost one third of available units (32%). Table 6 shows in further detail the number and proportion of the various types of business in the town, as at 1986.

TABLE 6 NUMBER OF RETAIL AND SERVICE BUSINESS OUTLETS IN ALTRINCHAM

	No.	%
Convenience Outlets		
Supermarkets and Food Stores	32	7
Confectioners, Tobacconists, Newsagents	7	2
Durable and Comparison Outlets		
Clothing and Footwear	78	18
Jewellers	11	2
Furniture and Furnishings	30	7
Electrical and Household Goods	33	7
Department Stores and Major Multiples	7	2
Others	66	15
Service Outlets		
Banks and Building Societies	19	4
Estate Agents	8	2
Financial and Legal Services	16	4
Restaurants, Cafes, Public Houses	40	9
Hairdressers, Travel Agents, Dry Cleaners etc	36	8
Others	24	5
Vacant Properties	33	7
Total Outlets	440	100

A survey in 1985 revealed that Altrincham's catchment area extends well beyond Trafford's boundaries, as far as Macclesfield in the south east, Northwich to the south and Warrington to the west. To the north the area is limited by the Manchester Ship Canal and the River Mersey.

The core of Altrincham's catchment area comprises the wealthy suburbs of Altrincham itself, Hale and Bowdon. It extends north and west over other suburban areas, such as Sale, Gatley, Cheadle and Bramhall, and country towns and rural areas such as Wilmslow, Bollington and Knutsford.

This catchment area has expanded and deepened

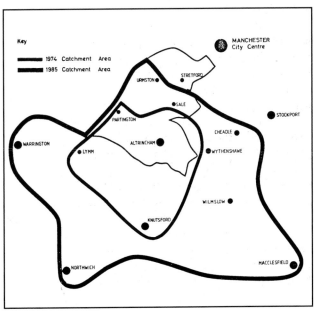

Fig. 21.8. **Altrincham Town Centre Shopping Catchment Area, 1974 and 1985.** *Trafford M.B.C.*

Fig. 21.9. **Sainsbury's**   *D.G.B.*

significantly over recent years, both reflecting and causing Altrincham's importance as a shopping centre of sub-regional importance. Between 1974 and 1985 the proportion of shoppers who travelled a mile or more to get to the town centre increased from 66% to 75%. Fig. 21.8 based on comparative questionnaire surveys carried out in 1974 and 1985, shows the geographical increase in Altrincham's catchment area over 11 years.

The 1985 survey revealed that shoppers in Altrincham are characteristically young and from the more affluent households (mainly professional and managerial groups). 56% of shoppers responding to the survey were under 35 years of age, and 58% were in social classes A,B, or C1. Most of those visiting the town to shop came direct from home and over half travelled by car. The vast majority came to purchase non-food goods. The survey recorded only one in ten shopping solely for food. The survey was carried out before the opening of Sainsburys, Fig. 21.9, and this proportion may have increased. Shoppers' satisfaction with Altrincham has remained high over the years. More shoppers now see Altrincham as their first choice shopping centre for non-food than 1974. For example, over 70% of shoppers responding to the 1985 survey regarded Altrincham as their choice centre for purchasing clothes or shoes.

The growth of Altrincham town centre cannot be stopped by planning action even if, as some believe, that were desirable. The Council aims to steer the next stages of growth into the underused land on either side of Denmark Street. The Council is aiming at growth in quality, not just size. The implications of this, and the chances of success, are looked at in the next chapter 'The Future of Altrincham'.

ALTRINCHAM AS A PLACE TO LIVE

The 1981 Census records a total of 61,000 people living in Altrincham, Hale and Bowdon. In comparison with other parts of Greater Manchester it is a predominantly prosperous community. Three quarters of the 22,000 households in the area own their own home and car. A quarter of them own two or more cars. A third are classified in Social Classes A and B, in which professional and managerial occupation groups predominate. Among the working population more than 10% are self employed. Unemployment is low by the standards of the remainder of Trafford and Greater Manchester as a whole.

A comparison of the characteristics of Altrincham, Hale and Bowdon with the remainder of Trafford is set out in Table 7.

TABLE 7   POPULATION AND HOUSEHOLD CHARACTERISTICS – 1981

	Altrincham, Hale and Bowdon	Rest of Trafford
Households owning their own home	73.0%	63.0%
Households owning two or more cars	25.3%	15.0%
Social Class A and B households	30.9%	21.0%
Working population self employed	11.5%	7.1%

South Manchester and north east Cheshire are attractive and popular residential areas. The demand for houses in these areas remains substantial even during the current period of economic difficulty. A considerable amount of new housing is planned for Altrincham, Hale and Bowdon and it is anticipated that the population of this area will grow around 5% to 64,000.

Chapter Twenty-Two

THE FUTURE OF ALTRINCHAM

NIGEL STOCKS

THE HAZARDS OF PREDICTION

Few of us can resist having our fortunes told, even though we know that the results will turn out at best to be ambiguous and at worst misleading.

Local trends are even more hazardous than national ones to predict. Altrincham, important to us, is a speck on the national scene. Our local concerns are easily swamped by whatever rolls in from over the horizon. Have we, the British, really rediscovered the secrets of industrial productivity and innovation? If so, will economic revival benefit us here in Altrincham, or will it lure our more ambitious and mobile residents away? How will we choose to spend our money and our time? Will the electronic revolution, much discussed and little understood, enable us to work more and more from home, like some 18th century handloom weaver, making office blocks redundant and rush hours a memory? Or will one of those jokers in the pack – war, pollution, or economic slump – suddenly appear on the table?

I shall concentrate on the possible short term changes, the seeds of which can already be seen. Here my position as a local planner gives me some advantage. And this is a good point at which to state that the thoughts expressed in this chapter are my own, and do not necessarily reflect the views of Trafford Metropolitan Borough Council. Some may think that the planning authority is in a position to make its views come true. Not so. It is the way we each individually choose to live that shapes our environment. In a democratic society, planning authorities must work within the determining social trends. We cannot for example plan our cities around buses and trains when for most family trips every family prefers to use a car; families without a car are eager to buy their first, and those with one look forward to owning two. We cannot plan our neighbourhoods around corner shops when most households are happy to enjoy the advantages of the superstore.

ALTRINCHAM AS A PLACE TO WORK

More people want to work, live, shop in Altrincham and have their businesses in Altrincham, than the town can easily absorb. Altrincham combines the advantages of a market town with those of a desirable suburb. The migration of people and jobs across the country from north to south, and from big cities to the shires has so far left Altrincham complacently unaffected as part of the prosperity that runs along the Greater Manchester/Cheshire border from Lymm to Prestbury. The question is whether such prosperity remains local and therefore transient, soon to be eroded by continuing regional decline, or whether Altrincham will be one of the bridgeheads for forces which will revive the north west. A revived region, and Altrincham's role in it, will look and feel different from what we are used to. If economic growth returns to the north west, it will not flow again from the mill and coal towns of Lancashire, or the docks of Liverpool and Manchester. Even the old industrial estates like Trafford Park, now the beneficiary of intensive planning and investment, are unlikely by themselves to cause revival. These leaders of past prosperity may share in future growth but they will not lead it a second time around. Our attitude to change will itself be one of the tests which decides whether revival occurs. If we insist that economical revival enter through and only through the traditional urban gates and in familiar industrial forms, we shall wait a long time. The latest planning legislation already blurs the distinction between offices, light industry and warehousing. The segregation of places of work from home and countryside is also likely to become less rigid.

Apart from Altrincham's attractiveness, and the versatile people who live in such a town, its outstanding 21st century asset will be its position. Altrincham is one of the main southern gateways, and probably the most attractive gateway, to the Greater Manchester conurbation. It stands near the crossroads of the national M6 motorway route from London and Birmingham to Manchester, and the regional east-west M56 corridor of potentially outstanding (but so-far under-estimated) development from Stockport and Manchester International Airport, through Warrington to Chester.

If economic growth comes again to the north-west, the chances are that it will take a decentralised pattern along those two axes. It will not take the form of smoke-stack industry. Much of it will be hard to recognise as industry at all and its foremost firms will for the most part not want to congregate in industrial estates. The most important enterprises in such new regional economy will be companies and institutions exporting ideas rather than goods to the rest of the world i.e. high value-added products in the form of research, information and services. Parts of this new hi-tech scene already lie close about us: the Science and Engineering Research Centre at Daresbury, ICI research laboratories at Runcorn and Alderley Edge, British Nuclear Fuels

Fig. 22.1. **High-Tech firms in West Broadheath.**

D.G.B.

Fig. 22.2. **Davenport Lane**, potholed and unmade, (the line of Watling Street) leading to Sinderland Road and the A56 to Manchester.

Salford/Trafford Groundwork Trust

Centre at Warrington, Ciba Geigy research centre at Wilmslow, Barclays Bank computer centre at Knutsford. The basic infrastructure is there to service new companies. Investor interest is mounting and attractive sites wait to be released for development.

Within Altrincham, work predominantly means, and will continue to mean, the town centre and Broadheath, Fig. 22.1. If economic growth as sketched out occurs, Altrincham will also grow as the natural office centre providing finance, insurance, travel facilities and consultancy to those who want more immediate service than can be obtained from Manchester city centre. Broadheath, once its current problem of poor access has been solved and its poor environment, Fig. 22.2, has been improved, is well placed along with Carrington and Trafford Park to attract the varied specialist industrial firms which will grow in the climate created by regional revival. Not a few of these may spring directly or indirectly from a new sense of enterprise among the staff and graduates of several centres of higher education within Greater Manchester, many of whom live in the suburbs of Trafford.

ALTRINCHAM AS A PLACE TO SHOP

Few shopping centres have experienced such rapid growth in status as Altrincham. In the 'Regional Shopping Centres in NW England' study by Manchester University in 1964, Altrincham was ranked in importance as equal to Sale, Leigh, Eccles, and Hyde and less important than Oldham, Wigan, Ashton, Bury and Crewe. In the study by consultants Roger Tym and partners, prepared for the major shopping Public Inquiry in 1987, Altrincham was ranked as one of the three major sub-regional centres of Greater Manchester, along with Bolton and Stockport, second only to Manchester City Centre.

Nor has the town centre grown aggressively, at the expense of other local centres. Sale, Hale, Halebarns and Timperley are overshadowed by Altrincham but continue to prosper. Growth of shopping facilities for Altrincham has so far been in terms of quality rather than quantity. In 17 years, the only appreciable additions to Altrincham have been the Petros precinct to the north and Sainsbury's at the south end of the centre. A far smaller development, but more characteristic of Altrincham's role as a centre for specialist quality shops, was the conversion of the cottages in Goose Green to make a pleasant shopping corner. In addition, considerable number of new stores aptly described as 'retail warehouses' have grown 'out of centre', notably in Broadheath.

A further 250,000 sq.feet of shops and services (*e.g.* banks, building societies, restaurants etc.) in the town centre, together with offices, a hotel and cinema are now planned to reduce the anomaly between Altrincham's retail status and small size. Even so, at under one million square feet of shops and services, the town centre will still be some 50% smaller than either Bolton or Stockport town centres. The recent surge of enthusiasm by developers to build shops in the south west of Greater Manchester has also produced proposals for 3 new 'out of town' centres, each of one million square feet, two within Trafford at Carrington and Trafford Park, and the third close by in Salford.

The two significant questions for the immediate future are

- will one (or more?) of these new out-of-town shopping centres be given planning permission, and if so, how far will that dent Altrincham's competitive status?

- in any event, how will an investment of 250,000 sq.feet in Altrincham affect the town, and in particular will it enhance its centre's success as a centre of quality?

At present, neither question can be precisely answered. The decision on the out-of-town shopping centres, following a major public inquiry lies with the Secretary of State for the Environment – and who can predict what a politician will decide? If he does grant permission for one (or more) such centre(s), the impact on Altrincham will be lessened if Altrincham achieves its expansion first. It is perhaps comforting that the eagerness among developers to expand Altrincham appears undiminished by the prospect of competition. Originally there were planning applications from five separate developers for the same piece of land but at the time of writing there is still much discussion about what is appropriate for the site.

Before turning to the second question on Altrincham's future as a shopping centre, it may help first to ask why it attracts such development interest. There are several reasons, of which three seem the most significant:

1. The strategic planning regime under the now abolished Metropolitan County Council for many years throttled the growth of shops within Greater Manchester, for fear of what the County Council saw as over-provision. This fear was mistaken, under-estimating the growth in expenditure and the steady shift of where shoppers lived, from the city centre to the edge of the conurbation. The result is under-provision, especially in the south west of the former Metropolitan County. This is now being made good.

2. Altrincham's catchment area in recent years has widened (Chapter Twenty-One). Shoppers have increasingly switched their custom both from their smaller neighbourhood centres and from Manchester City Centre, to Altrincham.

3. The catchment area is densely populated and comparatively wealthy. Wealthy people not only spend more but they buy more specialised and

Fig. 22.3. **Fashion shop**. Petros area with roof car park over.

D.G.B.

Fig. 22.4. **Small shops in Regent Road.**

D.G.B.

fashionable goods, Fig. 22.3. Shops naturally reflect their customers' tastes. Altrincham is not a mere collection of standard multiples but has a high proportion of independent traders, and a busy market. The fine grain, small-scale old-fashioned character of the town centre, Fig. 22.4, happily captures and expresses its upmarket retailing functions. Architecturally, Altrincham may not be a grand centre but it is a comfortable one in which to shop.

If this analysis is correct, it will be easier to answer the second question about Altrincham's future as a shopping centre. If no planning permission is given for an out-of-town shopping centre, there will be little to upset the steadily increasing commercial success of Altrincham. The danger is the opposite: that we shall find it difficult to handle the trade and its traffic. But if planning permission is given for an out-of-town centre, Altrincham's ability to retain its position as one of the three sub-regional centres of Greater Manchester will rely on the strength of its grasp of the profitable fashion and specialist trades. As shopping ceases to be entirely a chore and becomes an opportunity for an enjoyable day out for more and more people, who are able to choose which of a number of centres they will visit, the image of a pleasant Victorian market town becomes an increasingly precious commercial asset.

Any prediction of success within what is already a ferociously competitive market is conditional upon the success with which we conserve, improve and promote that market town image. To be successful, the expansion of the town centre must enhance not just its size but also its charm and convenience.

The reader can be his own prophet if he first secures answers to the following key questions. Will the expansion of Altrincham

• make it easier to reach the centre by car, and park there conveniently?

• provide a variety of opportunities for people to relax during and after shopping?

• be accomplished without pulling down chunks of those old streets which attracted Altrincham's customers in the first place, simply to make space for new shops and their traffic?

• be designed to ensure what is new fits seamlessly into what is old?

Readers who like their prophecies to turn out right can in this case influence the future by pressing for the answer 'yes' to these 4 questions

ALTRINCHAM AS A PLACE TO LIVE

Change among the houses is likely to be steady rather then dramatic. Residential Altrincham will almost certainly look much the same in 10 or 15 years time, but it will feel different. Rising property prices herald increasing pressures. Households are changing, becoming smaller, older and, in Altrincham more numerous. The way we want to live is changing: we put down shallower roots in any locality because we move house more frequently; more of us are happy to

Fig. 22.5. **Retirement flats (private).** Regent Road.   D.G.B.

138

live in flats, Fig. 22.5; we buy more and own more; with our cars, radios and televisions we are noisier neighbours; we have more leisure; we travel more and own more cars to travel in; sadly, we split our families more often so that what was one household then needs two smaller dwellings. These are mostly national trends which show no sign of coming to an end and from which Altrincham is not exempt. It is not possible to change our way of living in these ways and leave our domestic environment as it was. Old, established and built up though most of Altrincham is, it will adapt to these trends. However carefully we absorb and disguise the physical effects, it is the accumulation of little changes that determines the sense of a place.

It is safe to bet on more traffic. Growth of traffic and parking on suburban streets will be even more marked than that on the main roads. A family's first car is gone all day with the rush hour. It is the second car which takes children (who once walked) to school, and housewives (who once cycled) to shops. The third car is driven by the child him or herself to school (and goodness knows where or how in the evening). Cars affect landscape as well as roads. Large single family houses with one car give way to flats with several. Gardens turn into hard standing and vehicle manoeuvring space. Widened entrances with safe sightlines replace narrow gateposts. What was once a brief romantic glimpse of a driveway curving between shrubberies in the more spacious parts of Altrincham now opens up to show just how far grass, shrubs and eventually trees have yielded ground to building and tarmac.

The very elderly live longer and need a place to live. The Victorian and Edwardian terrace houses of Broadheath and around Stamford Park share one thing in common with the modern dwellings now built along Sinderland Road and Oldfield Road: they afford insufficient space for a 3, and sometimes even a 2 generation household. In any case, more women working away from home means fewer people able to look after an elderly relative. There will be even more sheltered homes and nursing homes. The large Victorian houses of Altrincham, otherwise so difficult to maintain, lend themselves for conversion or redevelopment, Fig. 22.6. The areas in which they stand inevitably become less domestic and more institutional.

The inexorably rising price of land sorts out who can afford to live where. Altrincham and its sister suburbs of Hale and Bowdon were recently dubbed in the Daily Telegraph as part of the 'golden triangle' of south Manchester. Slowly but persistently, house prices rising faster than elsewhere winnow residents down to those who can afford to stay—the wealthy, and in contrast, the Council or protected tenant. Those in the middle, especially if they have children, look elsewhere. In the past it has been possible to extend the built-up area by building new family housing on the next fields out. The built-up area around Altrincham is now reaching the edge of the green belt and pressure on this will increase. Whether we like it or not, the population of Altrincham will become socially more polarised. Gentrification, the process by which the wealthier colonise and do up the houses of the less wealthy, is already clearly evident. New Street in Altrincham, Victoria Road in Hale, Bowdon Vale, the streets around Stamford Park between Moss Lane and Hale Road east of the town centre, provide easy examples to spot, Fig. 22.7.

The rising price of land coupled with the end of the supply of new housing as the built-up area meets

Fig. 22.6. **Victorian house converted to nursing home,** with extension (to left of picture).

D.G.B.

the green belt, will lead to denser development within Altrincham. Owners, especially as they leave, will sell off larger gardens for development; builders will search out coach houses for conversion; developers will turn the larger houses into flats. It will be done ingeniously and skilfully – because the neighbours are watchful, the planning authority nags, and the product has to sell. But something has to give, and it will, for the most part, be the spacious landscape in the leafier parts of Altrincham. Tree Preservation Orders are useful instruments but are powerless against the laws of nature. When the forest trees planted by the Victorians die, as die they must, the space in which to replant will often not be found.

CONCLUSION

Economics is not the sole determinant of the way we live, but it is one of the main keys. Altrincham will not maintain its present relative prosperity if the wider region continues to decline. But Altrincham stands virtually where a regional revival will occur – if we encourage it. Altrincham town centre will then be one of the nearest principal service centres to the new area of industrial growth. Assuming we have the good sense not to lose quality while we grasp for quantity, Altrincham will grow both as an office centre and as a fashionable shopping centre. Residential Altrincham will be more crowded, more widely gentrified and in places more elderly. It will also be more expensive.

If this sounds uncongenial, it should not. The changes described are generally those of a wealthier society. We shall ourselves not be the same people. Perhaps we shall be more tolerant of each others' company, even if it is closer than Altrincham people have been used to in the past. There will be compensations. Notably the countryside, to which residents of Altrincham already enjoy good access, is likely to become more accessible and better suited to

Fig. 22.7. 'Gentrified' house,   D.G.B.
between Moss Lane and Stamford Park Road.

informal leisure as it becomes less preoccupied with the production of food. Altrincham particularly, already privileged by the improved Bollin Valley and the nearby National Trust estates at Dunham, Tatton and Styal, will also enjoy a scenic country footpath if the Council's intentions to convert the disused railway from Broadheath to Lymm come to fruition.

Finally, in contemplating the future it is worth remembering that though broad changes are often due to forces beyond our control, the way those changes are handled locally is largely in our hands.

Bollin Valley

Chapter Twenty-Three

CONCLUSION

DON BAYLISS

The first section in this chapter identifies the factors which explain why Altrincham, a small place of a few hundred people in AD1290, grew to be a town of over 40000 people and developed its present character. The factors which will be considered are: location, site and plan; the economy; transport developments; the landlords; local government; the people. The second part describes the modern townscape of central Altrincham, and the chapter concludes with a review of the 1990 celebrations of Altrincham's 700 years as a chartered borough.

LOCATION, SITE AND PLAN

Altrincham had a location near the Manchester to Chester road and the centre of the town lay at the crossroads of the Manchester to Ashley and Dunham to Stockport roads, and there were roads to Bowdon and Hale. This meant it was locally very accessible, which must have contributed to the success of the weekly market and annual fairs. Accessibility was later enhanced by the building of the Bridgewater Canal and the railways. The location of the town assured its easy contact with Manchester to which in the last century it became increasingly bound.

Altrincham's site lay east of an upland of well-drained soils important for farming. The town developed on a narrow, steep slope between the farmlands and the low boglands of Timperley Moss and Hale Moss. In the 19th century the upland farmland was replaced by spacious better-class housing. A broad heath became the site of an important industrial area, yielding rents and rates from a former wasteland, a little distance from the town. The lowlands (including the mosses when drained) provided sites for more modest housing, schools and recreation areas. Upland and lowland are now virtually completely built over. There have been, therefore, remarkable changes in land-use.

The plan of the mediaeval borough was attenuated in shape, Fig. 2.3 (Chapter Two) and Fig. 23.1. The curved streets of Church Street and Albert Place, suggest the northern part owed its shape to the curved paths of the previous village. The NE-SW alignment of the elongated grid of Market Street and George Street was, no doubt, that of the new Altrincham created in the Middle Ages. This proved to be a suitable compact area in which modern shopping and offices could develop. However, the centre of economic activity eventually shifted from the market place towards Stamford New Road and Railway Street after the

railway was built and then to George Street after 1975. Because of these recent shifts the town now lacks a well-defined centre.

THE ECONOMY

At the outset, the economy was based round two activities, market-trading and farming. The market continued from AD1290 to the present day, and the fairs lasted until after the mid-19th century. Small industries such as domestic textiles and smithing were noted as early as the 15th century. However, Altrincham went into a decline similar to that experienced by many urban places in the 15th century and regrowth did not begin until perhaps the late-16th century. Increased wealth between 1600 and 1760 led to the Great Rebuilding common to many Cheshire towns. In Altrincham, wealth came from wool, hemp and flax production and dairying. In the 18th century a worsted industry developed though most people were still employed in agriculturally-related work including vegetable production for the Manchester market. The profits from these activities together with the wealth of some incomers probably led to the second rebuilding in the second half of the 18th and the early 19th century. The rise of industrial Manchester caused competition which led to the collapse of Altrincham's domestic textile industry and its early 19th century factory textile industry. The town changed, for half a century, to being a supply centre for the food needs of Manchester and a residential and service centre for a population which lived in Altrincham but largely worked in the city, to which Altrincham was now bound. The pleasant site, the large range of religious denominations, schools and leisure pursuits gradually added to Altrincham's attractions. After World War II the town's retailing and service function greatly increased in scope. The central retail zone now occupies an area larger than the original mediaeval grid of streets and serves a widening catchment region. A new office zone is extending round the retail area like a halo. Public services, once functions of the local administration, are now provided by outside bodies.

After 1884, a huge industrial area developed at Broadheath (especially concerned with the manufacturing of machine-tools), some of the industries moving here from Manchester. As the markets of these large enterprises were not local but national and international, the fame of Altrincham spread. After World War II, the industrial sector has been in the doldrums but in 1981 was nevertheless still the greatest single employer. Broadheath activities as a whole have waned and now employ in total fewer people than are now employed in the many new offices and other commercial and service occupations of Altrincham centre. However, Broadheath is now diversifying into high-tech and service industries and retail warehousing. During its existence it has added greatly to the prosperity, architecture, growth and social character of the town.

TRANSPORT

An important factor for trade from early times was the route followed by Watling Street especially when this route was diverted through the town. While its presence did not prevent an early decline of the town, it no doubt helped the recovery of the town from the Elizabethan period and was important in later times when parts of this road and the Stockport road were turnpiked in the last half of the 18th century and stage coach services began. The canal of 1765 brought trade and goods, and within two years there followed the development of commuting by boat to Manchester. The demand of Manchester people to move out of the city (Chapter Eight) led to an expanding use of carriage and horse-bus transport and to the need for a railway. Altrincham after 1849 became for forty years solely a residential and service town. In the 1880's, it was the presence of good transport systems, especially for coal for power, which led entrepreneurs to appreciate the potential for development of Broadheath between the Manchester road, the canal and railways. From 1906 Altrincham became the terminus for tramways from Manchester, in the 20's a bus centre for private bus companies serving north Cheshire and, from 1929, for city services. The railways, trams and buses were the main transport factors in the town's growth. The car came too late to cause growth but is altering Altrincham's social character by providing increased mobility for the inhabitants and it also allows more visitors to be able to shop in the town. Altrincham is well-placed for vehicular access to major roads and motorways which will assist its commercial and industrial future. However, there are severe traffic problems due to a lack of a ring road system, and lack of parking spaces. The main effect of changes in transport systems was to facilitate in-migration and commuting and secure Altrincham ever more closely to the Manchester region.

THE LANDLORDS

The incumbents at Dunham owned most of the land for most of the time. They also owned the early courts and influenced later councils where local administrative policy decisions were made. They depended on rents and dues from the town for income. The de Masseys have to be given credit for selecting a location for the borough which proved to be

appropriate for the town for 700 years. The Booths were not able to prevent economic decline in the 15th century but later were involved in expanding the estate and in national politics in the 17th century, though any direct effect on Altrincham is not clear, except to increase the financial burden of the inhabitants. However, they were responsible for some building in the town and they drained the mossland and enclosed some heath. In giving Altrincham a new courthouse and buttermarket they created it a centre for several local courts and gave a good facility for a specialised dairy industry. In the 18th century improved estate management by the 2nd Earl of Warrington assisted Altrincham along the road to economic recovery. The Stamfords, at Dunham in the mid-18th century, made no objection to the building of the canal nor to the railway in the mid-19th, so far as is known. They built a fine church and encouraged (with some constraints) the development of Broadheath (Chapter Nineteen). They also generously provided several areas for recreation and housing. It is certain that their regulations exercised on architecture, construction and infrastructure on the estate lands were beneficial and have left a legacy of buildings of a high standard, referred to in Chapters Nine, Fourteen and Fifteen, which have made Altrincham very attractive as a place in which to live or to visit. The National Trust continues with this policy. Areas of the town not owned by the Dunham estate were not subject to stringent building

Fig. 23.1. **Growth of the built-up area, AD1290 - 1990**
1. In AD 1290 the town probably occupied the area of Church Street, Old Market Place and George Street.
2. There was decline of population and area over the next 400 years. However, Altrincham experienced the 'Great Rebuilding' of Cheshire towns in the 17th/early-18th century and a second rebuilding in the late-18th / early-19th century late-Georgian period. By 1835 the town was spreading south-westwards and also new hamlets had appeared at Broadheath, Sandiway and Sinderland Road to the north, but the centre was not as built up as in the 14th century.
3. Between 1835 and 1875 there was new building in The Downs, Newtown and the Barrington-Oakfield area near the railway stations. Between 1875 and 1907 there was a third rebuilding of public buildings, houses and shops, which gave the centre much of its present character. East of the railway, the Manor Road - Ashfield Road - Stamford Park area developed. South of the town, the Byrom Street - Brown Street area was built, and, to the north, housing for the Broadheath workforce. In the west, late-Victorian villas filled the land on each side of Dunham Road and around St. Margaret's.
4. Between 1907 and the mid-50's new private and council property filled remaining pockets of open land, north of the town, from the railway west to Oldfield Brow. Since the 50's there has been a fourth major phase of rebuilding in the town centre and a few new houses and two new schools have been built in the remaining open spaces. A fifth rebuilding is scheduled east of the present town centre.
N.B. The 19th-20th century dates are those of the Tithe Map and available O.S. map editions.

controls and here some poor housing resulted, most of which has had to be demolished.

LOCAL GOVERNMENT

Until mid-19th century the main regulator of life was the Court Leet, governing the borough under the aegis of the lord of the manor. The Court was composed of inhabitants who carried out quite onerous tasks to keep the town functioning, to regulate trade and farming and to preserve law and order. Due to a growing population, a shrinking number of burgesses and lack of legislative and financial power, this body was replaced by elected forms of government able to raise a rate. From mid-19th century the borough really ceased to exist politically in the original meaning of the term, and Altrincham was not to be a borough again until 1937. The ancient form of government was followed in sequence by the Local Board, Urban District Council, Municipal Borough Council, and, after 1974, Altrincham became part of Trafford MBC. Altrincham's town hall now stands redundant for executive decision-making.

THE PEOPLE

In AD1290, the borough is unlikely to have possessed only one social class, the burgess trader-farmers referred to in the charter, but also a range of other people, such as craftsmen, professional men, employees and mendicants. This range of occupations widened as the centuries passed; eventually the farming element was replaced by market gardeners who themselves eventually disappeared, as the land was covered by buildings.

In the late-18th, early-19th century a high class of people came into the town and with their associated servants, they were a contrast to the traders, clothiers, wharfingers, and farming residents. This polarisation of society was reflected in the zoning of groups into particular areas of the town, wealthy people in Higher Town, poorer in Lower Town. The proportion of the upper class declined when the railway brought in more middle and working class people and many of the upper class subsequently moved out.

Originally people only attended Bowdon Church. In the late-18th century non-conformity developed and at this time St. George's was also built but was not declared a parish church till 1868.

In numbers population declined from a peak immediately post- AD1290, to the 16th century, after which it rose, at first gradually, and, from the mid-19th century, rapidly. Over the 19th century as a whole, the effect of natural growth rate and the continuing large number of in-migrants led to a tenfold increase in population. Toward the end of the century two new social elements appeared: the large skilled workforce at Broadheath and the 'Cottontots', shippers and professional people who moved into the area around St. Margaret's Church. Many of these people were socially minded, and worked for the common good. During the 20th century, population more than doubled, leading since World War II to a wide range of social class, (with some emphasis at the upper end of the scale), having occupations in the professions, industry, retailing, other commerce, education, leisure, and catering for the elderly.

Fig. 23.2. **Cresta Court Hotel, where Woodlands Road meets Church Street.** Hamilton House and Lynnfield office blocks lie beyond

D.G.B.

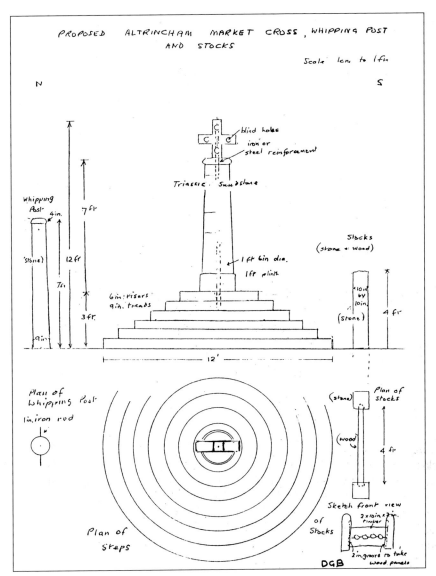

Fig. 23.3. Draft design for replica market cross, 1988. *D.G.B.*
The cross and other features were designed by the editor of this book. The
scheme was supported by Altrincham and Bowdon Civic Society and funding
was arranged by Mr J.A. Littler.

Fig. 23.4. Replica of market cross in process of erection. *D.G.B.*
And see front cover. Mason – Mr. C. Crosby of T. Crosby & Sons.

Fig. 23.5. **Tabley Court office block in Kingsway.**   *D.G.B.*

Fig. 23.6. **Arnold's yard at the back of the Unicorn.**   *D.G.B.*
St. George's to the north

DEVELOPMENT STAGES

From the early mediaeval period there have been several different Altrinchams;

(1) a growing village before 1290;

(2) a bustling mediaeval trading borough after 1290;

(3) a town in decline until the 16th century;

(4) a revitalised market town in the late-17th and early-18th centuries;

(5) a market town with a few factories after the canal came in the mid-18th century. There were many elegant houses in Higher Town but squalid cottages in Lower Town.

(6) a crowded market town with a dominant industrial sector in the late-19th and early-20th century after the railway was built, with great contrasts ranging between magnificent villas and areas of slum property;

(7) a modern, sophisticated, retail, office, industrial and residential town with a population of about 40,000.

Until mid-19th century the chief factor in the town's fortunes was the tight control over the town by the landlords and burgesses. After this date there were many complicated and interwoven factors including,

i.   new forms of transport,

ii. the effect of the industrial revolution in the Manchester area,

iii. new forms of administration after 1851 with eventual loss of independence in 1974;

iv. the growth and wane of heavy industry, to be replaced since W.W.II by an increase of service and residential functions.

All these in their turn have created the Altrincham we know today.

THE CENTRAL ALTRINCHAM TOWNSCAPE

The nature of the buildings which occupied the central area of the Altrincham of 1990 will now be described. The original borough is thought to have covered only the area from the George and Dragon at the north of Church Street, southwards round Old Market Place and along Market Street and George Street as far as Regent Road. Today the main central retail area does not reach as far north as the George and Dragon but lies to the south of Old Market Place around George Street, which was in the ancient borough, and Stamford New Road and Railway Street which were not, being late-19th century streets. Between Old Market Place and the George and Dragon there are two blocks of offices, Fig. 23.2, also the Cresta Court Hotel and a row of small shops of the east side of Church Street, with Victorian houses, St. George's Church, a car-exhaust fitters and a funeral director's on the west. Old Market Place, once the former chief place of the ancient borough is now designated a Conservation Area, Appendix 4. To mark the 700th anniversary of the Charter, a sandstone replica of the former market cross, Figs. 23.3. and 23.4, and some stocks and a whipping post were commissioned by Altrincham and Bowdon Civic Society and funded by contributions from Trafford MBC and establishments round Old Market Place. The cross was dedicated at a ceremony on 7 October 1990, by R.R. Frank P. Sargeant, Bishop of Stockport and the title of the three monuments was given by the Society, through the Mayor, James R. Haydock, J.P., to the people of Trafford.

The Unicorn almost closes the north end of the market place and on both sides is attractive old property on former burgage sites including the Orange Tree, an Indian restaurant, the fine listed Lloyds Bank (of the late-19th century and early-20th century rebuilding of much of this area), two furriers, a wine merchants and bar, (with a mediaeval framework showing 18th century rebuilding) and a kitchen designer's. Several shops on the east side are now due for demolition for a site for offices. Heavy traffic effectively divides the ancient market place, which would benefit from pedestrianisation. The old Roebuck pub lies on Victoria Street, perhaps the old road to Stockport, and down Kingsway is the attractive modern Tabley Court office complex, Fig. 23.5.

Behind the Unicorn off Albert Place, are auction rooms, car sales and repair, and a high-tech shop in a yard, Fig. 23.6, where the 'Sanjam Fair' has recently been pleasantly revived. Behind St. George's Church is quiet Church Walk, the parish hall and a training centre for the disadvantaged. At the end of Church Walk which formerly led to the town's openfield, is the C. of E. primary school and the recent flats of Townfield Gardens, and farther north are the large Victorian and early-20th century semis of Richmond Road area. To the west, on the Dunham Road, are the police station, the Unitarian chapel and a large garage. Market Street leads off to the south-west.

The alignment of Market Street and parallel George Street and their cross streets, are believed to be part of the new town of AD1290. Single-way traffic speeds down the narrow north end of Market Street (earlier called High Street) between some fine listed Georgian residences from the late-18th century town rebuilding, now mainly offices and specialist shops. On High Street, running transversely, is the National Trust Office and shop, and to the east, a multi-storey carpark and shop service area, Fig. 23.7. Continuing along Market

Fig. 23.7. **High Street with Altrincham's multi-storey car-park.**

D.G.B.

Fig. 23.8. **North end of Petros – Stamford Square.**

D.G.B.

Fig. 23.9. **Springfield Road with Elf offices on Woodlands Road beyond.**

D.G.B.

Fig. 23.10. **Barrington Road, looking towards Woodlands Road.** Housing with windows boarded up awaiting demolition and replacement by offices. 'Unisys' office block in distance.

D.G.B.

Fig. 23.11. **King's Court, off Railway Street, pleasant to relax in.**

D.G.B.

Street is the Town Hall of 1900 and the former St. Margaret's Institute, and several Victorian semis (some converted into offices, and another to be replaced with a block of flats). On the east side are a solicitor's, and office services. On the site of the former Volunteer barracks and training ground is the listed Market House of 1879 and the glassed market area of 1930. There is a colourful, noisy, busy market on Tuesdays, Fridays and Saturdays. The General Hospital, here, is now mainly concerned with old people. Parallel to Market Street runs Greenwood Street on which is part of the market area and shops such as a TV-firm, electrics, carpets and a cafe. Quieter Central Way also lies parallel, on which there are more hospital buildings and also a canework shop.

George Street is the busiest shopping area, created a modern shopping mall by the Petros development of the mid-1970's. Its buildings have a modern uncluttered outline and there are spacious rear service areas for supplies. North of Shaw's Road the development contains Stamford Square, Fig. 23.8., three

large department stores, branches of many multiples and high street shops, travel agents, banks and building societies and Norweb (the N.W. Electricity Board). A department store stands on the site of an old Wesleyan chapel and in front of it is Trafford's popular portable lottery office (what would Wesley have thought?). South of Shaw's Road much of the property is older and part of the east side of George Street is a Conservation Area. There are more multiples here, general stores, several travel agents, and a building society. The old Bricklayers Arms was recently saved from demolition (mainly by a petition). Near Regent Road is the covered Grafton Mall with cafe, furniture, opticians, newsagent, toy and fancy goods shops, with an attractive flower stall in its central 'foyer'. Above is the 10-storey Grafton office block which pierces the Altrincham skyline.

Bustling Shaw's Road and Cross Street link Market Street with George Street and Stamford New Road. Shops here are mainly non-multiples *e.g.* an 'ex-Army' shop which has been there since the War, books, fancy

148

Fig. 23.12. **Railway Street taken from the junction of the Downs (from the left), Ashley Road on right, and Lloyd Street (with car emerging).** Graftons office block on far left, 'Shanty Town' on right. D.G.B.

goods, pets, sports, clothing, opticians, confectionery, health foods and clothing shops, pizzeria, sausage shop, and an amusement arcade. Regent Road linking Market Street, George Street and Railway Street contains a travel agent and dry cleaners, clothes, charity, books, kitchenware, cheesery, antiques, chemist's shops, a clock and watch seller and repairer, a photo-processor and a take-away hot potato servery. The Grapes pub is on the south side.

There are one or two old alleyways across the main streets, one of which has a picture framer's in a cellar. Over many of the three four-storey Victorian shops in all the streets, the top storeys are frequently used for offices.

At the north-west end of the former line of George Street, Lower Kingsway has a terrace of small shops selling models, bicycles, leather goods; and the Malt Shovels. There is a well-designed new office block and some excellent large old semis on Springfield Road but these are overshadowed by the 6-storey Elf high-rise offices at the Woodlands Road end, Fig. 23.9. On the busy junction of this road with Barrington Road stands the recently built Methodist Church. Barrington Road is rapidly changing from a residential to an office area, Fig. 23.10.

Two important shopping areas lie outside the area occupied by the ancient borough; Lloyd Street-Ashley Road at the southern end of the old town and the heavily trafficked Stamford New Road-Railway Street, parallel to George Street. On Lloyd Street there are office supplies, a clothes shop, photograph processor, fitted furniture, a motor factors, a greengrocers, an estate agents, a security shop, hairdresser/boutique, a brightly lit lamp-and-shade shop, and the Park Hotel. The largest place is a supermarket. This together with some moderate-rise flats and two-storey old people's flats and centre were built on land cleared of old terraced property. South of Lloyd Street on Ashley

Fig. 23.13. **The ginnel behind 'Shanty Town' shops.** Formerly fronts of houses, overlooking site of Bowdon Station. D.G.B.

149

Road, Oxford Road and The Downs is another group of shops including a book-shop, fish and game merchant, hot food take-away, two restaurants (one Chinese), fancy goods, stationers, opticians, children's clothes, photographers, hobbies, a furniture store, flower shop, newsagent, antiques, furriers, a building society and the Messenger newspaper offices.

From Lloyd Street north-eastwards up Railway Street as far as the library on Stamford New Road most of the shops and offices on the west are in a Conservation Area except for the Grafton development. There is a range of 'high street-type' shops and offices including banks and building societies. Of two former banks near Lloyd Street one is now a restaurant, and another on the west side, a picture-framers, a handsome sandstone building in the 'Gothic' style. King's Court, Fig. 23.11, up a short passage, is an attractive renovated mall of small shops and a restaurant. On the opposite side of Railway Street is a row of small late 19th century property on to which rather unsightly shop fronts have been grafted to first floor height, known rather unkindly as 'Shanty Town', Fig. 23.12. The backs line a ginnel between Lloyd Street and Goose Green on which can be seen what were formerly brick fronts of houses with doors and windows, Fig. 23.13. They were probably cottages for railway workers and overlook

Fig. 23.14. **Looking along Stamford New Road towards Moss Lane crossroads.** Station buildings on left, Station Hotel and McDonald's on right.

D.G.B.

Fig. 23.15 **Bus-rail interchange.** Footbridge to right leads to Stamford Square (Petros area). Chester – Manchester diesel at the platform. Beyond the car-park is a bridge carrying Moss Lane over the railway.

D.G.B.

the site of Bowdon Station below (now a large muddy carpark) and are scheduled for demolition. Premises include the Express Advertiser office, sports shop, travel agency, fancy goods and clothing shop.

Towards Moss Lane, there are the gas showrooms, chief post office, travel agents, cafes and take-aways. There are three public houses, the Downs, the Railway and the Stamford. Over many of the shops there are offices of several types including insurance, design and development. Opposite Regent Road the passage-way to the east leads to Goose Green, which in the old days was at the edge of Hale Moss. Its cottages were recently renovated; a boutique, men's outfitters, children's wear, florist, foodshop and restaurant are now there; a bronze statue of two geese makes a central focus and the 'green' is now a pleasant corner and a Conservation Area. Setted Grafton Street leads down past the magistrates' court to the attractive old building lately occupied by the Altrincham Guardian press.

Where Cross Street-Moss Lane and Stamford New Road cross is probably the busiest junction in town, Fig. 23.14. Moss Lane contains two dress shops, a cafe, a men's outfitters, a photographer's, newsagents, wig shop/hairdresser's, an upholsterer's and Oxfam. On the north side is the very striking Stamford House office block of 1905. North of Moss Lane there are two travel agents, camera shop, cancer charity shop and electronics shop, the quiet refuge of the library with books upstairs and meeting rooms below and north of this, a supermarket and Station House office block. The bus-rail interchange with its row of waiting black taxi-cabs, and buses large and mini- is a busy place, Fig. 23.15. The fine free-standing listed clock-tower dates from 1880. The station buildings of 1905 lost their original verandah but otherwise are still attractive in mellow brick. This is the town's chief point for communications and will become more central following the planned town centre development east of this.

The present main zone of economic activity has shifted to the south and east of the old borough centre (Old Market Place) to George Street which was the eastern limit of the old town. Whether the proposed new development of shops, offices, cinema, hotel and other facilities in the area of ¼ million sq.ft. east of Stamford New Road and Railway Street on former railway property, Fig. 23.16, will cause a new central focus to develop farther east remains to be seen.

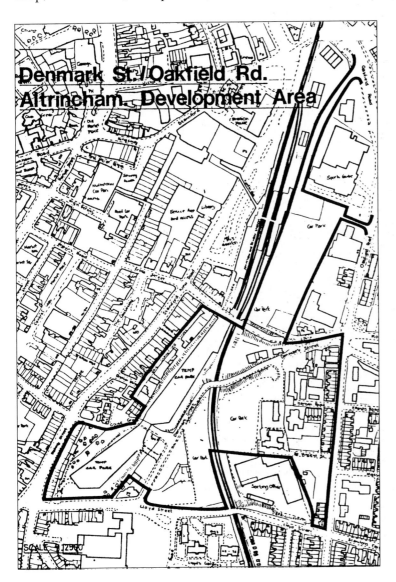

Fig. 23.16 **The area for development.** The first phase lies south of Moss Lane. It is almost equal in size to the existing shopping centre. In the editor's view, intending developers to date, can be criticised for wishing to cram too many shops and offices into this zone to the detriment of existing premises. There is the opportunity to create good civic space including a replacement for the former Stamford Hall, provide a heritage centre, and more residential property, including some for the elderly.

THE 1990 700 YEAR CHARTER CELEBRATION YEAR

One of the reasons for compiling this book was to mark the 700th year of the granting of Altrincham's Royal and Borough charters and as 1990 passed during preparation of the book it is appropriate to record the exceedingly fulsome celebrations of that year in the town.

This short acount, however, cannot do justice to the co-operation between, and efforts of, many organisations, voluntary, uniformed and others, and individuals, concerned in a most memorable series of events in 1990. Only a few of these can be mentioned and apologies are due to people and groups whose contribution should have been recorded. What was remarkable and much appreciated was the support, monetarily and in spirit given to Altrincham by Trafford MBC councillors and officers especially through Mr M.S. Havenhand, Director of Leisure Services and his colleagues, Mrs Julie Kiersey (formerly Miss Julie Clarke) and Mr M. Gledhill.

The programme for the year was co-ordinated by the Provost and Court Leet. The Provosts concerned were Mr J. Buckley, 1988-89, Mr J. Trickett, 1989-90, and Mr W.R. Firth, 1990-91. Arrangements were overseen by a Celebration Council, meeting on a monthly basis, on which many town organisations were represented as well as Trafford MBC and the National Trust. Its officers were Mr W.R. Firth, Chairman; Mrs. C. Crosbie, Vice-Chairman; Mr K. Cooper, Secretary; and Mr G. Hayes, Treasurer, Fig. 23.17. Its President was Sir Fergus Montgomery, M.P. It was supported by the late Lady Jane Grey and Messrs. Oliver and John Turnbull representing the former family ('Barony') at Dunham, and the National Trust (which is the present incumbent), represented on the Council by Mr P. Browning.

W.R. Firth

Fig. 23.17 Inaugural Meeting of the Celebration Council. Left to right: Mr K. Noble, Town Crier; Mr. W. Firth, Chairman; Sir Fergus Montgomery, M.P., President; Mrs C. Crosbie, Vice-Chairman; Superintendent D. Arrowsmith; Mr G. Hayes, Treasurer; Councillor G. Marland, Mayor 1988-89; Ch. Insp. M. Bolland; Mr K. Cooper, Secretary.

SOME OF THE EVENTS:

A colourful inaugural pageant with 'mediaeval knights', Fig. 23.18, attended by the Mayors of the surrounding boroughs.
A series of concerts arranged by Mr J. Littler of the Civic Society.
A competition for 'Young Town Criers'.
A series of lectures and and an exhibition describing the history of Altrincham arranged by the History Society.
A market traders' celebration.
Several church services including a Celebration Mass at St. Vincent's.
The painting of a large picture depicting scenes from

Fig. 23.18 Mediaeval 'knights' in an inaugural pageant.

W.R. Firth

Altrincham's history by Mrs M. Norris of the Society of Artists, Fig. 23.19.

Co-operation between the Celebration Council and Altrincham Festival Committee in Festival Week.

A large embroidered panel (now in St. Margaret's Church) showing important buildings of the town, worked by ladies of the Embroiderers Guild, Fig. 23.20.

A mediaeval day on Devisdale followed by a sumptuous banquet in the hall of Altrincham Boys Grammar School, Fig. 23.21.

Erection of a market cross, stocks and whipping post by the Civic Society.

Fig. 23.19 Painting by Mrs M. Norris.   *M.N.*

A. Taylor (Courtesy of Cheshire Life)

Fig, 23.20 **Embroidered Panel**

Fig. 23.21 Mediaeval 'banquet' at   *D.G.B.*
Altrincham Boys Grammar School.

Fig. 23.22 **Bollin Morris**   *D.G.B.*

Displays of dancing by the Bollin Morris and many other groups, Fig. 23.22.

Displays of project work on historical themes by schoolchildren in many schools, Fig. 23.23., and in the Library, Fig. 23.24.

Excavation of Timperley Old Hall by South Trafford Archaeological Group, Fig. 23.25.

Numerous activities by uniformed and youth organisations. Activities in the parks, such as brass band concerts, arranged by the Council.

The Mayors of Trafford, Councillor A. Coupe (1989-90), Fig.23.26, and Councillor J.R. Haydock (1990-91), Fig. 23.27, Trafford officers, and the Court Leet, Fig. 23.28, graced many events by their presence.

The year stimulated Trafford MBC to produce brochures, office-paper, decorated pavements in George Street, signs on lamposts and illuminated signs across roads recording the celebrations. Christmas cards and other stationery also celebrated the year and carried symbols such as the Massey silver lion, or coat-of-arms.

The celebrations were followed by a ball at the Cresta Court Hotel. Finally a cavity was made in the front wall of Altrincham Town Hall (shown in Fig. 23.29, being inspected by Mr M.S. Havenhand), and on 23 July, 1991, the Mayor of Trafford, 1991-92, Councillor Mrs Lydia Burton, inserted a 'time capsule', which contained records of several of the events of 1990 and other evidence of town life, to be opened 100 years hence.

D.G.B.

Fig. 23.23. Navigation Road School. Project work showing models of 'Venus' and, behind the boy, a coal barge

Trafford Leisure Services

Fig. 23.24 Deputy Mayor, 1990-91, Councillor Mrs Lydia Burton examines school project work in Altrincham Library

Fig. 23.25. *Below Left* **STAG Excavation of Timperley Old Hall.** A young Town Crier in the foreground.

Fig. 23.26. *Below Right* **STAG H.Q.** Visit by Councillor A. Coupe, Mayor 1989-90, and Mayoress with the youngest Town Crier.

A. Lockett

A. Lockett

Fig. 23.27 **Councillor J.R. Haydock, J.P., Mayor 1990-91,** at the opening of Altrincham History Society's Exhibition, July 1990. Others present left to right: Dr.C.A. Sparkes, Councillor M.E. King, Dr. D.G. Bayliss, Mr W.R. Firth (Provost 1990-91), Town Crier – Mr K. Noble.

H.E.B.

Fig. 23.28 **Some members of Altrincham Court Leet.**
(Left to right) Standing: Mr K. Noble, Town Crier, Alderman N. Dutton, Burgess G. Leybourn-Needham, Burgess C. Jackson, Burgess D. Mardon, Alderman R. Bishop, Burgess G. Cain, Alderman J. Buckley (Provost 1988-89), Alderman W. Pilkington.
Seated: Alderman A. Jackson, Barony Bailiff B. Massey, Barony Steward W.L. Pollard, Alderman J. Trickett (Provost 1989-90), Burgess D.G. Bayliss. For Provost W.R. Firth, 1990-91, see Figs.23.17 and 23.27.

H.E.B.

Fig. 23.29 **Mr M.S. Havenhand inspecting the time capsule cavity in Altrincham Town Hall.**

Trafford Leisure Services

REFERENCES AND ACKNOWLEDGEMENTS

Main printed sources used in several chapters:

Ingham, A., Altrincham and Bowdon with Historical Reminiscences of Ashton upon Mersey, Sale and surrounding Townships, 1897.

Leech, H.J., Tales and Sketches of Old Altrincham and Bowdon, 1880.

Nickson, C., Bygone Altrincham, Traditions and History, 1935. Rep. E.J. Morten, 1979.

Ormerod, G., The History of the County Palatine and City of Chester, 3 vols., 2nd Edn. London, 1892.

Victoria County History, Cheshire vols. Oxford, 1979.

C.R.O. = Cheshire Record Office, Chester.

Chapter One   Background

Anglo-Saxon Chronicle, Everyman Edn.

Bagley, J.J., ed., History of Cheshire series. Cheshire Community Council.

Dodgson, J. McN., The Place Names of Cheshire, part 2. Eng. Place Name Soc. Cambridge, 1970.

Morris, J., ed., Domesday Book of Cheshire. Phillimore, 1978.

Sylvester, D., and Nulty, G., The Historical Atlas of Cheshire. Chester, 1958.

Chapter Two   Foundation of the Borough

Beresford, M.W., New Towns of the Middle Ages. Lutterworth, 1967.

Beresford, M.W., and Finberg, H.P.R., English Mediaeval Boroughs, A Handlist. David and Charles, 1973.

Morris, J., ed., op.cit.

Acknowledgements: National Trust; Dr P. McNiven, Rylands Library, Manchester University; Mr I. Sharman, Keele University; Dr S.H. Rigby, Manchester University. Mlle. Hamel, University of Caen; for sources and translations. Trafford MBC for borough charter.

Chapter Three   The de Masci Baronage

Barraclough, G., ed., The Charters of the Anglo-Norman Earls of Chester, c.1071–1237. Lancashire and Cheshire Record Society, 1988.

Bates, D., Normandy before 1066. Longman, 1982.

Prestwich, M., Edward I. Methuen, 1988.

Public Record Office.

Warrington Public Library Archive section, Massey Papers.

Acknowledgements: Rylands Library.

Chapter Four   Estate and Township from 1290 to the mid-19th Century

Dore, R.N., History of Hale. Sherratt, Hale Civic Society, 1972.

Dunham Massey Hall, National Trust Guide.

Faulkner, P., Flashback, A Pictorial View. Faulkner, 1988.

Higham, N.J., Settlement and Land-use in one Cheshire Township, c.AD 1000-1400. The Manchester Geographer, vol. 17, 1986.

Leycester, Sir P., Antiquities of Cheshire. 1673.

Postan, M.M., The Mediaeval Economy and Society. Pelican, 1978.

Swarbrick, J., Dunham Massey Hall. Trans, Lancashire and Cheshire Antiquarian Society, vol xlii, 1927.

Book of Abstracts, AD1286–1704 and other Dunham Massey Estate papers: Rylands Library.

Bowdon parish records, Altrincham Library.

Census Reports, 1801-51, Manchester City Reference Library.

Tithe Map and Commutation Award, 1835, C.R.O. Copies of these and Hearth Tax returns by Mrs J. Hardman (in Altrincham Library).

Articles in the Bowdon Sheaf, published by the Bowdon History Society.

Acknowledgements: Dr P.H.W. Booth, Liverpool University; Mrs J. Williams, M.A.; Mrs J. Littler; Miss P. Faulkner; Mr R.N. Dore, M.A.

Chapter Five   The Borough from 1290 to the mid-19th Century.

Aiken, J.A., Description of the Country from Thirty to Forty Miles round Manchester, 1793. 2nd Edn, 1795. Rep. 1968.

Bagley, J.J., Life in Mediaeval England. Batsford, 1971.

Carus-Wilson, E.M., The First Half-Century of the Borough of Stratford-Upon-Avon. Econ. Hist. Rev., Ser.2, vol. xviii, 1965.

Leycester, Sir P., op.cit.

Rigby, S.H., Late Mediaeval Prosperity, and other papers. Econ. Hist. Rev., Ser.2, vol xxxix, No.3, 1986.

Dunham Estate papers: National Trust and Rylands Library.

Local Board of Health Map and Schedule, 1852: Altrincham Library.

Tithe Map and Schedule, op.cit.

Town Directories.

Acknowledgements: Mr R.N. Dore, M.A., Prof J. Denton and Dr S.H. Rigby; Manchester University Department of Geography Library; Dr P.H.W. Booth; Dr A.R.

Rumble, Department of English, Manchester University; Miss Belinda Cousens, Mr Peter Veitch, Mr C. Alford and Mr P. Chapman, National Trust; Dr P. McNiven, Rylands Library; Mr B.D. Morrison; Mrs J. Littler; Miss P. Faulkner; Mr R.J. Rees, M.A.

Mr R.N. Dore has helped considerably over Chapters One to Five. He is President of the Lancashire and Cheshire Antiquarian Society, and of Altrincham History Society. He is author of several books including 'The Letter Books of Sir William Brereton' for the Lancashire and Cheshire Record Society and several papers in journals.

Chapter Six   The Court Leet

Gallimore, M.T., The Development of the Seignorial Courts of the Liber Burgus of Altrincham from 1290 A.D. Unpub. law thesis, Manchester Polytechnic.

Rawlinson, Sir R., Report to the General Board of Health. HMSO, 1851.

Report from the Commissioners on Municipal Corporations in England and Wales: Report on the Borough of Altrincham. (C.H. Wilkinson). 1834.

Suit Roll for the Borough of Altrincham, 1786–92, Altrincham Library.

Town's Meeting Minute Books, Altrincham Library.

Webb, J., English and Local Government. London, 1907.

Acknowledgments: Members of Altrincham Court Leet, Altrincham Guardian Newspaper.

Chapter Seven   Local Government since 1851

Altrincham Official Guide, 1970.

Dore, R.N., History of Hale. Sherratt, op. cit.

Male, K.O., Altrincham Town Centre, A Policy for Re-development, Improvement and Conservation.

Morrison, B.D., Looking Back at Altrincham. Willow, 1980.

The Borough of Altrincham Charter Celebrations, 1937 booklet.

Year Books: Altrincham U.D., Municipal Borough, and Trafford Metropolitan Borough Councils.

Acknowledgements: Superintendent D. Arrowsmith, M Division, G.M. Police; Mr B.E. Chapman (decd.); Mr E. Graham Thomas; staff in the Legal Section of the Estates and Valuation Department, Trafford MBC; Mr K.A. Goulding, C.Eng., MICE., MIHT.

Chapter Eight   Population Growth and Character

Armstrong, W.A., Stability and Change in an English County Town: A Social Study of York, 1801–1851. Cambridge, 1974.

Briggs, A., Victorian Cities, London, 1963.

Dixon, F., The Manchester South Junction and Altrincham Railway. Oakwood, Exeter, 1973.

Dore, R.N., Manchester's Discovery of Cheshire: Excursionism and Commuting in the Nineteenth Century. Trans. Lancashire and Cheshire Antiquarian Society, No. 82, 1983.

Harrison, W., "History of the Manchester Railways, 1882". Pub.- Lancashire and Cheshire Antiquarian Society, 1967.

Patmore, J.A., The Railway Network of the Manchester Conurbation. Trans. Institute of British Geographers, No 34, June, 1964.

Rawlinson, Sir R., op.cit.

Thompson, F.M.L., The Rise of Suburbia. Leicester, 1982.

Census Enumerators' Reports, 1841–71, C.R.O.; Sale Library and Altrincham Library.

Directories and Gazetteers, e.g. Pigot, (Cheshire, 1834, Manchester and Salford, 1838); Slater, (Northern Counties, 1848, Manchester and Salford, 1851); White (Cheshire, 1860); Morris (Cheshire with Stalybridge, 1874).

Draft conveyances – 59/5, Nos. 1-50; 51-81; 143-197; Stamford papers, Rylands Library.

Acknowledgements: Miss S. Morgan and Dr J.K. Walton; Rylands Library.

Chapter Nine   Places of Worship

Balshaw, C., Stranger's Guide to Altrincham, 1858. Rep. E.J. Morten, 1973.

St George's Parish Magazines.

Heywood, Rev. J.A., A History of the Church and Parish of St. Margaret's, Dunham. (Unpub).

Abbott, E.M., The History of the Diocese of Shrewsbury, 1850-1986. Catholic Printing Co., Farnworth.

Merrell, Mrs. C.M., The Methodist Heritage of Altrincham. Merrell, 1986.

The Methodist Church 1932 Union Celebrations Altrincham and District Handbook.

Beasley-Murray, P., and Wilkinson, A., Turning the Tide. Bible Society, 1984 (Baptist Church).

Walker, C.M., A Short History of Altrincham Baptist Church, 1872-1972 (Unpub.), 1972.

Spiritualist National Union Archives.

Goring, J., and R., The Unitarian. R.M.E.P., 1984.

Acknowledgements: St. George's – Mrs J. Littler and Mr J.A. Butters; St. Vincent's – Provost, J. Burgon, V.F., Unitarian – Thomas Pitfield (picture); Welsh Presbyterian – chapel archives.

Chapter Ten   Some Services

Garrard, J., The Great Salford Gas Scandal of 1887. Salford University, 1987.

Pugh J., Story of Altrincham General Hospital, 1870-1970. Richard Symonds and Assocs.

Lloyd's Hospital, 1862. Pamphlet in Altrincham Library.

James, R.W., To the Best of our Skill and Knowledge. Pub. Chief Constable of Cheshire.

Fire Station, Princes Road. Cheshire C.C. Official Opening Pamphlet, 1962.

Swale, W.E., Forerunners of the North Western Electricity Board. N.W. Elec. Board 1962.

Acknowledgements: Mr R.F. Bonner, G.M. Fire Service Museum Archives; Station Commander P.J. Smethurst (Fire); Superintendent D. Arrowsmith, M Division, G.M. Police; Mr W. Wilson; Mr J.J. Minshall, Police Museum Archives; Mr R.B. Sumner, Borough Engineer and Surveyor, Trafford MBC.; Mr D. Burfoot and Mr Swettenham, N.W. Water Authority; Mr B. Goude, Norweb; Mr Sharville, Altrincham General Hospital; Mr M. Bingham, Mr A. Payne, North Western Gas Archives.

Chapter Eleven   Education
Groves, N.S., Church of England Day Schools, 1895-1914. Unpub. M.Ed. thesis, Manchester University.
Lawson, J., and Silver, H., Social History of Education in England. Methuen, 1973.
Lea, J.T., History of the Development of the Mechanics Institutions. Pub. Research in Librarianship, 1968.
Rogers, C.D., History of Charity Schools in Bowdon. Unpub thesis, Department of Ed., Leeds, 1966 (copy Altrincham Library).
School Log Books.

Acknowledgements: Mrs O'Connor, Navigation Road School; Mrs Shakeshaft for use of log-books for St. George's, St. Margaret's, and St. John's schools; Mrs M. Tyler.

Chapter Twelve   Altrincham at Leisure
Altrincham Garrick Society Souvenir, 1932.
Altrincham Guardian Newspaper records.
The Bowdon Sheaf, Bowdon History Society.
Timperley Cricket Club Centenary Year Handbook.

Acknowledgements: Mr L. Pollitt; Mr D. Lane; Mr K.G. Bailey; the authors of several articles in The Bowdon Sheaf, published by the Bowdon History Society.

Chapter Thirteen   Transport
Grayling, C., The Bridgewater Heritage. Bridgewater Estates plc., 1983.
Mullineux, F., The Duke of Bridgewater's Canal. Eccles and Dist. Hist. Soc., 1959.
Kirby, A.K., Tramways of Altrincham and Sale. Tramway Revue, vol. 14, No. 106. Summer, 1981.
Yearsley, I., and Groves, P., The Manchester Tramways. Transport Publishing Company, Glossop, 1988.
North Western. Pub. Manchester Transport Museum Society and the Omnibus Society, 1972.
Ogden, E., North Western. TPC, Glossop, 1981.
Bolger, P., An Illustrated History of the Cheshire Lines Committee. Heyday, 1984.
Dyckhoff, N., The Cheshire Lines Committee - Then and Now. Ian Allen, 1984.
Dixon, F., The Manchester South Junction and Altrincham Railway, op. cit.
Griffiths, R.P., The Cheshire Lines Railway. Oakwood, 1958.

Acknowledgements: Mr D. Walton, Altrincham Electric Railway Preservation Society; Mr W. Wilson; Mr J. Edwards; Mr A.D. George, Manchester Polytechnic.

Chapter Fourteen   Housing Development Since 1801
Bamford, F.W., Mansions and Men of Dunham Massey. F.W. Bamford, 1991.
Kemp, P., Higher Downs, Altrincham. Bowdon History Society, 1985.
Linotype and Machinery Ltd., Works and Industry of Linotype and Machinery Ltd., n.d.
Rawlinson, Robert., Report to the General Board of Health, op.cit.
Rodgers, H.B., Altrincham; A Town of the Manchester Conurbation. Town Planning Review, October, 1952, with amendments and extensions, July 1962.

Altrincham Municipal Borough Council documents, e.g. Housing Acts, 1936-52; Housing Repairs and Rent Act, 1954; The New Street Compulsory Purchase Order, 1956. Evidence of the Medical Officer of Health, 1956.
Census Report, 1851, Altrincham Library.
Town's Meeting Minute Book, 1825-59, Altrincham Library.
Trafford Metropolitan Borough Council papers; Denmark Street and Oakfield Road Area, Altrincham Town Centre Development Brief. July, 1987.
Development Guidelines, The Downs etc., 1974.
The Release of Land for Housing Development. Broadheath, Sinderland and Timperley Brook District Plans, 1981.

Acknowledgements: Trafford Leisure Services.

Chapter Fifteen   Buildings
Kemp, P., op.cit.
Morrison, B.D., op.cit.
Pass, A.J., Thomas Worthington, Victorian Architecture and Social Purpose.
1860 History and Gazetteer of Cheshire.

Chapter Sixteen   A Burgage in the Market Place
Aiken, J., op.cit.
Balshaw, C., Stranger's Guide, op.cit.
Bishop's Transcripts of St. Mary the Virgin, Bowdon. C.R.O., Chester.
Bowdon Parish Registers, Altrincham Library.
Brunskill, R.W., The Illustrated Handbook of Vernacular Architecture. Faber and Faber, 1987.
Brunskill, R.W., Timber Building in Britain, Gollancz, 1985.
Leycester, Sir P., op.cit.
Richardson, J., The Local Historian's Encyclopaedia. Hist. Pub., 1986.

Census returns, 1841–81, Sale Library,
Dunham Massey rentals and surveys, Rylands Library,
Hearth Tax and Land Tax returns, Wills, Marriage Bonds

and Licences, C.R.O.
Directories, e.g. Kelly's and Pigot's, Altrincham Library.
Local Board of Health Map, 1852, Altrincham Library.
Tithe Map, 1835, Altrincham Library.
Trans, Lancashire and Cheshire Antiquarian Society, Altrincham Library.
1st Edition 1" O.S. sheet 26, 1842/96, David and Charles.
1:500 O.S. map of Altrincham, 1876, British Library, London.

Acknowledgements: John Archer, David Holmes, Richard Mallinson, Department of Architecture, Manchester University; Miss G. Matheson, Rylands Library; Mr J. Fuggles, Miss Belinda Cousens, Mr P. Veitch, Mr C. Alford, Mrs M. Pegg, National Trust; Mr R. Fleming; Mr D. Brough; Mr and Mrs B. Whitby; Mr M. Crosby.

Chapter Seventeen   Past Personalities of Altrincham
Kemp, P., op. cit.
Nicholls, Lindsell and Harris Bi-centenary Records.
Bowdon History Society, articles in the Bowdon Sheaf.
Cheshire Life Magazine.
Records at Dunham Massey Hall.

Chapter Eighteen   Past Families
Hardman, Janet., A Study of Altrincham and its Families in 1801 and 1851. J. Hardman, 1989.

Altrincham Poorhouse Accounts.
Bowdon Farish Records.
Decennial Census returns.
Land Tax Assessments; Tithe Map and Commutation Award Schedule; (copies by the author are lodged in Altrincham Library).
Wills in the C.R.O.

Chapter Nineteen   The Industrial Development of Broadheath
Malet, H., Coal, Cotton and Trade. Neil Richardson, Manchester, 1982.
Sparkes, C.A., History of Horizontal Boring Machines with special reference to the Manchester Engineering Companies of Pearns, Richards and Kearns. Unpub. M.Sc. thesis, UMIST, 1988.
The Town and Trade of Altrincham. Mackie, 1897.
The Story of the Churchill Machine Company. Pillans and Wilson, Edinburgh.
Tydeman, W.J., George Richards and Co. Ltd., Ass. Brit. Mach. Tool Maker, vol. xxix, No. 149, July/Sept., 1947.

Leaflets – Discover Broadheath. Salford/Trafford Groundwork Trust, 1988; repr. Altrincham History Society, 1991.
        – Tilghman's Ltd., George Richards and Co. Ltd., Leaflet No. 87.
        – Staveley Group, 1951.
Acknowledgements: to the companies concerned.

Chapter Twenty   Altrincham in World War II

Acknowledgements: Trafford Leisure Services.

Chapter Twenty-One   Altrincham Today
Chapter Twenty-Two   The Future of Altrincham
Acknowledgements: The Borough Engineer and Surveyor's, Planning, and Leisure Services Departments of Trafford MBC.

Chapter Twenty-Three   Conclusion
Acknowledgements: Early O.S. maps - Geography Department, Manchester University; Mrs L. Ryan, Chairman, Altrincham and Bowdon Civic Society; Mr W.R. Firth.

Appendix 1   Glossary
Acknowledgements: assistance from Dr. P.H.W. Booth for checking and amending.

Appendix 2   List of Mayors
Mrs J. Littler; Miss J. French; Trafford MBC.

Appendix 3   Altrincham and Broadheath Firms
Dr C.A. Sparkes.

Grateful thanks are extended to persons, and owners and occupiers of all property photographed, with apologies for any infringement of privacy. Acknowledgement for the use of illustrations is indicated, with apologies for any omissions or incorrect detail.

Thanks for assistance are also due to:

Mrs G. Fitzpatrick, formerly of Altrincham Library Local History Section for providing source material and illustrations from the excellent local collection and to Trafford Leisure Services for facilities, and permission to reproduce illustrations.

Mr D. Rendell for advice on, and for processing, many illustrations printed in the book.

APPENDIX 1

GLOSSARY

acre – a statute acre is 4840 sq. yards = 0.405 hectare; a Cheshire acre = 2.12 statute acres. An acre in 'the fields' (in Altrincham's Charter) would be probably in strip form, though not necessarily in one strip.

amercement – a fine.

Angevin dynasty – The Plantagenets, from Henry II to Richard II, i.e. from 1154 to 1399.

bailiff – (i) a chief officer who managed the lord's Estate; (ii) the chief officer of the borough court, elected by the burgesses.

bakehouse – an important monopoly source of revenue for the lord.

barony – a large tract of land held by a baron from an overlord by suit and service, e.g. the provision of several knights in the time of war. The de Masseys had to provide 5 knights. The Barony of Dunham Massey adjoined the baronies of Stockport and Halton.

boon – a service or duty for which the lord normally had to compensate the tenant with food and drink.

borough – In mediaeval times a borough was created by a charter, with distinctive laws and governing body, a characteristic being that it contained freemen with burgage land.

burgage – a plot of land in the borough on which a burgess's house was usually built.

burgess – a man or woman who owned land called a burgage in a borough.

charterer – a tenant holding land by the lord's charter.

common pasture – a right to graze animals in the open commons such as the mosses, heaths and woodlands, and on the common arable lands after harvest.

copyholder – a tenant who held land by the custom of the manor, by copy of the court roll. The terms of the copyhold tenure varied from place to place.

Court Baron – in Altrincham a 3-weekly court which tried petty offences, also held at the end of the View of Frankpledge or Court Leet proceedings.

Court Leet – a manor court held once or twice a year distinguished by the right to elect constables, other officers and juries and oversee administration. It also tried petty offences.

Dark Ages – in this book, AD 410 (when the Romans left), to AD 1066, the Norman Conquest.

demesne – the lord's property in a manor; some parts may have been held in the form of strips intermingled with those of peasants and farmed for him; it could also be a 'home farm'.

enclosure – in common field areas, arable land was unenclosed until after harvest when it would be enclosed temporarily for grazing animals on the stubble. Parts of wastes might similarly be enclosed temporarily. The term also refers to permanent enclosure when many common open fields and wastes were enclosed when farming practices changed from 'openfield' farming to that carried out in fenced fields.

escheat – property that falls to the feudal lord for want of an heir, or other reason.

ession – an amercement (fine) for not attending court.

estreat – written details of an amercement.

feoff, enfeoffment – grant of possession of property in perpetuity.

fine (fyne) – in old usage, the final settlement of a case.

guild merchant – a guild for merchants, a 'closed shop' which regulated trade, with its own apprenticeship arrangements and quality and quantity controls.

halmote – a manor court.

haybote – wood for building hays or heys.

hay/hey – an enclosure for hunting, restricting the movement of animals; in farming, a clearing e.g. from woodland; a fenced area.

heriot – formerly on decease a man's armour had to be returned to the lord; later, a death duty.

hide – notionally 120 statue acres of arable land; a measure for taxation purposes, not used in Cheshire after 1086.

housebote – wood for building houses.

implead – to be tried for an offence.

lastage – a toll for attending market.

liberties and free customs – privileges of men of free status, such as freedom from certain tolls and dues.

manor – the holding of a Norman lord; it could be a whole place (vill/township), part of one, or several small places together. It would include the buildings and all lands associated and its lord would command the allegiance of all in it. In the Altrincham area many small vills were reckoned to be individual manors. 'Sundreland' and 'Bagelei' 'vills' were grouped together and reckoned to contain manors belonging to 3 or 4 lords. In contrast, Dunham was one huge manor, which contained several vills belonging to one lord.

mark – 13s 4d (66p)

mediaeval period – in the Middle Ages; here the term refers to the time from 1066 to Tudor times (mid-16th century).

Mercia – Anglian kingdom of central England with a northern boundary originally on the Mersey; capital Tamworth. Important kings – Penda and Offa.

messuage – house with associated building and land.

moiety – usually a half portion of an estate.

motte-and -bailey – the motte was a mound on which a keep or stronghold was built, at first of wood, later of stone; this was surrounded by a palisade and ditch. It was separated from a neighbouring large palisaded enclosure, the bailey, in which the lord's followers lived. Both might be surrounded by a ditch.

multure – a due or toll for grinding corn.

Palatine – describing a county such as Cheshire which had its own government separate from the rest of England.

pannage – the right to graze pigs. In woods pigs ate acorns and beech mast.

passage – a toll for travelling on highways or ferries.

peasants – manorial tenants who paid rent and frequently performed services for the lord. Those who were unfree were called villeins, niefs or serfs.

perch – a Cheshire linear perch was 8 yards whereas a statute perch is 5½ yards.

Portmote – the court of a borough. Some Portmotes continued into the 19th century but others were earlier merged with Court Leets.

Provost – in former times an official elected by the people of the manor, usually responsible for the husbandry of the commons. Some towns used the term for their chief citizen. Chief officer of Altrincham's modern Court Leet, elected from the burgesses for one year.

reeve – usually a man of villein status elected to organise the daily business of a manor.

Roman period – AD 43 – AD 410.

Romano-Britons – native Celts or British who adopted some Roman culture and practices.

selion or strip – component of openfield, theoretically an acre of land which could be ploughed in a day by a team of oxen and a communal plough; grouped into patches or 'furlongs'. In a traditional community, they were allocated in rotation among the inhabitants and the lord (forming part of his demesne).

serfs – see villeins.

settlement – in the context of this book i. any inhabited place, ii. the process of colonising a district, iii. (marriage) a dowry.

stallage – a toll for trading in a market.

suit and service – a list of tenants of the manor who were obliged to attend the manor court.

temporal lord – a lay, secular or civil lord.

tenterframe – a wooden framework on which cloth was attached to numerous hooks around the edges to be stretched and bleached in the open air. Sometimes many frames were grouped together covering a large area.

township – an area consisting of a settlement and its surrounding lands, perhaps originally largely self-sufficient agriculturally when population was very small. (A number of small rural townships might form a large manor, such as the Manor of Dunham Massey).

turbary of the heath – the right to dig turves of peat for fuel and roofs.

View of Frankpledge – In many parts of England this was a court review of behaviour of the inhabitants with miscreants presented by the Constables. This did not happen in Cheshire and several other western counties where it was the name for a manor court with limited criminal jurisdiction, or, later, a roll-call of tenants.

vill – township.

villeins – unfree inhabitants of a manor, bound by service to the lord.

virgate – a quarter of a hide.

Watling Street – the Roman road from London to Wroxeter; locally the name given to the road from Chester to York.

APPENDIX 2
LIST OF MAYORS OF ALTRINCHAM

Provided by Mrs J. Littler and Miss J. French and Trafford MBC.

1452 Edward Massey	1656 John Ashley	1710 John Smith	1764 John Birch
1483 Richard Massey	1657 Robert Hesketh	1711 Edward Garnett	1765 Thomas Moore
1547 Roger Booth	1658 Thomas Hesketh	1712 John Cooke	1766 William Rigby
1552 John Royle	1659 Henry Smith	1713 Thomas Royle	1767 Thomas Warburton
1555 John Norris	1660 Robert Lingard	1714 Robert Lupton	1768 William Leicester
1556 John Ryle	1661 John Palden	1715 Robert Frith	1769 John Walthew
1557 John Ryle	1662 William Rowlinson	1716 Charles Crosswell	1770 William Parkinson Ju
1558 Ralph Massey	1663 James Doe	1717 Robert Leather	1771 William Taylor
1559 Ralph Massey	1664 George Birch	1718 John Ashley	1772 George Cooke
1560 William Ardron	1665 George Parker	1719 James Hardey	1773 Isaac Worthington Ju
1561 George Newton	1666 John Coe	1720 Richard Royle	1774 John Ratcliffe
1562 George Newton	1667 James Brookes	1721 James Robinson	1775 John Derbyshire
1563 George Newton	1668 George Aldcroft	1722 Samuel Holt	1776 George Lupton
1565 Ralph Massey, Sen.	1669 George Hardey	1723 John Smith	1777 William Howard
1588 George Aldcroft?	1670 William Leicester	1724 John Hardey	1778 Thomas Duncalf
1614 William Rawlinson	1671 George Vaudrey	1725 Joshua Grantham	1779 Edward Darbyshire
1616 Alexander Vaudrey	1672 Richard Wright	1726 William Leicester	1780 John Austin
1618 Robert Lingard	1673 George Cook	1727 Fernando Laughton	1781 William Pooks
1619 Richard Brereton	1674 Robert Lingard	1728 Richard Berry	1782 Vernon Poole
1620 Edward Bent	1675 George Parker	1729 William Taylor	1783 Oswald Leicester
1621 Randle Wright	1676 Thomas Doe	1730 William Royle	1784 John Clough
1622 George Birch	1677 John Ashley	1731 Richard Leigh	1785 Charles Poole
1623 William Rowlandson	1678 Henry Hesketh	1732 John Birch	1786 Robert Mills
1624 William Hesketh	1679 William Delves	1733 James Fletcher	1787 John Eccles
1626 William Hesketh	1680 Richard Wright	1734 George Smith	1788 Robert Leicester
1627 Robert Parker	1681 George Birch	1735 George Warburton	1789 James Staples
1628 Robert Lingard	1682 Henry Smith	1736 George Royle	1790 Aaron Brundrett
1629 James Leycester	1683 James Brookes	1737 Henry Smith	1791 Thomas Howard
1630 Randle Wright	1684 John Burgess	1738 John Worthington	1792 James Walthew
1631 Peter Rowlinson	1685 James Ashley	1739 Aaron Eccles	1793 Timothy Brownel
1632 George Birch	1686 Thomas Hesketh	1740 Joshua Grantham	1794 James Gratrix
1633 Richard Brereton	1687 Joseph Pierson	1741 Thomas Royle	1795 William Parkinsc
1634 Richard Brereton	1688 George Hardey	1742 John Smith	1796 John Atherton
1635 Jeffry Coe	1689 John Leather	1743 Richard Nield	1797 Samuel Howard
1636 George Vaudrey	1690 Jeffrey Stockley	1744 Robert Frith	1798 Samuel Hardey
1637 Lawrence Leicester	1691 Jeffrey Stockley	1745 George Ashton	1799 George Burgess
1638 Richard Wright	1692 Robert Lingard	1746 George Burgess	1800 George Worthing
1639 George Ashton	1693 Robert Leicester	1747 Benjamin Irlam	1801 Peter Leicester
1640 Robert Linguard	1694 Timothy Taylor	1748 John Leigh	1802 Samuel Walker
1641 William Hesketh	1695 William Hesketh	1749 Richard Royle	1803 William Ashley
1642 William Rowlinson	1696 Henry Smith	1750 George Twyford	1804 William Smith
1643 Henry Cartwright	1697 James Hardey	1751 Joseph Grantham	1805 Thomas Royle
1644 Henry Cartwright	1698 George Aldcroft	1752 George Robinson	1806 John Postles
1645 George Parker	1699 John Eccles	1753 Peter Bailey	1807 Thomas Carter
1646 John Bent	1700 Jeremiah Brundrett	1754 Thomas Royle	1808 Abner Partington
1647 George Birch	1701 George Birch	1755 James Wainwright	1809 William Royle
1648 William Leicester	1702 George Leicester	1756 Samuel Lamb	1810 Thomas Darbyshi
1649 George Vaudrey	1703 William Grantham	1757 Richard Crouchley	1811 John Mitchell
1650 Richard Brereton	1704 John Bent	1758 The Hon. Booth Grey	1812 Samuel Hope
1651 Richard Brereton	1705 William Higginson	1759 Isaac Shaw	1813 John Austin
1652 Richard Brereton	1706 John Higginson	1760 Nathaniel Priestner	1814 Isaac Davenport
1653 Henry Bradshaw	1707 Robert Ashley	1761 Charles Cresswell	1815 John Mitchell
1654 Richard Wright	1708 George Smith	1762 Robert Ashley	1816 John Barratt
1655 Peter Parker	1709 James Warburton	1763 Edward Cooke	1817 William Ashley

1818 John Drinkwater
1819 Joshua Ashcroft
1820 Samuel Bruckshaw
1821 Samuel Renshaw
1822 Timothy Brownell
1823 Samuel Street
1824 Samuel Clarke
1825 John Faulkner
1826 John Hope
1827 Richard Irlam
     Grantham
1828 John Clarke
1829 John Adshead
1830 Nathaniel Pass
1831 Robert Shelmerdine
1832 John Lupton
1833 Charles Poole
1834 Richard Poole
1835 Isaac Harrop
1836 Isaac Harrop
1837 William Hamilton
1838 Isaac Gaskarth
1839 Joseph Arstall
1840 Isaac Gaskarth
1841 Joseph Bruckshaw
1842 William Collier
1843 William Collier
1844 William Renshaw
1845 James Royle
1846 James Matthews
1847 Joseph Hall
1848 George Massey
1849 Richard Broadbent
1850 Richard Broadbent
1851 Mark Pierson
1852 Mark Pierson
1853 George Berry
1854 Samuel Barratt
1855 John Davenport
1856 William D. Nicholls
1857 William D. Nicholls
1858 John Mort
1859 John Mort
1860 John Howard
1861 Charles Balshaw
1862 James Street
1863 Thomas Balshaw
1864 Samuel Delves
1865 Samuel Delves
1866 Samuel Delves
1867 James Astle Kelsall
1868 James Southern
1869 Humphrey Davis
1870 Joseph Gaskarth
1871 Joseph Gaskarth
1872 Matthew Fowden
1873 John Shelmerdine
     Mort
1874 Samuel Burgess
1875 Edward Neild
1876 William Greenwood

1877 William Greenwood
1878 John Siddeley
1879 Joseph Gaskarth
1880 James Byrom
1881 George Smith
1882 Henry Balshaw
1883 Henry Balshaw
1884 Benjamin Riley
1885 George Bowen
1886 Joseph Gaskarth
1887 James Hamilton
1888 William Griffin
1889 Eustace George
     Parker
1890 Joel Foden
1891 William Agar
     Renshaw
1892 John Dale
1893 William Griffin
1894 William Griffin
1895 David Morrison
1896 Frederick Raymond
     Barber Lindsell
1897 James Grimble
     Groves
1898 James Grimble
     Groves
1899 Samuel Thompson
1900 James William
     Byrom
1901 William Agar
     Renshaw
1902 William Agar
     Renshaw
1903 Edward Thomas
     Cleathero
1904 Alfred Golland
1905 Alfred Golland
1906 Alfred Golland
1907 Samuel Birtles
1908 Harold Gaskell
     Syers
1909 Godfrey William
     Bonson
1910 William Shield
1911 Gerald Whitwham
1912 William Cooke
     Renshaw
1913 George Faulkner
     Armitage
1914 George Faulkner
     Armitage
1915 George Faulkner
     Armitage
1916 George Faulkner
     Armitage
1917 George Faulkner
     Armitage
1918 George Faulkner
     Armitage

1919 Henry Francis
     O'Brien
1920 William Walton Baker
1921 Harry Gordon Cooper
1922 Arthur Broadbent
     Ireland
1923 William Henry Veno
1924 Thomas Clarke
1925 Robert Reid Duncan
1926 David Stanley
     Morrison
1927 James Kayley
1928 Arthur Gray Pickard
1929 Arthur Percy Hill
1930 Alfred Pailthorpe
1931 William Waterhouse
1932 William Waterhouse
1933 William Waterhouse
1934 William Waterhouse
1935 William Waterhouse
1936 William Waterhouse
1937 The Rt. Hon. Roger
     Grey, Earl of Stamford
1938 William Waterhouse
1939 William George Henry
     Biddle
1940 Thomas Clayton
1941 Edgar Webb
1942 Albert Weston
1943 William Harold
  · Walker
1944 Richard Holcombe Lee
1945 Sidney Newns Garner
1946 William Bradley-Jones
1947 James Sumner Pearson
     (died in office)
April
1948 Alfred Whitely
May
1949 James Herbert
     Cosgrove
1950 Arthur Vesey
1951 J. Leonard Warren
1952 Raymond S. Watson
1953 Frank Gibson
1954 Thomas Baxter
1955 G. Anthony Haigh
1956 Edward J. Horley
1957 Edith M. Fitton
     (First Lady Mayor)
1958 Robert M. Kelsall
1959 James L. Baxendale
1960 Edward M. Chorlton
1961 Ian M. MacLennon
1962 Lillian M. Smith
1963 Raymond Street
1964 George Harmer
1965 Wilfred Yates
1966 Ethel M. Hoyle
1967 George Hoyle

1968 Derek Harper
1969 Roy Hall
1970 M. William Hiett
1971 J.B. Dunn
1972 Stephen Williamson
1973 Raymond Littler....

.... who was the last
mayor of Altrincham.

In 1974 Altrincham
became part of the new
Metropolitan Borough of
Trafford. All local mayor-
alties were discontinued
and merged into a single
office of 'Mayor of Traf-
ford'.

Mayors of Trafford MBC:
1974 C. Warbrick
1975 G.H. Carnall
1976 H. Pyper
1977 C.S. Fink
1978 J.B. Humphreys
1979 M.E. King
1980 R.G. Haigh
1981 S.G. Brownhill
1982 D.F. Sullivan
1983 J. Taylor OBE
1984 Mrs. M. Hinchcliffe
1985 R. Mee
1986 F.H. Eadie
1987 W. John Golding
1988 G. Marland
1989 A.R. Coupe
1900 J.R. Haydock
1991 Mrs. L. Burton

APPENDIX 3
ALTRINCHAM AND BROADHEATH FIRMS
Provided by Dr C.A. Sparkes to accompany Chapter Nineteen.

A list of Altrincham and Broadheath manufacturers, and some other industrial firms, past and present, including the date established where known and the products.

Alliance Colour Chemicals. Dyers.
Altrincham Electric Supply Company. 1897. Electric power generation.
Altrincham Gas Company. 1846
Automatic Scale (ASCO). 1915. Weighing machines.
Baldwin and Francis Ltd. 1952. Flame-proof switchgear.
Bannermans. Textiles.
Belmont Manufacturing Co. Textiles.
Blackwell National Roofing Company.
Borax Works. 1860. CIRA iron founders.
Broad, Jesse. Printers.
Broadheath Saw Mills. Turned timber components.
Box M.E. 1920. Road surfacing.
Budenberg Gauge Company. 1912. Pressure gauges.
Cartwright and Sons. Vehicle bodybuilders.
Castings P.I. 1950. Investment castings.
Cast & Steam Packing.
Cheshire Printers. Printing.
Churchill Machine Tool Company. 1906. Grinding Machines
Clare Collet. 1919. Drilling chucks.
Davidson, J. (Broadheath) Ltd. Scrap Merchants.
Derbyshire & Sons. 1931. Sand castings.
Eagle Engineering and Motor Co. 1896. Motorcyles and cars.
Dowding & Mills (Northern) Ltd. Motor rewinding.

Essex Tool & Gauge. 1940. Jigs and fixtures.
Hampson Carpets.
Harmand Engineering. Centrifugal pumps.
Home Edward. 1918. Electrical controls.
Hudson & Matthews. Motor cycle side cars.
Industrial Colloids. 1932. Detergents.
J.B. Electrics. 1942. Electrical and mechanical repairs.
Kearns. H.W. 1907. Machine-tools.
Lancashire Road Roller. Roadway contractors.
Leathers (Altrincham). 1888. Leather packings.
Linotype and Machinery. 1897. Printing machines.
Lord Brothers. 1922. Tin containers.
Luke and Spencer. 1877. Abrasive wheels.
Luxiproducts. Nursery goods.
Madan,. Charles. 1882. Steam injectors.
Meldrum Brothers. Refuse destructors.
Northern Automatic Screw. 1946. Turned components.
O'Briens. Oil merchants.
Parker J.F. 1924. Scrap metals.
Radium (Broadheath). 1902. Leather dyes.
Record Electrical. 1911. Graphic recorders.
Richards, George. 1884. Machine-tools.
Rotalac. 1935. Extruded plastics.
Ruby Motor Cycle Company. Motor cycles.
Smith & Coventry. Machine-tools.
Thornton & Pickard. 1896. Photographic materials.
Tilghman Ltd. 1870 Shot blast plant.
Vicrete Products (Altrincham). 1949. Pre-cast concrete.
Wallpaper Manufacturers. 1935. Wallpaper.
Whitelegg, F.V. Engineering pattern maker.
Whitelegg, J. & Son (Altrincham) Ltd., Sheet metal.

APPENDIX 4
LISTED BUILDINGS AND CONSERVATION AREAS

LISTED BUILDINGS

Some of the buildings mentioned in this book are 'listed' by the Department of the Evironment and must be maintained as they are and cannot be altered without permission. The listed buildings in the area of the ancient township of Altrincham are all classified as Grade II:

St. George's Church
St. John's Church
St. Margaret's Church (II*)
Unicorn Hotel incorporating former Town Hall
Old Market Place: No's: 2, 2A, 4, 4A, 16.
Old Market Place: Lloyds Bank
Market Street: No's: 1, 1A, 3,5,7,10,12,14,16
Stamford Estates Office
Market House
Kingsway: No's 1,4,6 and part of no. 8
Clock tower on station forecourt
Norman's Place: No's 2,4,6,8 and The Elms and Richmond House
The Downs: No's 32 and 34, 36 to 44 even, 56 to 62 even
Sandiway Road: No's 1-11 odd and 13-21 odd
Lloyd's Bank and Post Office, Broadheath
Luxi-Leisure Ltd., the 1833 warehouse adjacent to the former coal wharf.

Other worthy buildings which are not 'listed' at present: The Town Hall of 1900, Budenberg's, Bricklayer's Arms, Packet House, the 'Guardian' building, buildings around Old Market Place, e.g. No. 6 and 8 and others opposite such as the Orange Tree.

CONSERVATION AREAS

The Town and Country Planning Act of 1971, according to Trafford MB's Development Control Guildelines, imposed "a duty on the local planning authority to decide which areas of special architectural or historic character should be preserved or enhanced." These powers were extended in 1974. While much attention should be given to conservation (several of the listed buildings are found in such areas) it was realised that there would be new development but this should be appropriate. There were two types of area: Core Areas, where the most stringent policies would operate, and Fringe Areas which surround and protect the Core Areas.

The basic guidelines are as follows.

land-use – should remain primarily residential;
open space – development would not generally be permitted;

the form of development – standard and design should be high in quality and buildings should normally be of only two or three storeys;
preservation – demolition of buildings would generally be resisted;
improvement – rehabilitation of old buildings would be encouraged;
tree preservation and planting – existing stock should be maintained and more planted;
residential density – in core areas, there should be only detached dwellings at 0-3 per acre; rural fringe 1-3 per acre; urban fringe, various types of dwelling ranging from 3-5 per acre for detached houses to 6-10 per acre for flats;
car parking – each new dwelling to have provision for 2-3 cars, depending on location.

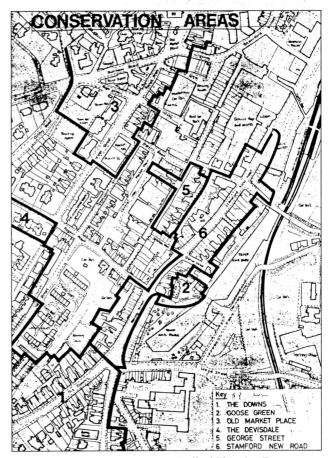

Trafford Planning Department

The six Conservation Areas in Altrincham.

APPENDIX 5
CONTRIBUTORS

Foreword
R.N. Dore, M.A., author of several books and papers on Cheshire history. President, Lancashire and Cheshire Antiquarian Society and Altrincham History Society.

Chapters One, Two, Four, Five, Thirteen, Twenty-Three
D.G. Bayliss, M.A., Ph.D.
Contributor to several history journals. Chairman, Altrincham History Society; Committee member, Altrincham & Bowdon Civic Society. Member of Altrincham Court Leet.

Chapter Three
I. Sharman
Researcher in mediaeval history, Keele University.

Chapter Six
R. G. Higginbottom, M.A.
Member of Altrincham Court Leet; Vice-President, Altrincham WEA.; Vice-Chairman, Altrincham History Society; Committee member, Altrincham and Bowdon Civic Society.

Chapter Seven
Miss J. French
Formerly employed on the staff of Altrincham Municipal Borough Council and Trafford Metropolitan Borough Council.

Chapter Eight
A. Daber, M.A.
Former post-graduate student, Lancaster University. Registrar, Quarry Bank Mill, Styal, Cheshire.

Chapter Nine
G.D. Fairley
Member, St. George's Church.

C.K. Lewis
Former Headmaster, St. Margaret's C. of E. and Altrincham C. of E. Aided Primary Schools.

Very Rev. Canon J. Burgon, V.F.
Provost of Canons and Dean of Deanery, St. Vincent's Church.

Rev. W.J. Moxon
Vicar, St. John's Church.

Mrs C.M. Merrell
Class leader, Altrincham Methodist Church; teacher; author 'The Methodist Heritage of Altrincham', 1986.

Mrs J.E. Morgan, B.A.
Member, Altrincham Baptist Church. Ex-teacher, recently freelance writer and editor with Lion Publishing.

Mrs M.M. Kettle
Member, Welsh Presbyterian Church.

R.C. Evans
Elder of the Devonshire Road Evangelical Church.

Rev John Midgley, M.A., M.Ed., B.D.
Former minister Dunham Road Unitarian Chapel. Recently Development Officer of the General Assembly of the Unitarian and Free Christian Churches.

Mr R. Gentle and Mrs M. Jaques
Members, First Church of Christ Scientist.

Mrs M.E.J. Baverstock-Bosley
President, Altrincham National Spiritualist Church.

Chapters Ten, Eleven
Mrs H.E. Bayliss
Co-author of a study of population in West Yorkshire; Secretary, Altrincham History Society. Committee member, Altrincham and Bowdon Civic Society.

Chapter Ten
W.L. Pollard, Lt.Col.
Founder and Steward, modern Court Leet. Committee member, Altrincham and Bowdon Civic Society.

Chapters Twelve, Seventeen
B.D. Morrison, FRICS, FRIVA.
Author of several publications; President, Altrincham Society of Artists.

Chapter Thirteen
R. Dunning
Archivist, Manchester Transport Museum Society.

A.M. Davies
Researcher in public transport systems.

A. MacFarlane
Secretary, Altrincham Electric Railway Preservation Society.

Chapter Fourteen
Mrs G. Fitzpatrick, B.A., A.L.A. Formerly Senior Assistant Librarian, Trafford Leisure Services, Altrincham

Library, with responsibility for Reference and Local History collections. Author of 'Altrincham Past and Present'. Willow, 1990.

Chapter Fifteen
E.R. Fleming, RIBA.
Consultant: Hartington, Fleming and Worsley, architects.

Chapter Sixteen
Mrs J. Littler
Researcher in local and family history; transcriber of Dunham Rentals. Committee member, Altrincham History Society.

Chapter Eighteen
Mrs J. Hardman
Researcher in family and local history. Author and publisher of 'A Study of Altrincham and its Families in 1801 and 1851'and 'A Study of Timperley and its Families in 1801 and 1851'.

Chapter Nineteen
C.A. Sparkes, M.Sc., PhD., C.Eng., FIMechE., AMCT.
Retired Managing Director of H.W. Kearns & Co., Ltd. Consultant to machine-tool and other companies.

Chapter Twenty
J.A. Littler, former Chairman of Whitwham and Company, Wines Ltd., President, Altrincham and Bowdon Civic Society; Secretary, Altrincham Chamber of Commerce, Trade & Industry.

Chapters Twenty One and Twenty Two
N.R. Stocks, BA., ARICS., Dip.TP., MRTPI,
Former Chief Planning Officer, Trafford MBC.

INDEX

Willow Publishing
Willow Cottage, 36 Moss Lane, Timperley,
Altrincham, Cheshire, WA15 6SZ

© Don Bayliss, 1992

Printed by the Commercial Centre Limited,
Clowes Street, Hollinwood, Oldham.

The authors' royalties from this publication
have been donated to local charities